SOLUTION POWER

SOLUTION POWER

Ten Tools You Can Use To
Solve Any Problem
At Work And At Home

Kevin Pufall
and
Reagan Pufall

SKR Pufall, LLC
Omaha, Nebraska

Copyright © 2003 Kevin Pufall & Reagan Pufall

Printed and bound in the United States of America. All rights reserved. No part of this book may be reproduced in any form without the prior written permission of the publisher except by a reviewer who may quote brief passages in a review.

Published by SKR Pufall, LLC
PO Box 390567   Omaha, NE 68139-0567
(877) 923-2557   www.pufall.com

ISBN 0-9714486-0-4

LCCN 2002094617

Dedication

To our mother Sally: counselor, speaker, entrepreneur, teacher, politician, homemaker, and actress. Friend to many, inspiration to all, and the best mom in the world.

My Nana Sally

Loving, funny, loves antiques.
Dreams of fantasy things
and a loving world.
Who wants to
make up things
and have fun.
Who wonders
if other people
know how to have fun.
Who fears nothing.
Who likes dresses
and grandkids.
Who believes
in life after death.
Who wishes
for peace and joy.
Who would like
to see her two kids
young again.
We love you.

Emily Pufall, granddaughter
Age 9, 1995

Contents

The Ten Tools	9
Getting Started	
Introduction	**11**
Key Concepts	13
The First Tool	
Insight	**17**
Your Problem-Solving Personality Type	18
See Problems in a Positive Light	40
The Second Tool	
Response	**51**
The Problem-Solving Responses	54
Advantages of the Strong Responses	59
From Weak to Strong	73
The Third Tool	
Clarity	**95**
Gain Internal Clarity	95
Analyze the Problem	121
The Fourth Tool	
Focus	**135**
Focus on Having a Problem	136
Focus on Overcoming Obstacles	143
Focus on Achieving Your Goal	149
Focus on Attaining Fulfillment	155

The Fifth Tool
PRIORITY   165
- The Priority Pyramid   167
- Building the Pyramid   171
- Create Your Fulfillment Action Plan   179

The Sixth Tool
DISCOVERY   195
- Share Solutions   197
- Use Discovery Resources   202

The Seventh Tool
TEAMWORK   209
- Delegation Teamwork   211
- Partnership Teamwork   222
- Your Life Team   229

The Eighth Tool
CREATIVITY   235
- Prepare to be Creative   236
- Creativity Techniques   242

The Ninth Tool
DETERMINATION   265
- Courage   266
- Persistence   276

The Tenth Tool
RELEASE   285
- Separating   286
- Letting Go   295

Afterword   303
Appendices   305
List of Anecdotes   309
Index   313

The *Solution Power* Tools

1. Insight
Discover Your Strengths & See Problems in a Positive Light

2. Response
Act with Strength

3. Clarity
Understand Problems Clearly & Completely

4. Focus
Keep Moving in the Right Direction

5. Priority
Choose the Right Problems

6. Discovery
Find & Use Existing Solutions

7. Teamwork
Delegate & Partner

8. Creativity
Invent Your Own Brilliant Solutions

9. Determination
Overcome Problems Through Courage & Persistence

10. Release
Separating & Letting Go

Getting Started

Introduction

Get The Most From Your Solution Power Toolbox

How much happiness and satisfaction will you experience in your personal life? How much success and fulfillment will you achieve in your career? The answers to these questions depend largely on your ability to solve problems. If you have difficulty solving problems, life can be a frustrating struggle. If you learn to solve problems effectively, and even take advantage of problems by turning them into opportunities, life can become an exciting and rewarding adventure.

So becoming a better problem-solver is not just a handy skill, it is essential to a fulfilling life. How can you become a more effective problem-solver?

One challenge is that there are so many kinds of problems to solve. They come in all sizes, from minor difficulties to major crises. Problems may appear suddenly and demand immediate solutions, or they may develop slowly and require ongoing, gradual solutions. Some problems arise at work as you perform your job and build your career, while others arise in your personal life as you develop relationships and grow as an individual. Problems may be technical, requiring solutions based on specific expertise and training, or they may be emotional, requiring solutions based on insight and communication.

The good news is that you can solve every problem you will ever encounter by using the ten problem-solving tools presented in this book. That's because these tools are the fundamental strategies of problem-solving. They are the universal techniques for generating great solutions to problems of all kinds. Every good problem-solver uses at least some of these tools, and the best ones use them all.

In reading this book you will discover that you have already been using some of the *Solution Power* tools. You will gain insight into why you are naturally inclined to use those particular tools, and will learn how to use them even better.

You will also discover the benefits of using the tools you have not used very often in the past. Most people tend to rely on just two or three problem-solving tools. However, the more tools you learn to use, the greater success you can achieve, because you will have at hand the particular tool that is best-suited to solving any problem that arises.

This book is both a toolbox and a user's manual. It presents the ten *Solution Power* problem-solving tools along with instructions on how you can use them most effectively. As with any set of tools, the more you use them the more skilled you will become. By mastering all ten, you will become a master of solving problems in all aspects of your life.

INTRODUCTION

KEY CONCEPTS

This book is about the *tools* you can use to find *solutions* to your *problems*. Since these terms are fundamental to the *Solution Power* system, we will begin by defining them.

WHAT IS A PROBLEM?

A problem is when you want something you don't have.

Try out this definition. Think of some problems you are facing right now and then describe each one by completing the statement, "I want _____." For example:

Instead of saying:	Say:
"I'm in terrible shape!"	"I want to be healthy and physically fit."
"My business is a failure!"	"I want to increase my net profits."
"My marriage is miserable!"	"I want a happy and loving marriage."
"I hate this lousy job!"	"I want a better job."
"My yard looks awful!"	"I want a beautiful lawn."

This approach to defining problems automatically focuses your attention on the positive outcome you want, which is more useful than focusing it on the negative situation that currently exists. Describing a problem in terms of the goal you desire immediately shifts your thoughts toward finding a solution that will achieve it.

WHAT IS A SOLUTION?

A solution is how you get what you want or change what you want.

When you want something you don't have, you feel a natural desire to change the situation. The difference between what you want and what you have creates emotional tension. This tension is what motivates you to solve the problem.

The most common approach to problem-solving is to figure out how to get what you want. Once you get it, the feeling of tension is replaced with a feeling of satisfaction. The problem is solved. Most of the tools in this book will help you accomplish this kind of "I got what I wanted" solution.

Another approach is to carefully reconsider what you want. If you realize you don't really want the thing that you don't have, you can let go of the desire for it. The problem simply vanishes. The feeling of tension is replaced with a feeling of peace of mind. Some of the tools in this book will help you achieve this kind of solution as well.

So a solution is any plan, action, idea, realization, or information that enables you to make what you have match what you want.

WHAT IS A TOOL?

A tool is anything you can use to achieve a solution.

The *Solution Power* tools are strategies, skills, and insights that you can use to build solutions to problems of all kinds. They are effective techniques of thought, emotion, and behavior. We call them tools to emphasize that they are just as practical and useful as physical tools like a hammer, a magnifying glass, or a surgical scalpel.

The key is to adopt the tools as problem-solving habits. **Your ability to solve problems depends on how you habitually think, feel, and behave when a problem arises.** Many people have unwittingly developed habits that make it harder for them to understand their problems clearly and solve them effectively. This book will help you identify any unproductive problem-solving habits you may have and replace them with new habits that employ the *Solution Power* tools.

Once you turn the tools into habits you will carry them with you everywhere you go, in a mental problem-solving toolbox. When a problem arises, you will naturally reach into your toolbox to find the best tool for solving that particular problem.

Learning to use these tools will give you a great advantage in life. Even though the ability to solve problems is tremendously important, the fundamental techniques of effective problem-solving are rarely taught. Most problem-solving training focuses on highly specific solutions to problems like how to swing a golf club, potty train a child, or use a software program. Such advice is useful but its value is limited to a narrow range of problems. The *Solution Power* tools operate on a deeper level, so they can be used to solve problems of all kinds.

Solution Power is packed with ideas on how to apply the ten tools to your individual problem-solving needs. You don't have to use every single one of them right away. Pick three or four techniques, write them down, and make a commitment to use them consistently until you have built them into strong problem-solving habits. Then come back and choose a few more.

Let's get started! Congratulations, you are already on your way to a life of solution-finding success!

THE FIRST TOOL

INSIGHT

DISCOVER YOUR STRENGTHS &
SEE PROBLEMS IN A POSITIVE LIGHT

The INSIGHT tool:

1. Helps you identify and develop your natural problem-solving strengths, and
2. Gives you a more positive and useful understanding of the problems you encounter in life.

The first step is to discover and understand your problem-solving personality type. We each have our own distinct personality, so we each solve problems differently. And that's great! There is no single "right way" to solve problems. Everyone has a tendency to rely on the two or three *Solution Power* tools that come naturally to them. Some people are gifted with CREATIVITY, some are drawn to TEAMWORK, and some achieve great success with DETERMINATION. Which tools you find most comfortable and effective depends on your individual personality. Knowing your natural problem-solving strengths allows you to develop them even further. It also enables you to identify and learn to use the problem-solving tools that do not come naturally to you. In addition, discovering your personality type will empower you to make changes in your personal life and your career, so that how you live is better-suited to who you are and what you do best.

The second part of the INSIGHT tool is learning to see problems in a positive light. Unfortunately, many people treat problems as irritating nuisances, discouraging obstacles, or frightening dangers. These negative perceptions make it difficult to solve problems in a timely and effective manner. INSIGHT will help you treat problems as useful messengers, powerful allies, and welcome guests in your life, allowing you to solve them with confidence and optimism.

YOUR *SOLUTION POWER* PROBLEM-SOLVING PERSONALITY TYPE

Your personality type is your baseline, your reference point in the journey of successful problem-solving. You can discover your type by completing the questionnaire on the next three pages. For each question, check the box next to the answer that best describes you. If both answers are sometimes true for you, pick the one that you lean toward or that is true more often. You will get the most accurate results by moving through the questions fairly quickly rather than analyzing them at length.

Relax and have fun with it! There are no right or wrong answers, and no better or worse answers. Each personality type has its own unique strengths and advantages.

1. Are you Individual or Social?

A. When faced with a problem, are you more likely to:

- ☐ Tackle it on your own, and only look for help from others if you really get stuck.
- ☐ Start gathering ideas, encouragement, and assistance from others right away.

B. Do you see yourself as generally:

- ☐ Self-reliant.
- ☐ Outward-reaching.

C. Which of these do you believe is most true:

- ☐ "If you want something done right, do it yourself."
- ☐ "Two heads are better than one."

D. What bothers you more, people who:

- ☐ Always rely on others to solve their problems.
- ☐ Obstinately suffer alone when help is available.

E. Are you more likely to say to yourself:

- ☐ "Asking for help means admitting I can't solve my own problems."
- ☐ "Hiding my problems from others would be pointless and isolating."

F. Do you feel that:

- ☐ Solving your problems on your own shows that you are strong, responsible, and resourceful.
- ☐ Sharing your problems with others shows that you are open and supportive, a team builder.

___ **Individual score**   ___ **Social score**

2. Are you Linear or Intuitive?

A. When faced with a problem, are you more likely to:

- ❏ Work through it one step at a time.
- ❏ Follow your instincts and impulses.

B. Do you see yourself as generally:

- ❏ Logical and analytical.
- ❏ Open-minded and insightful.

C. Which of these is more often true:

- ❏ "Don't put the cart before the horse" and, "Build from the ground up."
- ❏ "Rules are made to be broken" and, "Foolish consistency is the hobgoblin of small minds."

D. What bothers you more, people who:

- ❏ Don't follow instructions, try to fix what isn't broken, and flit from one idea to another.
- ❏ Plod along doing the same old thing the same old way and resist spontaneous ideas.

E. When first using new software, do you usually:

- ❏ Refer to the instruction manual or "help" function.
- ❏ Just start using it and figure out how it works by experimenting.

F. What advice would you more likely give for solving problems:

- ❏ "Begin at the beginning, gather information, and evaluate your options."
- ❏ "Question your assumptions, play with ideas, and listen to your gut."

___ **Linear score**   ___ **Intuitive score**

3. Are you a Thinker or a Doer?

A. When faced with a new problem, are you more likely to:
- ❏ Take a step back.
- ❏ Jump right in.

B. Which of these is more often true:
- ❏ "Look before you leap" and, "Measure twice, cut once."
- ❏ "He who hesitates is lost" and, "Nothing ventured, nothing gained."

C. What frustrates you more, when people:
- ❏ Jump the gun and take off in all directions before a good plan has been put in place.
- ❏ Sit around analyzing something over and over instead of just getting to work on it.

D. Is it more important to:
- ❏ Get it right.
- ❏ Get it done.

E. What do you find more satisfying:
- ❏ Analyzing the situation and designing a good plan.
- ❏ Working efficiently and completing a task or project.

F. When you are solving a problem, do you:
- ❏ Explore options to make sure you have found the best possible solution.
- ❏ Come up with a good solution and put it into action.

___**Thinker score**   ___**Doer score**

For each of the three pairs of traits, put a check next to the one on which you scored higher:

- ❏ **Individual**   *or*   ❏ **Social**
- ❏ **Linear**   *or*   ❏ **Intuitive**
- ❏ **Thinker**   *or*   ❏ **Doer**

Now put a check mark next to the problem-solving personality type that includes those three traits:

Thinkers:
- ❏ **Individual Intuitive Thinker**
- ❏ **Social Intuitive Thinker**
- ❏ **Individual Linear Thinker**
- ❏ **Social Linear Thinker**

Doers:
- ❏ **Individual Intuitive Doer**
- ❏ **Social Intuitive Doer**
- ❏ **Individual Linear Doer**
- ❏ **Social Linear Doer**

You may find that you are a blend of two personality types. For example, if you are clearly an Intuitive Thinker, but your score on Individual versus Social was split 3 to 3, then you are a blend of Individual Intuitive Thinker and Social Intuitive Thinker. Go ahead and check both of them, as they will each provide useful insights into your natural problem-solving gifts.

Most people have the easiest time deciding they are either Thinkers or Doers, which is why the personality types are presented in those two groups. Descriptions of each type are on the following pages. Find yours and "try it on." It will help you see the strengths you can rely on, and the particular challenges you may face, when confronting problems.

You can also read about the other personality types. You will probably recognize your relatives, friends, and coworkers. This will give you insight into the problem-solving styles of the other people in your life and why they may react to problems very differently than you do.

All personality types are equally desirable and valuable. Every one of them is capable of solving problems effectively, even if they take very different approaches to doing so.

The Problem-Solving Personality Types

Thinkers

Individual Intuitive Thinker

- ➢ At your best you are **"The Innovator."** Using your inner resources of insight and ingenuity, you create new and better solutions to old problems, and enjoy tackling challenging new problems. You are at your best when gathering information and playing with abstract concepts. You particularly enjoy the analyzing and designing phase; once you figure out the solution you are not too interested in the humdrum work of implementing it. You thrive on variety and challenge, and are bored by repetition. A favorite phrase: "Here is the solution!"

- ➢ Beware of being seen as "The Flake." Remember that your great solutions won't be implemented or appreciated if you do not communicate them effectively to others. Share your solutions clearly and in concrete terms, or else Social people may see you as eccentric or aloof, and Linear Doers may perceive your stream of ideas as ineffective and disruptive.

- ➢ You are naturally gifted with the CREATIVITY and CLARITY tools. You can readily master FOCUS and the research aspect of DISCOVERY. Developing TEAMWORK and DETERMINATION may be your biggest challenge.

- ➢ It is easy for you to team up with Social Intuitive Thinkers and Individual Intuitive Doers. When solving problems with Social Linear Thinkers, learn to appreciate their ability to keep others organized. If you create a great new process, they will make sure it is implemented properly. When solving problems with Social Linear Doers, learn to appreciate their ability to make sure the team gets things done. They are naturally good at doing the follow-through work you find tedious.

Social Intuitive Thinker

➢ At your best you are **"The Brainstormer."** Using your natural skills for communication and innovation, you work well with others to create brilliant new solutions to tough problems. You are at your best when discussing a problem and possible solutions with others. Doing so stimulates your thinking, and you also have a knack for helping others tap into their own creativity. You particularly enjoy batting around sudden inspirations and clever plans; it feels like play to you. You thrive on variety and group projects, and are bored by repetition and working alone. A favorite phrase: "Let's figure this out!"

➢ Beware of being seen as "The Interrupter." Remember that not everyone shares your enthusiasm for discussing new ideas. Balance your drive for spontaneity and innovation against the need others feel for predictability and consistency. Exercise self-restraint, or else Linear Doers may see your ideas as scattered and disruptive, and Individuals may perceive your communication style as invasive and distracting.

➢ You are naturally gifted with the TEAMWORK and CREATIVITY tools. You can readily master the networking aspect of DISCOVERY, and can achieve RELEASE with support from those whose judgment you trust. Developing PRIORITY and DETERMINATION may be your biggest challenge.

➢ It is easy for you to team up with Individual Intuitive Thinkers and Social Intuitive Doers. When solving problems with Individual Linear Thinkers, learn to appreciate their ability to keep the discussion organized and on track. If you generate great new ideas, they will fit them into the overall design or plan. When solving problems with Individual Linear Doers, learn to appreciate their ability to implement the ideas created by the group. The ultimate success of the team may hinge on their actions.

Individual Linear Thinker

- At your best you are **"The Planner."** Using your natural skills of analysis and concentration, you develop thorough and effective solutions for even the most complex problems. You are at your best when organizing information and developing sequential action steps. You particularly enjoy the planning phase. You are also good at measuring progress and evaluating results, but are not too interested in sharing responsibility with others. You thrive on challenges in a structured environment, and are not fond of lengthy, unfocused discussions. A favorite phrase: "Here is the plan!"

- Beware of being seen as "The Hermit." Remember that your thorough plans and meticulous work won't be appreciated if you do not communicate them effectively to others. Present your plans in a clear, flexible manner, or else people who are Social may see you as aloof, and Intuitive Doers may perceive your plans as constraints on their desire to experiment.

- You are naturally gifted with the CLARITY and DETERMINATION tools. You can readily master FOCUS and the research aspect of DISCOVERY. Developing TEAMWORK and CREATIVITY may be your biggest challenge.

- It is easy for you to team up with Social Linear Thinkers and Individual Linear Doers. When solving problems with Social Intuitive Thinkers, learn to appreciate their ability to use group discussions to stimulate fresh thinking and new ideas. You don't need to enjoy these meetings, just listen for the real breakthroughs and take careful notes. When solving problems with Social Intuitive Doers, learn to appreciate their flair for leading group experimentation even when it deviates from your plan. Your plan will become even better if you incorporate their discoveries into your analysis.

Social Linear Thinker

➢ At your best you are **"The Organizer."** Using your natural skills of organization and communication, you keep others focused on achieving effective solutions to complex problems. You are at your best when explaining complex ideas in a clear manner and helping diverse people work consistently toward a common goal. You particularly enjoy working out the details of a solution with others, measuring progress, and monitoring compliance, but are not too interested in performing routine tasks alone. You thrive on working with others to meet challenges in a structured environment, and can be irritated when individuals go off on their own tangents. A favorite phrase: "Let's stick to the plan!"

➢ Beware of being seen as "The Bureaucrat." Remember that your ability to keep people organized and on task can become a negative if it prevents innovation and growth. Exercise some flexibility, or else Intuitive types may see you as stifling their ability to create needed change, and Doers may perceive your rules as roadblocks to getting things done efficiently.

➢ You are naturally gifted with the CLARITY and TEAMWORK tools. You can readily master DETERMINATION and the networking aspect of DISCOVERY. Developing CREATIVITY and RELEASE may be your biggest challenge.

➢ It is easy for you to team up with Individual Linear Thinkers and Social Linear Doers. When solving problems with Individual Intuitive Thinkers, learn to appreciate their off-the-wall ideas. Select their best ideas and include them as new guidelines or procedures in your process. When solving problems with Individual Intuitive Doers, learn to appreciate their impulse to try new ideas and methods, even if they bend the rules or depart from the current plan. You can improve the program by using their best discoveries.

Doers

Individual Intuitive Doer

➢ At your best you are **"The Experimenter."** Using your inner drive for exploration and innovation, you create new and better solutions. You are at your best when tackling a tricky problem. Trying out different approaches to see what works almost feels like play. You particularly enjoy hands-on work and learning from the results you get. Lengthy meetings and detailed planning sessions seem like tedious time wasters. You thrive on variety and tackling new challenges, and you find repetition boring. A favorite phrase: "I wonder if this would work?"

➢ Beware of being seen as "The Screw-Up." Remember that not all of your experiments will work out, and not everyone will appreciate your eagerness to jump ahead and bend the rules. Exercise self-restraint and openly explain your experiments, or else Social types may see you as erratic or distant, and Linear Thinkers may perceive you as disobedient or inconsistent.

➢ You are naturally gifted with the CREATIVITY tool. DETERMINATION will be a particularly important and powerful tool for you. Developing TEAMWORK and CLARITY may be your biggest challenge.

➢ It is easy for you to team up with Social Intuitive Doers and Individual Intuitive Thinkers. When solving problems with Social Linear Doers, learn to appreciate their ability to keep people organized and productive, even if they resist your ideas. If you communicate on their terms, they will effectively implement the solutions you discover. When solving problems with Social Linear Thinkers, learn to appreciate their ability to maintain focus and consistency. In the end you will achieve more if your discoveries are applied in an organized structure.

Social Intuitive Doer

➢ At your best you are **"The Inspirer."** Using your natural skills for communication and experimentation, you support and motivate those around you to help you create brilliant new solutions to tough problems. You are at your best when participating in new approaches and discussing results. You have a knack for helping others adopt an open-minded approach to solving a problem. You thrive on variety and group projects, and are bored by repetition and working alone. A favorite phrase: "Let's find a better way!"

➢ Beware of being seen as "The Disrupter." Remember that not everyone shares your enthusiasm for trying new things. Balance your drive for continual experimentation against the need others feel for consistency and careful planning. Exercise self-restraint, or else Linear Thinkers may see you as a loose cannon, and Individuals may experience your suggestions as interrupting their ability to concentrate.

➢ You are naturally gifted with the TEAMWORK and CREATIVITY tools. You can readily master the networking aspect of DISCOVERY. Developing CLARITY and PRIORITY may be your biggest challenge.

➢ It is easy for you to team up with Individual Intuitive Doers and Social Intuitive Thinkers. When solving problems with Individual Linear Doers, learn to appreciate their ability to concentrate and stay on task. Remember that many problems can only be solved with prolonged effort along a single path. When solving problems with Individual Linear Thinkers, learn to appreciate their ability to prepare thorough plans and enforce consistency. Your experimentation is valuable, but group problem-solving does require underlying organization. If everyone were as freewheeling as you, things could get pretty chaotic.

Individual Linear Doer

➤ At your best you are **"The Bulldog."** Using your natural inner ability to stay focused and achieve solid results, you pound through even the toughest problems. Nothing distracts you and nothing stops you. You are at your best when making good progress on the problem in front of you, and particularly enjoy the satisfaction of getting a problem solved and done with. Wasting time on lengthy discussions bores you. You thrive when focused on one problem at a time in a setting that allows you to stay on task. A favorite phrase: "Problem solved!"

➤ Beware of being seen as "The Fly on the Window." Remember that tenacity can be a great strength, but if you are on the wrong path to a solution, you can waste a lot time pounding your head against a dead end. Gain the perspective to notice when progress has stalled, and to step back and look for a better way. Communicate in an open and friendly manner, or else people who are Social may see you as hardheaded or aloof, and Intuitive Thinkers may perceive you as stubborn or closed-minded.

➤ You are naturally gifted with the DETERMINATION tool. You can readily master RESPONSE and the research aspect of DISCOVERY. Developing TEAMWORK and CREATIVITY may be your biggest challenge.

➤ It is easy for you to team up with Social Linear Doers and Individual Linear Thinkers. When solving problems with Social Intuitive Doers, learn to appreciate their flair for group experimentation even when it disrupts your work. If you follow some of their better suggestions, you can solve the problem better and faster. When solving problems with Social Intuitive Thinkers, learn to appreciate their skill at using group discussions to generate new ideas. Just wait until they finally agree on a plan and then make it happen.

INSIGHT

Social Linear Doer

➤ At your best you are **"The Captain."** Using your natural skills of organization and achievement, you get those around you working in unison to solve tough problems. You are at your best when helping diverse people move together toward a common goal. You particularly enjoy having the problem solved and done with. You thrive on working with others to produce real results in a structured environment, and get irritated when individuals either want to slow down for discussion or go off on their own tangents. A favorite phrase: "This way, everybody!"

➤ Beware of being seen as "The Lemming." Remember that just because everyone is moving in the same direction does not mean you are moving toward the best solution. Your ability to keep people working can become a negative if it prevents solid planning up front and periodically pausing to evaluate progress. Exercise some flexibility, or else Intuitive types may see you as being rigid, and Thinkers may perceive you as hasty or inefficient.

➤ You are naturally gifted with TEAMWORK, and DETERMINATION will be a particularly important and powerful tool for you. Developing CREATIVITY and CLARITY may be your biggest challenge.

➤ It is easy for you to team up with Individual Linear Doers and Social Linear Thinkers. When solving problems with Individual Intuitive Doers, learn to appreciate their ability to discover new ideas, even when their experimentation disrupts progress in the short run. If you incorporate their discoveries into the group effort, you will achieve better and faster results. When solving problems with Individual Intuitive Thinkers, learn to appreciate their off-the-wall ideas. Pick the ones that will really work, and get everyone using them right away.

Understanding the Personality Types: Two Problem-Solving Examples

Example 1, at work: You are told that production in your unit must be increased.

Individual Intuitive Thinker: You return to your workstation. As you gaze into space, you mentally explore what might be slowing you down and different ways to improve your output.

Social Intuitive Thinker: You get the unit together and say, "Let's put our heads together and figure out what's slowing us down and how we can increase production." You ask for ideas.

Individual Linear Thinker: You return to your work station and chart your unit's workflow from start to finish, looking for production bottlenecks. You draft a better step-by-step process.

Social Linear Thinker: You get the unit together and say, "Let's walk through our production process from start to finish, identify current bottlenecks, and build a more efficient process."

Individual Intuitive Doer: You return to your work station and start experimenting with different ways of doing your work, observing whether each approach results in improved production.

Social Intuitive Doer: You get the unit together and say, "Let's try out some new ways to get our work done faster." You all start experimenting together, and you observe the results.

Individual Linear Doer: You get right back to your work and start pounding out production faster than ever. You will meet the new production target even if it means working harder and longer.

Social Linear Doer: You get everyone together and announce, "We need to increase production. If we all boost production speed by 5% and work a little overtime, we can do it, and we will do it!"

Example 2, at home: You realize your house is messy and needs to be kept cleaner.

Individual Intuitive Thinker: You sit at the kitchen table and gaze out the window. You mentally explore reasons why the house gets messy and different ways to keep it cleaner.

Social Intuitive Thinker: You gather your family and say, "Let's put our heads together and figure out how why the house gets messy and how we can keep it cleaner." You encourage ideas.

Individual Linear Thinker: You sit at the kitchen table, list each cleaning task in each room of the house, and create a schedule of weekly cleaning assignments for each family member.

Social Linear Thinker: You gather your family and say, "We need to keep this house clean. Let's list each cleaning task and figure out who is going to do what."

Individual Intuitive Doer: Each time you clean the house, you experiment with different cleaning processes and methods to see what works the best.

Social Intuitive Doer: You encourage your family members to try new approaches to cleaning, and you experiment with different incentives to discourage them from making messes and to improve their participation in cleaning.

Individual Linear Doer: You resolve to clean more frequently and to work harder and faster when you do. You will do whatever it takes to keep the house clean.

Social Linear Doer: You gather the family and say, "Enough is enough. We will stop making messes and we will clean more regularly. Here is a list of the consequences for making messes and your new cleaning assignments."

GET THE MOST FROM YOUR PERSONALITY TYPE

Lead with your natural strengths. Have you noticed something that almost all successful people have in common? They concentrate on getting the most out of their strengths and don't waste much time worrying about their weaknesses. People are more likely to succeed when they do what they are naturally good at, which usually is also what they enjoy doing. So the first step in becoming a problem-solving expert is to identify which tools come naturally to you, get really good at using them, and rely on them as your go-to techniques for solving problems.

For example, if you are naturally Intuitive, check out the CREATIVITY tool for some great techniques that you can use to generate even bigger and better ideas. Thinkers will get good tips on performance improvement from CLARITY. If you are a Doer use DETERMINATION, and if you are Social review TEAMWORK. You get the idea. Become a true expert at using the tools with which you are most comfortable, and no matter what life throws your way you will have a solid problem-solving foundation you can rely on.

A surprising number of people never become experts with the tools that should come naturally to them because they have negative feelings about their own problem-solving personality type. These feelings can begin in childhood. For example, a Linear person raised in an Intuitive family may grow up perceiving herself as dull, while a Thinker raised in a family of Doers may be typecast as inefficient or even lazy. The other major cause of a bad problem-solving self-image is pursuing a career that is ill-suited to one's personality type. For example, an Individual person who enters a profession requiring continual interaction with team members or customers may end up seeing himself as awkward and inept, while an Intuitive person in a job requiring repetitive work and attention to detail may feel unreliable or even incompetent.

This is no way to go through life! Remember that every personality type is equally valuable and equally capable of solving challenging problems. Life is too short and too precious to spend it feeling bad because your natural gifts do not match your upbringing or your employment. You have to be comfortable in your own skin. Be proud of your personality type! Go ahead and tell people the kind of problem-solver you are. You can say, "One thing about me is that once I tackle a problem I never give up," or, "Explain the problem to me and I bet I'll have a couple of interesting ideas for you tomorrow." Feel good about who you are. And for goodness' sake don't ever apologize for being "uncreative" or "impractical" or whatever negative label someone may have planted in your mind. If there is some approach to solving problems that does not come easily to you, that just means there is some other approach for which you have a natural gift.

By identifying your personality type you have already gained increased awareness of your natural inclinations and abilities. Don't take them for granted! Top performers in any field, whether athletes, sales people, artists, doctors, or teachers, are never content to get by on their natural talent; they are those who continually work to improve their skills so they can achieve ever better results. Similarly, you can improve your natural problem-solving gifts by consciously practicing the specific insights and techniques in this book that will develop them to their fullest potential.

So gain a clear understanding of your natural problem-solving strengths, take pride in those strengths, and then concentrate on learning the insights and techniques that will make you a true expert in those areas.

Find a supportive environment. Don't try to fit your square peg into a round hole. In other words, don't spend your life in situations that are ill-suited to your problem-solving personality type. If you are highly Intuitive, don't pursue a career that rewards routine consistency rather than innovation. If you are a Thinker, don't spend your vacations caught up in nonstop action with a group of Doers. If you are strongly Social, don't work for a company that makes you spend hours figuring out a problem by yourself because if you take ten minutes getting a great solution from an experienced coworker you will get in trouble for "visiting during work hours."

If you are not a good fit with your current surroundings, whether at work, in your social life, or at home, you will not be as happy and successful as you could be. On some level, you will feel that you don't belong, you will feel misunderstood, and you will not perform as well as expected. Either the peg has to change or the hole has to change. Either you have to change who you are, or change the situation you are in.

In *Solution Power*, we will encourage you to *grow* as a problem-solver. We will urge you to *expand* the number of tools you are comfortable using. But we will never suggest you should abandon *who you fundamentally are.* You gotta be you! Trying to be someone you're not rarely succeeds. For example, Social Linear Doers who have a knack for leadership often become highly visible role models because of their natural ability to motivate others to achieve great solutions. However, an Individual Intuitive Thinker who tries to imitate that same approach to leadership will probably be uncomfortable and unconvincing in his attempt to be a "back slapper" and a "hard driver." He will only achieve maximum success if he has the self-awareness and confidence to use his own true strengths of innovative thinking and effective planning as his primary methods of problem-solving leadership.

If you feel you are stuck in a situation where *who you are* simply does not match *who you are expected to be*, then you have a problem. But that's fine, because you are reading a book about how to solve problems! You will either find a solution by using tools two through nine, or you will learn how to resolve the situation by using the tenth tool, RELEASE. In other words, you will either find a way to become comfortable and successful in your current situation, or you will learn the best way to leave it behind and move to an environment better suited to who you are.

So one big advantage of clearly understanding your problem-solving personality type is that it helps you make smart choices in your career and in your personal life. You can choose roles for yourself that allow you to achieve happiness and success by using your natural problem-solving strengths.

Appreciate and benefit from all the other personality types. While some people feel bad about their own problem-solving personality types, other people have the opposite difficulty. They think their approach to solving problems is the "right way" or the "only way" and they look down on those who take a different approach. People who think like this miss out on a lot of great opportunities.

You will definitely do better as a problem-solver if you can see the value of the other personality types. Don't fall into the trap of judging others negatively just because they think and act in ways that are unfamiliar to you. Some Intuitive Thinkers look down on Linear Doers as prosaic and dull, while some Linear Doers dismiss Intuitive Thinkers as unproductive and frivolous. Gaining better awareness and understanding is the surest cure for such unproductive prejudices. Familiarity with the different personality types reveals that each has its own different, but equally effective, approach to solving problems.

Most important, you will discover some personality types who are naturally good at using the tools that do not come easily to you. Realize that for different kinds of problems, different tools may be needed. You will come to understand that those who are most different from you are actually the most valuable to you, because their strengths are complementary to yours. If you are a truly confident person, you will seek to **make your opposites into your partners**, because as a team you will have the combined natural abilities to solve almost any problem. Forming such partnerships allows you to achieve a level of success in life and at work far beyond the reach of those who go it alone and reject approaches different than the ones they find familiar.

THE VALUE OF PROBLEM-SOLVING DIVERSITY

The insecure leader tends to hire people similar to himself, because he feels comfortable with them. They don't threaten his assumptions or his habitual ways of thinking and behaving.

However, the truly confident leader deliberately hires a variety of personality types, including those whose approach to problem-solving is different from his. These are the most successful leaders, because they assemble teams that combine diverse strengths, making them able to solve all types of problems.

I was once asked to interview for a position at a company whose leadership team consisted entirely of Doers. They assumed I was a Doer too, and by their comments they made it clear they had no patience with what they saw as the slow and indecisive behavior of Thinkers. Although I have learned many of the skills of the Doer, and can function as a Doer when I need to, I am still basically a Thinker by nature and knew I did not belong in that organization. I also knew their narrow approach would not serve them well.

Sure enough, over the next few years they stumbled from one crisis to another due to a lack of proper planning and analysis. Any organization needs a balanced team of Doers and Thinkers to get it done *and* get it done right.

-Reagan

Learn to use all ten tools. If you become an expert in using your natural strengths, create roles for yourself that suit your personality type, and seek partnerships with those whose natural strengths differ from yours, life will be good. But it can get even better! The final step is to keep adding more tools to your *Solution Power* toolbox until you achieve proficiency with all ten of them.

This is using your personality type as a foundation rather than as a limitation. A natural Thinker, for instance, who masters some of the problem-solving techniques of a Doer can solve a wider range of problems with extraordinary effectiveness.

ADOPTING NEW PROBLEM-SOLVING TOOLS

As a business leader I find it natural to use the Social approach to solving problems. Using tools like DISCOVERY and TEAMWORK to solve challenging problems at work helps foster a sense of participation, ownership, and group identity among my staff.

In my personal life I tend to act as an Individual. When I encounter a tough problem my instinct is to keep it private and deal with it on my own. Several years ago, though, I saw that a good friend of mine took a different approach. When he ran into a rough spot in life, he would talk about it with his friends. I saw that it gave him good emotional support and great ideas for how to handle the situation. I realized that his approach got better results than mine did, so I decided to try using it myself.

Since then, when I encounter a tough challenge or setback in my personal life, I remind myself to reach out to those I trust for advice and support. It still does not come naturally to me, but the more I do it the more it becomes a comfortable habit rather than a conscious effort. And my wonderful friends and family consistently provide me with warm encouragement and valuable suggestions.

-Reagan

In the fifth chapter you will learn to identify and tackle the highest-level problems, the ones you will gain the most from solving. Solving these high-level problems will require new and more powerful techniques, so you will naturally want to experiment with more tools. Learning to use all ten tools will give you the confidence to take on problems that may seem insurmountable to you now. As you master the tools you will transform problem-solving from a reactive method of escaping from trouble into a proactive process for building a rewarding life, and you will turn more and more problems into opportunities.

SEE PROBLEMS IN A POSITIVE LIGHT

Now that we have considered the different problem-solving personality types, we can see that different people relate to problems in very different ways. For example, a Doer may see a problem the way a running back in football sees a linebacker: as an obstacle he needs to get around or knock down in order to reach the goal line. But a Thinker may perceive the same problem as an archaeologist would view the ruins of an ancient city: as an intriguing mystery to solve.

However you relate to problems, the important thing is that you make the "relationship" a positive one. Seeing problems as frightening, irritating, or discouraging creates a negative state of mind that hinders effective problem-solving. The ideal relationship is to perceive problems as opportunities, as situations that you can turn to your advantage. This allows you to solve them more quickly and easily, and with the best possible outcome.

SEE PROBLEMS AS NECESSARY AND VALUABLE

Recall, from the Introduction, the definition of a problem: *a problem is when you want something you don't have.*

All people have wants. You might want:

- A million dollars
- Warm clothing for your children
- To perform at the Grand Ole Opry
- True love
- To grow the biggest vegetables in town
- Peace and harmony throughout the world
- Another cookie

Even a humble servant of God, who has devoted her life to helping the poor and who wants little in the way of material possessions or personal comfort, has a deep desire to provide for the needs of those who are suffering most. It follows, then, that **to live is to want, and to want is to have problems.**

This link between wanting something and having a problem can cause anxiety. Some people have a fearful relationship with problems, perceiving them as dangerous and threatening. Other people are not necessarily afraid of problems, but they see them as unpleasant, as an annoyance or bother that should be avoided. In either case, these people instinctively realize that problems arise from wants, and all too often they seek to have fewer problems by *wanting less.*

This is a classic case of the medicine being worse than the disease. For example, if you want a million dollars and you don't have it, then you have quite a challenging problem. The easiest way to solve it is to simply decide you do not really want that much money after all. But if you make that choice, then you are never going to get a million dollars! Eliminating the desire for something that you really want should be your *last* resort for dealing with the problem, not your *first*.

If you are not money-oriented, replace the "million dollars" in this example with some other major "want" that you find highly desirable. It might be sending your children to a top-ranked college, becoming a scratch golfer, achieving a closer relationship with God, or running in the Boston Marathon. The point is, if you followed the strategy of avoiding big problems by deciding to *want less* then you would be guaranteed to never get any of these wonderful things. You would end up living a small and timid life. In order to experience a robust and fulfilling life you have to want big things that you don't have, and that means you will have to challenge yourself with solving the problem of how to get them.

Consider the following examples of people who achieve fulfillment by tackling tough problems:
- The entrepreneur who eagerly takes on the multitude of problems that come with starting and running a new business, not only for the potential financial rewards but also from the spirit of adventure and personal satisfaction.
- Everyone who embraces parenthood, choosing the endlessly complex and demanding problems of raising children over the relative simplicity of considering only their own needs.
- The rock climber who finds joy and fulfillment in an activity that consists of solving one difficult and dangerous problem after another, and who continually seeks out challenges of increasing intensity.
- The artist who struggles each day with the mysterious and subtle problems of creating meaning and beauty.
- The business executive who builds a career by advancing into positions with ever greater responsibility for solving ever tougher problems, and who accepts a position as CEO of a struggling company for the sheer challenge of turning it around.

For example, when Henry Ford first got started he had a huge problem. He wanted every working person in America to be able to own an automobile, and at that time only a small number of very wealthy people could afford them. In addition, he had no factory, no workforce, and very little capital. What an enormous problem! What is interesting, of course, is that it was entirely voluntary. He created this tough problem for himself by choosing to want something really big. As he contemplated the enormity of this challenge, he could easily have solved it at a personal level simply by deciding he didn't want to do it after all. But then he would have lived a small and timid life. Instead, he tackled the problem, became incredibly successful, and forever changed the world.

This does *not* mean that *all* problems are good or that you should just run around getting mixed up in as much trouble as possible. It is important to recognize which desires are most important to you: the achievements, experiences, and possessions that will give you true fulfillment in life. These are the "wants" you should never surrender just to avoid the difficulties you may encounter in seeking to attain them. The FOCUS and PRIORITY tools provide an effective process for identifying and pursuing these high-value goals. They will also help you identify which of your current wants are *not* truly important to you. Setting aside these low-priority wants will allow you to dedicate your problem-solving time and effort more effectively. The RELEASE tool provides techniques for letting go of these time-wasting problems before you get too tangled up in them.

The goal is to recognize and avoid *unnecessary* problems, and to recognize and pursue *valuable* problems. Valuable problems arise naturally from growth; they are signs of progress. As long as you keep pushing yourself to accomplish more, to learn more, to have more, to see more, and to grow more, you will encounter an endless series of challenging problems. And that's great!

Consider what it would be like to have a life with no problems, particularly the biggest, toughest problems most of us face:

- Learning how to walk, talk, and ride a bicycle
- Handling the fear of your first day of school, and of having to make new friends
- Learning math, spelling, and how to draw a cat that your teacher can actually recognize as a cat
- Dealing with the perils of teenage romance

- Facing the fear of leaving home and living life on your own
- Choosing a spouse, and building a successful marriage
- Learning to be a good and loving parent
- Getting a job, and learning to do it well

Stop for a moment and imagine a life without these challenging problems. Read the list over again, and picture a life in which most of these problems are avoided. Would anyone choose such a life? Of course not! Solving problems like these is a necessary part of the human experience. In fact, **facing and solving big problems is a vital part of a worthwhile life.** Make a commitment to yourself to never diminish your aspirations just to avoid a tough problem.

SEE PROBLEMS AS OPPORTUNITIES

Is there any difference between a problem and an opportunity? Perhaps just this: **a problem becomes an opportunity the moment you decide to turn it to your advantage.** This does not require any change in the outside world; it happens entirely within your own mind. All it takes to turn any problem into an opportunity is to stop complaining about it or idly wishing it would go away, and instead start figuring out how to get the most out of solving it. In the space of a heartbeat you will now be pursuing an opportunity. This will allow you to solve the problem more quickly and easily, and with the best possible outcome.

Many people will doubt this statement. You can probably think of a few problems that are so dreadful it would seem shocking or inappropriate to label them opportunities. However, the vast majority of the problems we encounter can readily be seen and treated as opportunities. This applies even to some very serious problems, such as:

- Getting fired or laid off
- Suffering a terrible disappointment
- Getting divorced

If you think about it you can probably bring to mind any number of cases in which people have looked back on events like these and said, "That was the best thing that ever happened to me." People have turned being fired into an opportunity to start their own company, go back to school, or pursue the career of their dreams. People have turned the pain of disappointment into an opportunity to gain the strength and maturity that enabled them to go on to build a great life. If some people had never suffered through a painful divorce, they might still be trapped in an unhealthy relationship and would have lost the opportunity to blossom and fulfill themselves as individuals. **It is all a matter of how you perceive the problem and react to it.** It can become a permanent, painful scar or it can become an exciting opportunity that opens new doors in your life.

But what about those rare and terrible problems that seem to have no positive side at all? The truth is that there are people who have treated even the most terrible calamities as opportunities. Remarkable people have been able to treat profound problems like becoming paralyzed, experiencing the death of a loved one, or being a prisoner of war as opportunities for growth, insight, and achievement. This does not diminish the enormity of these terribly painful and unimaginably difficult experiences. Instead, it shows the incredible resilience of the human spirit. Does that mean you would ever *choose* to experience such a thing? Of course not. Can everyone react so positively to such a calamity? Probably not. But the fact that some admirable individuals have been able to do so teaches us that we can certainly choose to see the everyday problems of our own lives as opportunities rather than as unmitigated disasters.

This does not imply that you can turn all of your problems into happy, fun-filled experiences. Sometimes problems really stink. Here are some examples of stinky problems:

- Your computer crashes, and you realize you just lost several hours of unsaved work.
- You come down with the flu when you have lots of important work that really needs to get done at the office.
- Your car breaks down. This is especially stinky if you are far from home, it's the middle of the night, and it's pouring rain.

Even if you have a great attitude toward problems, none of these situations is likely to make you break out in a smile. But you will at least be able to keep them in perspective by adopting the attitude, "It's not the end of the world." After all, getting upset and bent out of shape would just make the experience worse. And even though you may not be able to see them as delightful opportunities, you can at least look for a way to get *something* positive out of them. For example:

- When you redo the lost work, you may be able to do it a bit better.
- When you get the flu, you could put a reminder in your calendar to get a flu shot next year, and you might learn that your office does not actually fall apart when you miss a couple of days.
- When your car breaks down you could learn the importance of regular automotive maintenance, or maybe the lousy experience will finally push you to find a better-paying job so you can buy a new car.

You get the idea: the problem still stinks, but at least you make some progress as a result of solving it.

If you can't see anything else positive about a problem, you can always tell yourself, "Well, here is an opportunity for me to grow stronger as an individual." If nothing else, simply surviving the problem will teach you how resilient you are, giving you greater confidence. As Nietzsche said, "What does not destroy me, makes me stronger." That thought might not make the problem more fun, but it can give you a sense of self-assurance and determination that will make it more bearable.

SOMETIMES PROBLEMS STINK, AND THAT'S OKAY

At one time I was in-house legal counsel for an insurance organization. Each week I would meet with the outside attorneys who represented us in litigation. Our lead litigation attorney was an excellent lawyer and also had a great sense of humor. One week, as we started discussing the first case on the agenda, he smiled grimly and said, "I have to tell you, we have a great big stinking dangerous problem in this case." I had recently attended a rather dopey feel-good seminar on the power of positive thinking, so I interrupted him, saying, with mock sincerity, "Wait, you have to remember that there are no such things as problems, there are only opportunities to learn." He thought about that for a moment and replied, "Well then, we have a great big stinking dangerous opportunity to learn."

That just cracked me up. After that, whenever we ran into a really tough problem, we would say, "Uh-oh, looks like we've got an 'opportunity to learn' on our hands."

-Reagan

However, many problems truly can be turned to your advantage, leaving you better off than you were before the problem arose. You just have to develop the habit of looking for the opportunity that is hidden within whatever problem you are facing. This is discussed in greater detail in the FOCUS chapter. For now, start using this simple technique: whenever you feel apprehensive about tackling a problem, or you begin to despair during the solution-finding process, take a moment and complete the following statement: "This is a great opportunity to ____." Say it out loud, and complete the sentence by sincerely stating a positive advantage you will gain from the experience. Don't be cynical or sarcastic. No matter how bleak a problem seems, just spending a few moments identifying how you can turn it to your advantage will give you a boost of energy, motivation, and sense of direction.

> **SEEING PROBLEMS AS OPPORTUNITIES**
>
> I had been working as in-house legal counsel for an insurance organization for about two years, when, much to my surprise, I was offered a promotion to Chief Operating Officer, the number two executive position in the company. Since I knew nothing about business leadership and had spent all my adult life learning the craft of a lawyer, moving out of law and into management would take me well outside my comfort zone. The situation felt like a problem, but my instincts told me this was a rare opportunity for personal and professional growth, so I accepted.
>
> At first it was a struggle, but a key insight proved to be the turning point in mastering my new role: as legal counsel, my job had been to spot risks and advise the organization on how to *avoid* them, but as Chief Operating Officer, my job was to spot risks and lead the company in *pursuing* them. **Leaders must learn to see that some risks are opportunities to be pursued rather than hazards to be avoided.** Of course, you must also develop the ability to identify which risks are the most promising ones to pursue, because some are better opportunities than others!
>
> -Reagan

You can reinforce your self-identity as someone who treats problems as opportunities and is good at solving them simply by telling other people that is who you are. You can say, at work or to your friends, "I like to solve problems, come to me if you ever want help." One of the surprising things about life is that people usually believe what you tell them about yourself. Another surprising thing is that *you* will usually end up believing what you tell people about yourself! Simply telling people that you are happy to tackle tough problems and are good at solving them will go a long way toward making it true. Begin looking around for problem-solving opportunities, instead of just waiting for them to pop up.

CREATE WIN/WIN SOLUTIONS

A healthy attitude toward problems is easier to attain when you adopt a generous, rather than a selfish, approach. Look for solutions that benefit everyone affected by the problem. Too many people see life as a win/lose proposition, meaning that in order for them to win someone else has to lose. They believe that all the good things in life – such as love, wealth, security, joy, and pleasure – are in limited supply, and that for their share to get bigger, someone else's share has to get smaller. People who take this approach to solving problems look for solutions that put them ahead of other people, whether by making themselves better off or by making other people worse off. These people live their lives in an atmosphere of competitive tension, surrounded by people who will seize any chance to turn the tables on them and make them the loser.

Why make life so hard for yourself? Adopt the win/win approach to living. People who think win/win realize something the win/lose thinkers never understand: there is no limit to the good things in life, and if we work together we can all have more than each of us can ever get by striving alone. People who adopt this approach spend their lives in a zone of generosity, surrounded by people who will help them win in every situation. This is particularly useful when you are using the problem-solving tools DISCOVERY and TEAMWORK. So whenever you are tackling a problem, solve it for as many people as possible.

CONCLUSION

You are already a problem-solver, perhaps a very effective one. But as with any other skill, problem-solving can be strengthened and developed. Since succeeding in life depends so much on successfully solving problems, you should develop your natural talents to their greatest possible extent.

To a large degree, your ability to solve problems depends on your attitude toward them. Dwelling on past failures, current difficulties, or future calamities only breeds pessimism and anxiety. Focusing on past accomplishments, current opportunities, and future successes generates optimism and energy.

Insight: Summary

Your Problem-Solving Personality Type

- **Discover your personality type.** Identify your natural strengths and learn what you can do to become an even more effective problem-solver.
- **Get the most from your personality type.** Rely on and improve your natural strengths, create an environment that is compatible with who you are, appreciate the other personality types, and learn to use all ten tools.

See Problems in a Positive Light

- **See problems as necessary and valuable.** Recognize and avoid unnecessary problems; recognize and pursue fulfilling problems.
- **See problems as opportunities.** A problem becomes an opportunity the moment you decide to turn it to your advantage. People have found ways to turn even terrible calamities into opportunities.
- **Create win/win solutions.** Look for solutions that benefit everyone affected by a problem. Seek to increase everyone's share of the good things in life rather than simply dividing the current supply.

THE SECOND TOOL

RESPONSE

ACT WITH STRENGTH

We have seen that there are a number of different problem-solving personality types. We have also seen that problems can be perceived in a number of different ways, such as irritants, opportunities, threats, challenges, or calamities. So it is no surprise that when a problem arises people respond in many different ways, such as analyzing the problem logically, trying to ignore it, tackling it with enthusiasm, flying into a rage about it, or running away from it.

We call these reactions problem-solving RESPONSES. There are four types of RESPONSES, each of which consists of a physical reaction combined with an emotional reaction. Becoming aware of how you habitually respond to problems, and consciously developing new and better habits for how you do so, will make encountering problems less unpleasant and upsetting, and allow you to solve them more effectively.

Physical Reactions

People's physical reactions to problems can be categorized into two types:

- **Active.** An Active reaction is characterized by more physical movement, and by movement that is rapid and energetic.
- **Still.** A Still reaction is characterized by less physical movement, and by movement that is slower and more measured.

One is not necessarily better than the other. For example, suppose two people face a sudden crisis. One of them panics, becoming highly agitated, unable to direct his thoughts or control his feelings, and takes off running. The other one leaps energetically and enthusiastically into action, tackling the problem vigorously and bringing the situation under control. These are both Active reactions.

Now suppose two other people are confronted with a serious problem. One of them reacts by becoming paralyzed with fear, frozen in place and unable to think coherently. The other stays calm and collected, analyzes the problem accurately, and develops an effective solution. These are both Still reactions.

These examples demonstrate that either type of physical reaction can be effective or ineffective for solving problems. It depends on what emotion is generating the physical reaction. For example, a feeling of fear can generate an ineffective Active reaction of fleeing or an ineffective Still reaction of paralysis. On the other hand, a feeling of confidence can generate an effective Active reaction of enthusiastic energy or an effective Still reaction of serene concentration.

Since it is the emotional aspect of a RESPONSE that determines whether a physical reaction will be productive or counterproductive, let's take a closer look at the emotional reactions.

EMOTIONAL REACTIONS

For the purpose of problem-solving, emotions can be categorized as either Strong or Weak. The Strong emotions are those that give us the most help in solving problems, while the Weak emotions are less helpful, or even get in the way. These labels refer to how *useful* the emotions are, not to how *intense* they feel. For example, we can experience "strong" sensations of fear, anger, or despair, but the *Solution Power* system places these emotions in the Weak category because they are relatively ineffective for solving problems.

Strong Emotions
- **Confidence:** Courage, Decisiveness, Assertiveness
- **Curiosity:** Interest, Wonder, Adventurousness
- **Determination:** Commitment, Perseverance, Tenacity
- **Optimism:** Faith, Hope, Trust
- **Desire:** Motivation, Ambition, Aspiration
- **Love**: Affection, Friendliness, Empathy
- **Worthiness:** Pride, Self-respect, Honor
- **Serenity:** Patience, Composure, Acceptance
- **Generosity:** Forgiveness, Thoughtfulness, Benevolence
- **Happiness:** Joy, Gratitude, Cheerfulness
- **Enthusiasm:** Passion, Excitement, Inspiration

Weak Emotions
- **Fear:** Panic, Anxiety, Timidity
- **Pessimism:** Despair, Cynicism, Suspicion
- **Anger:** Hostility, Malice, Aggression
- **Inadequacy:** Insecurity, Neediness, Submissiveness
- **Sadness:** Grief, Disappointment, Bitterness
- **Frustration:** Futility, Ineffectiveness, Irritation
- **Selfishness:** Greed, Jealousy, Possessiveness
- **Regret:** Guilt, Shame, Sorrow
- **Apathy:** Laziness, Indifference, Uninterest

There are many ways in which Strong emotions are more useful than Weak emotions for solving problems. We will review these in detail, but first let's see how the physical and emotional reactions combine to form the four problem-solving RESPONSES.

THE *SOLUTION POWER* PROBLEM-SOLVING RESPONSES

		PHYSICAL REACTION	
		Active	Still
EMOTIONAL REACTION	Strong	**Strong & Active**	**Strong & Still**
	Weak	**Weak & Active**	**Weak & Still**

Here are descriptions of the four RESPONSES, with examples of each:

STRONG & ACTIVE

With this RESPONSE problems are solved quickly and effectively through energetic action.

- A Strong & Active RESPONSE can be **dynamic and forceful**. Emotions like passion, decisiveness, aspiration, and assertiveness can produce this energized, take-charge, results-oriented approach. This is particularly useful for getting a lot of problems solved in a hurry, or for tackling a tough problem that might otherwise seem intimidating. This expansive, outward-focused approach can also provide inspiration and a sense of direction for those around you.

- Another version of the Strong & Active response is **exuberant and playful**. Emotions like enthusiasm, happiness, joy, adventurousness, and excitement create a mindset of exploration and experimentation. This approach makes problem-solving enjoyable and entertaining, turning work into recreation. It also generates a warm and inviting atmosphere that encourages communication and cooperation.

- Strong & Active can also take the form of **relentless and unswerving** drive. Emotions like desire, commitment, motivation, and tenacity can generate this state of unstoppable individual achievement. This is an ideal state for problems that will require prolonged, energetic effort, especially when you must solve problems without assistance from others. It is particularly effective when facing the most challenging or threatening problem situations.

Doers usually find that Strong & Active RESPONSES come naturally to them, while Thinkers frequently discover that experimenting with these RESPONSES leads to significant improvement in solution-finding success.

Strong & Still

With this RESPONSE, problems are solved thoroughly and efficiently through focused, measured effort.

- A Strong & Still RESPONSE can take the form of an **intellectual and analytical** state of mind. Emotions like curiosity, interest, patience, and perseverance produce this calm, thoughtful approach. This is particularly useful for understanding complex problems clearly and solving them thoroughly. It is often associated with solving technical, scientific, or mathematical problems, but it can also be used effectively for problems requiring creative breakthroughs and inspired innovation.

- Another version of Strong & Still is **meditative and spiritual**. Emotions like serenity, gratitude, love, thoughtfulness, and acceptance help create a state of internal focus, balance, and harmony that taps into the intuitive power of the subconscious mind. This also generates an openness to others that facilitates understanding and empathy, leading to improved communication and effective teamwork.

- Strong & Still can also mean being **firm and resolute**. Emotions like determination, confidence, pride, ambition, and perseverance can generate this state of unshakable inner strength. This is an ideal state for problems that require prolonged attention and effort, especially when solving the problem will require facing opposition and adversity. It also provides self-sufficiency and discipline you'll need for situations in which you must solve problems on your own.

Thinkers often use Strong & Still RESPONSES such as these by nature, while Doers frequently discover that by adding these RESPONSES they greatly expand their problem-solving options.

Weak & Active

This RESPONSE produces a lot of activity, but the activity is ineffective or counterproductive, so the problem does not get solved or does not get solved very well.

- One version of the Weak & Active RESPONSE is driven by fear, in which a person's self-control is overwhelmed by a powerful impulse to run away. All animals share an instinct, when faced with a threat, to either fight, flee, or freeze. This is the "flee" reaction. Of course, it makes sense to flee from a problem that poses an immediate threat, such as a fire. However, people who lack effective habits for coping with problems often try to "run away" from problems as a form of avoidance.

- Another variation of Weak & Active is the "fight" reaction. The emotion that generates this reaction is hostility. Instead of running away from a perceived threat, the person goes on the offensive, lashing out at the problem. The role of hostility in problem-solving is discussed later in this chapter.

- A Weak & Active RESPONSE can also take the form of agitation, in which people "throw a fit," "make a scene," or "have a cow" when faced with a problem. This kind of tantrum behavior may be the most common version of the Weak & Active RESPONSE. It seems to arise from a combination of emotions such as anxiety, inadequacy, irritation, laziness, hostility, and doubt. A person may react this way to a problem that seems pointless and unnecessary, or that he simply does not want to deal with. It is also common among people who have not developed skills for coping effectively with problems.

When a Doer reacts to a problem with a Weak emotion, a Weak & Active RESPONSE often results.

Weak & Still

With this RESPONSE problems are not solved, or are not solved very well, due to a lack of effective action.

- A Weak & Still RESPONSE can take the form of the "freeze" reaction from the instinct to fight, flee, or freeze. When overpowering feelings of anger, panic, suspicion, or fear are turned inward, the result is paralysis. This reaction causes people to become frozen in a state of emotional tension that clouds their thinking and prevents productive action.

- Another version of the Weak & Still RESPONSE occurs when emotions like apathy, laziness, futility, or sadness lead to an absence of direction, energy, and motivation. A person may respond this way to a problem that seems unimportant or uninteresting to him, or to a problem he believes is beyond his ability to solve. People also respond this way to problems during times when they are depressed or lack compelling goals.

- Weak & Still can also be characterized by insecurity or uncertainty. This variation arises from emotions like timidity, inadequacy, neediness, or submissiveness. People may respond this way to unfamiliar problems, or problems they lack the skill and knowledge to tackle with confidence. People also respond this way when they are unsure of themselves or are emotionally dependent on others. Problems cause them to feel jittery and anxious, making it difficult for them to concentrate on solutions. They prefer to stick with what is familiar and avoid trying anything new, making it harder for them to replace unhealthy habits with healthier ones.

When a Thinker reacts to a problem with a Weak emotion, a Weak & Still RESPONSE often results.

Advantages of The Strong Responses

Focus

Weak emotions keep you focused on having problems. Strong emotions help you focus on finding solutions.

Let's do an experiment. Choose a problem you are currently facing. Perhaps you are unhappy with your health or your physical fitness. Maybe you have a problem at work, in your marriage, or with your children. Perhaps there is a problem in your community that you care deeply about. Maybe you have financial woes.

Now direct your attention at what it feels like to have that problem. Think about how unpleasant, inconvenient, or unfair it is, and how much worse it might get. Consider who is at fault for causing the problem, and whom it is hurting. Focus on *having* the problem, not on any potential solution. Really get into it; don't keep it at a distance.

As you concentrate on the problem, become aware of the emotions you feel. You will probably experience several different emotions as various aspects of the problem cross your mind. Don't judge or control the emotions, just notice them and remember them, or better yet, write them down. Close the book now and spend a few minutes on this exercise.

That wasn't much fun, was it? It might be a good idea to take a moment and get that experience out of your system before continuing. Stand up and walk around a bit, straighten your back and stretch, take some nice slow, deep breaths, and think about something pleasant. Here's a happy thought: after reading this book, you will experience those emotions much less frequently!

Refer back to the list of Strong emotions. Notice that the emotions you felt while focusing on the problem are not on that list.

Now look at the list of Weak emotions. This is where you will find the emotions you felt. You might have written "nervous" instead of "anxiety," or "depressed" instead of "sadness," or "furious" instead of "anger" but the feelings are the same. We can see that **focusing on having a problem generates Weak emotions.**

Time for the enjoyable part of the exercise! Use the same problem, but this time don't dwell on *having* the problem. This time envision *getting it solved.* Start thinking about different things you could do to solve the problem. Then visualize yourself putting those solutions into action and making good progress. Finally, picture yourself successfully solving the problem. Don't worry about "being realistic," just imagine how it would feel to have the problem completely solved. You are in fabulous physical shape, your kids are all happy and successful, and your spouse is loving and considerate. Or you have received a great promotion, you are debt-free, and your business is running at a 50% net profit. Or the poor in your community are being fed and housed, the schools are being improved, and the parks are getting cleaned up. Imagine it as vividly as you can. Again, take note of the emotions you feel. Close the book now and spend a few minutes on this exercise.

Wasn't that a wonderful experience! Turn again to the list of Strong emotions. Did this exercise give you courage or hope? Did you get a sense of adventure or motivation? Did you feel the warmth of love or forgiveness? Perhaps you experienced joy, serenity, or a sense of pride. Or maybe your vision of success gave you renewed enthusiasm or determination. Whichever particular feelings you experienced, we can see that **focusing on solutions generates Strong emotions.**

You may have felt some Weak emotions when you first started focusing on solving the problem. It is natural to experience Weak emotions when you are about to tackle a tough problem. You might start out feeling anxious, angry, frustrated, sad, or irritated. But as you focus less on having the problem and more on finding a solution, the Weak emotions fade and are replaced with Strong emotions.

You experienced all of these emotions because there is a strong link between where you focus your attention and how you feel. This link operates at a subconscious level and it works in both directions: when you focus on solutions, you tend to feel Strong emotions, so **when you feel Strong emotions, you tend to focus on solutions.** Later in this chapter we will provide specific techniques for generating Strong emotions.

Let's take a look at how this linkage works in daily life. First, think of people you know who are habitually anxious, angry, pessimistic, sad, selfish, or lazy. Have you noticed that when these people have a problem, it is difficult to get them interested in possible solutions? Instead, they dwell on the problem itself, making themselves even more anxious, angry, pessimistic, and so forth. Now, think of people who are habitually confident, optimistic, motivated, happy, enthusiastic, or determined. When these people encounter a problem, they start looking for a solution almost immediately. Can you imagine a truly confident, optimistic, and motivated person sitting around dwelling on her problems? It just doesn't happen. Not only do Strong emotions naturally direct us toward finding solutions, they also guide us toward creating the kind of lives that we want for ourselves.

When you imagine your ideal future, do you imagine yourself feeling insecure, disappointed, angry, apathetic, and anxious? Of course not! We all aspire to create lives in which we enjoy Strong emotions like enthusiasm, pride, serenity, joy, love, and confidence. So why not start living that life *right now*. Learning to react to problems with Strong emotions immediately starts turning your envisioned future into reality.

Personal and Professional Growth

People who use Weak emotions to solve problems limit their growth as problem-solvers. Strong emotions help you learn new problem-solving skills and ideas.

Weak emotions cause people to resist change and close their minds to new ideas. For example, when people are angry they often refuse to listen to suggestions or opinions from others? It is hard for them to learn anything while they are angry, because they are intent on expressing their hostility *toward* others, rather than receiving new information or ideas *from* others. In fact, the moment they start to consider new facts or open their minds to a different perspective, their anger starts to fade away.

When a Weak emotion has its grip on you, it doesn't want to let go. When you are angry, that powerful feeling of anger wants to continue. The same is true for emotions like panic, despair, and indifference. Even though these are unpleasant emotions, it is hard to give them up when they have you under their spell. On some level, you know that opening your mind to a different way of thinking and feeling could replace panic with serenity, despair with hope, and indifference with enthusiasm. Perversely, from the depths of the Weak emotion, you don't want this to happen! So you keep yourself closed off from any facts or ideas that might change your state of mind.

As was noted previously, people who habitually react with Weak emotions tend to focus on having problems and resist focusing on finding solutions. They also tend to focus on their own individual thoughts and feelings. Think again about people you know who are habitually anxious, angry, pessimistic, sad, selfish, or lazy. Have you noticed that these people tend to resist anything you say that might help them see things in a more positive light? They often lack curiosity, and have little enthusiasm for learning in general. On the other hand, people you know who are habitually confident, optimistic, motivated, happy, enthusiastic, or adventurous are almost certainly interested in learning new things and open to considering different points of view. One of the great advantages of Strong emotions is that they naturally encourage us to continue to learn and grow. The more new ideas and skills we learn the better problem-solvers we become.

Ending Procrastination

Weak emotions feed a cycle of procrastination. Strong emotions break the cycle.

Weak emotional reactions often cause people to avoid dealing with problems promptly. This, of course, is procrastination. As any procrastinator knows, most problems do not go away on their own. They eventually reach crisis stage, causing unpleasant consequences for the procrastinator. Why don't these unpleasant experiences break the habit? In part it is because procrastination provides certain "rewards" that reinforce the cycle of behavior:

- In the short run, procrastinating allows the person to avoid thinking about and dealing with what he perceives to be an unpleasant problem.

- Sometimes he gets bailed out by others. When they see that important work is not getting done, or that the procrastinator is heading for trouble, his coworkers, friends, parents, spouses, and others may step in and solve the problem. The procrastinator feels that he has benefited by having the problem solved with little effort on his part.

- Sometimes a problem simply disappears by chance before the procrastinator has to deal with it. This further teaches the procrastinator not to solve problems promptly, because he has avoided expending the effort that would have gone into solving the problem in a timely manner. Even if this only happens one time out of ten, it still stands out in the procrastinator's memory because of the relief he feels when a problem miraculously vanishes.

- Delaying the problem-solving process relieves the procrastinator of having to consider multiple possible solutions. Many potential solutions, particularly the ones that require advance preparation, become impossible as time passes. To the procrastinator, this simplifies the situation. He will use the only option still available when time is running out, even if it is a lousy one. He may actually feel rewarded by not having to investigate and choose among a number of good alternatives.

- Problems that are not solved by others or which do not go away on their own inevitably reach a crisis point, and the procrastinator often feels a sense of panic as a result. This panic translates into a powerful sense of urgency – a big "push" – that energizes and motivates the procrastinator to finally solve the problem. Reliance on this negative motivation relieves him of the responsibility to develop self-motivation and time-management skills.

- When the crisis is finally over the procrastinator experiences a great sense of relief. He learns that *facing his problems* feels terrible, but that *solving his problems in a last minute crisis* leads to great relief. He is now fully primed to repeat the cycle the next time he encounters a problem.

Procrastination has many disadvantages as a problem-solving technique:

- Failure is a lot more likely. Fewer problems get solved, and they often don't get solved very well.
- Although other people may, at least for a time, step in and solve problems for the procrastinator, they will eventually get tired of bailing him out. This can strain his personal and workplace relationships, as friends, relatives, and co-workers start to distance themselves from the procrastinator and his endless series of crises.
- When others do bail out the procrastinator by solving a problem for him, it makes him even more dependent on them to solve his problems.
- Since the procrastinator's last-minute solutions are often temporary fixes, the same problems are likely to return again and again.
- The procrastinator is likely to get hooked on the adrenaline rush of performing under last-minute pressure, becoming dependent on it as a source of motivation. This causes him to bounce from crisis to crisis with little progress in between. As his dependence on "motivation by crisis" increases, he finds it harder and harder to solve problems in a timely manner.
- The procrastinator ends up caught in the rat race, living reactively rather than proactively. Solving any particular problem is usually just a return to zero, relieving some immediate stress but not achieving real progress.

Procrastinators often feel intensely unpleasant Weak emotions like panic, regret, guilt, shame, frustration, and inadequacy. They may try to overcome the habit by heaping blame and abuse on themselves, and vowing to never be so stupid again. However, as every procrastinator knows, this does not help. If indulging in self-recrimination could break the cycle, there would be no procrastination, because procrastinators do plenty of that already.

Any successful strategy for overcoming procrastination must be based on Strong emotions. Replacing Weak emotions with Strong ones like confidence, motivation, forgiveness, serenity, and enthusiasm counteract the impulse to procrastinate. Later in this chapter we will discuss techniques you can use to successfully make the transition from Weak to Strong. If procrastination is an issue for you, try using these techniques to generate a Strong RESPONSE the next time you find yourself tempted to ignore an important problem or postpone tackling it.

SELF CONTROL

People who use Weak emotions are governed by outdated instinctive reactions. Strong emotions keep *you* in charge.

Any problem can feel like a threat. It might pose a threat of suffering physical pain or a threat of experiencing emotional pain like disappointment or grief. It could pose a threat that you will lose something of value or that you will not get something that you wanted. Even a technical or procedural problem at work carries the threat that you might experience the unpleasant sensation of failure or face the disapproval of your supervisor.

As was mentioned earlier, we have powerful ancient instincts for how to react when faced with a threat: fight, flee, or freeze. These are the same instinctive reactions that drive the behavior of wild animals when they are threatened. Have you ever been walking through a field when a rabbit suddenly bursts out of hiding and races away? The animal had perceived your approach as a threat, and at first locked itself into the "freeze" reaction, instinctively seeking to hide. As you got closer the rabbit's tension steadily increased, until it grew unbearable and activated the "flee" reaction. And if you could have somehow chased the poor creature down and cornered it, you might even have ended up bitten or scratched as it finally resorted to the "fight" reaction.

We humans are programmed to follow these same reactions because they were useful for solving the kinds of problems that humans encountered in the distant past when our instincts were developing. Those problems were often sudden and simple, and could be solved through immediate action. For example, when one of our ancestors confronted a problem in the form of a hungry cave bear, these instinctive reactions could help him hide by locking him into complete immobility, give him a boost of adrenaline so he could run away at maximum speed, or embolden him to attack it in defense of his clan.

However, in our modern culture we rarely encounter hungry cave bears. Our problems are more likely to be sustained and complex, rather than sudden and simple. For most modern problems the fight, flee, or freeze reactions are simply not effective solutions. You cannot effectively hide from, run away from, or attack and destroy problems like a heavy workload at your job, communication issues with your spouse, or a leaky kitchen faucet. In fact, attempting to use any of these solutions for such problems is likely to make the situation even worse.

But many people are still dominated by these ancient instinctive reactions. For people who habitually react with Weak emotions like fear, pessimism, insecurity, or anxiety even small problems can feel like threats. Because these Weak emotional reactions focus on and magnify the threatening aspects of problems, they trigger the impulse to fight, flee, or freeze. These people end up being controlled by their circumstances because these powerful instincts overwhelm their ability to consciously choose how they will respond to problems.

SOLUTION POWER

> **STRONG RESPONSE HABITS AND SELF-CONTROL**
>
> During my freshman year of college there was a fire in my dormitory. I was sound asleep, but when the fire alarm went off, all the safety training that had been drilled into me during the previous twelve years of school immediately kicked in. I rolled out of bed onto my hands and knees, then scooted over to the door and pressed my hand against it. It did not feel hot, so I opened it slightly. Thick smoke billowed in along the ceiling. But, just like in the fire safety movies, there was a layer of clear air that extended about two feet above the floor.
>
> I opened the door and crawled through the common area toward the stairway. I was the only one crawling! I saw running legs flying by, and heard shouting and screaming through the blanket of smoke above me. The other students were dashing around in a blind panic, ramming into walls, furniture, and each other. Some even fell over, landed in the layer of clear air, and then immediately jumped to their feet and resumed running around in the smoke!
>
> When I reached the stairway, I stopped and repeatedly shouted, "Drop to the floor and crawl toward my voice." Finally, one fellow dropped to his hands and knees and zoomed past me like a caffeine-crazed crab. At that point the firefighters arrived, and I left the building. Fortunately, although some students were hospitalized, no one died.
>
> In retrospect, I realized that the other students could not control their instinctive impulse to "flee" because they had not developed behavioral habits in advance for coping with the unfamiliar and dangerous situation of being in a burning building. I had a Strong RESPONSE simply because I had consciously focused on the fire safety lessons we had all been taught in school. I had repeatedly visualized how I would respond to a fire. These mental rehearsals gave me a ready-made solution, an emotional and behavioral habit for dealing with the situation.
>
> This experience taught me the value of developing effective problem-solving habits in advance, so they will be ready in a time of crisis. Just as I was able to rely on the techniques of fire safety, you will be able to rely on the *Solution Power* problem-solving techniques when you encounter a serious problem. The more you turn them into your natural RESPONSE habits, the easier it will be for you to react with strength in the face of adversity.
>
> -Kevin

People who are dominated by their instinctive Weak reactions are also relatively easy for other people to control. Once others learn that someone predictably reacts to problems with an uncontrollable impulse to run away, hide, or lash out it is easy for them to manipulate that person's behavior. For example, you have probably seen marriages in which one spouse has learned to control the other by "pushing their buttons" in order to produce a particular emotional reaction.

You will be a more effective problem-solver if you can master these outdated instincts and develop more controlled, intelligent, and productive ways for handling the kinds of problems you face in the modern world. This self-mastery can be achieved by adopting Strong RESPONSES.

Strong emotions put you in control because, as we saw earlier, they help focus your attention on potential solutions rather than on the problem itself. This helps you to see problems more as opportunities rather than as threats. It is simply not possible for the fight, flee, or freeze reaction to be triggered while you are generating emotions like confidence, optimism, curiosity, serenity, or determination. If you can develop the habit of responding to problems with powerful feelings like these, you will no longer be subject to uncontrollable panic or anger, and will be able to consciously guide your actions toward any desired goal.

USING ASSERTIVENESS INSTEAD OF HOSTILITY

Hostility sometimes solves problems, but often creates new problems in the process. Assertiveness usually solves problems better, without creating new ones.

An especially useful contrast can be drawn between the Weak emotion of *hostility* and the Strong emotion of *assertiveness*. Since both of these emotions can generate forceful words and action, it is easy to confuse them. However, hostility is Weak because it is an expression of anger, while assertiveness is Strong because it is an expression of confidence. Many kinds of problems, particularly those that bring you into conflict with others, benefit more from assertiveness than from hostility. These situations often arise when you know what should be done, but someone else is refusing or failing to take the appropriate action. Let's take a closer look at these two emotions and how they compare for solving problems.

Hostility is the "fight" reaction from "fight, flee, or freeze." It arises from the instinct to strike back at anything that feels like a threat. The Weak & Active version of hostility includes making threats, refusing to listen, blaming others, making exaggerated statements, and criticizing individuals rather than discussing the situation. Often, the hostile individual loses control of his temper, or threatens to do so. There is also a Weak & Still version of hostility, which is often called *passive aggression*. This takes the form of sullen and destructive inaction. Most of us know people who routinely respond to problems with one of these versions of hostility. At home this might be a spouse or parent who reacts to family stress by sulking and using the silent treatment or by yelling, stomping around, and perhaps even resorting to physical violence. At work this includes the manager or coworker whose primary reaction to problems is to blow up, or to silently sabotage other people's projects.

Assertiveness can be defined as *confidence in action*. It is aimed at constructively overcoming opposition or inaction in order to solve a problem. Assertiveness is characterized by speaking clearly and directly, by making accurate statements of fact, and by focusing on finding solutions and achieving goals. An assertive individual is willing to listen and to engage in dialogue, but will not be delayed or deterred by idle talk. The strength of assertiveness comes from maintaining emotional control, from being forceful while staying calm and cool.

Hostility is an example of how Weak emotions can put others, or no one at all, in charge of your life. It is tempting to resort to hostility because in many ways it is like a drug. Boiling anger produces a surge of adrenaline and an intoxicating sense of power. But like an addictive drug, hostility produces a short-term high followed by long-term misery. People who are habitually hostile may *feel* powerful when they lose their temper, but in reality they lack even the power to control their own emotions. They are controlled by their impulses, and others can learn to manipulate them by triggering those impulses.

By contrast, when you act assertively you maintain self-control. Assertiveness always works *for* you; it cannot be turned against you. This self-control also gives you less to feel bad about later. People often regret acting with hostility, but rarely regret acting assertively.

Because hostile behavior arises from the "fight" instinct, it carries the threat of emotional or physical violence. Hostility says, "I am stronger, so I will dominate you." Someone who is the target of hostility often feels demoralized and belittled, and will likely harbor enduring hostility toward the aggressor. Since hostility is an attack, it implies that there will be a winner and a loser in the conflict. In fact, sometimes *both* sides end up feeling like losers.

Assertiveness says, "Because my cause is just, I will prevail." At times, your assertiveness may cause others to feel uncomfortable, especially if their personal behavior or professional performance has been poor or inappropriate. However, because you are acting with respect they are much less likely to feel personally attacked or to harbor a grudge than they would be if you used hostility. They may even feel thankful that they have been given the opportunity to right the situation in a way that does not demean them. The beauty of assertiveness is that the door is left open for both parties to feel that they have won, or at least that no more was lost than necessary.

From Weak to Strong

So, how will you make the empowering transformation from Weak to Strong? The first thing is to get started now. Your RESPONSES to problems are habits. They are habits for how you think, feel, and behave when you encounter a problem. Replacing old Weak RESPONSE habits with new Strong RESPONSE habits will require sustained effort. So don't wait until you are in the middle of a really tough problem to try to change deeply ingrained behavioral patterns. Instead, start using the following insights and techniques on a daily basis. In time, you will automatically react with strength when you encounter a tough problem.

The rest of this chapter provides detailed information on how to adopt Strong RESPONSE habits. It may seem a bit complicated when you first read it, but it is actually pretty simple to use. It's like riding a bicycle: you have to give it conscious attention at first, but it quickly becomes a matter of habit. Once you adopt a few key ideas and get the hang of some simple techniques, you will find yourself naturally responding to problems with greater confidence and effectiveness.

Realize that You Choose Your Response

Suppose you applied for a promotion at work that was very important to you, both emotionally and financially. Then you learned that someone else had been selected. It is likely that you would feel a surge of Weak emotions like disappointment, anger, or frustration.

What happens next would depend on how you chose to respond to the situation:

- A Weak & Still RESPONSE could lead you to communicate less with your supervisor and your coworkers, and to work less confidently and enthusiastically. You could end up being perceived as sullen and unproductive, making it less likely that you would earn a future promotion. You could even decide not to apply for any other promotions in order to avoid any risk of repeating the unpleasant experience.
- A Weak & Active RESPONSE could lead you to become short-tempered with your boss and antagonistic toward the coworker who won the promotion. You could end up being perceived as bitter and hostile, making it less likely that you would earn a future promotion. You might work yourself up to quitting abruptly, even if you had a good position with career opportunities.
- A Strong & Still RESPONSE could allow you to accept the loss with grace, congratulating the person chosen and seeking input from your supervisor on what you could do to earn the next opening. You would likely be perceived as reasonable, confident, and professional, and would be more likely to earn a future promotion.
- A Strong & Active RESPONSE could allow you to transform your disappointment into determination, tackling your work with renewed energy and demonstrating strong team spirit. You would likely be perceived as enthusiastic and committed, and would be more likely to earn a future promotion.

The important thing to realize is that if you were in this situation it would be *your choice* which of these paths to follow. In fact, in any problem situation, *you choose* your RESPONSE. You either make the choice consciously, or you allow the choice to occur on the subconscious level. The rest of this chapter is about how you can take control of the choice, and make it wisely and effectively.

Manage weak emotions. As you will recall from INSIGHT, a rewarding life includes tackling challenging problems. And when you tackle challenging problems, you will inevitably experience some Weak emotions. For example, if you test your limits by trying new things – speaking to an audience, skydiving, getting married – you will encounter fear. If you take action against suffering – stopping child abuse, easing hunger, aiding the homeless – you will experience anger and sadness. If you strive to achieve any ambitious goal, you will deal with frustration and doubt.

Therefore, pursuing a life strategy of *avoiding* Weak emotions would result in missing out on many rewarding experiences. The key is learning to *manage* Weak emotions, so you can handle them, benefit from them, and then move on to a Strong RESPONSE.

Unfortunately, many people believe that they do not have any control at all over their Weak emotions. In fact, they believe that their Weak emotions have control over *them*, and over how they respond to problems. For these people, their RESPONSES aren't choices, they are chain reactions:

1. A problem arises.
2. The problem "makes them" feel an emotion.
3. The emotion "makes them" respond in a certain way.

This means that they allow their lives to be governed by circumstances beyond their control. The emotions they feel are generated by whatever problems happen to arise, and those emotions dictate how they respond. This mindset is revealed in statements like:

- "My boss yelled at me this morning, and it *made me* act crabby the rest of the day."

- "My first presentation went so badly that it *made me* too afraid to do another one."
- "Seeing the toys all over the living room floor *made me* yell at the children."

In reality, no person or event can *make you* respond in a certain way. Instead of saying, "My boss yelled at me, and it *made me* act crabby," it would be more accurate to say, "My boss yelled at me, I *felt* angry, and then I *chose* to act crabby." A statement like this may sound odd. After all, who would *choose* to act crabby? Weak RESPONSES like these don't feel like choices because we don't choose them consciously. But if we don't consciously intervene and make a deliberate choice about how to respond, then we leave that choice to whatever emotional impulse we happen to be feeling in the moment. We allow a Weak emotion like anger to directly dictate how we behave, such as acting crabby.

Solution Power provides a five-step process for taking conscious control of this choice, so that you can consistently choose a Strong RESPONSE to a problem even if you are feeling Weak emotions:

1. Recognize that you have a problem
2. Use Weak emotions as motivation
3. Avoid a Weak RESPONSE
4. Choose a Strong RESPONSE
5. Generate the Strong RESPONSE

1. RECOGNIZE THAT YOU HAVE A PROBLEM

In order to generate a Strong RESPONSE to a problem, you first have to recognize that you *have* a problem. Learning to promptly recognize that a problem has arisen allows you understand and solve it more quickly and completely.

Unfortunately, some people respond to their problems by trying to deny that they exist. For example, they may disregard obvious warning signs, such as conflict in their marriage, their kids getting into increasingly serious trouble, or unpleasant noises coming from their car engines. This same pattern of denial can be seen in people who stubbornly refuse to go to a doctor even when it appears they may have a serious illness. They sometimes delay so long before getting an examination that by the time they get a diagnosis it is too late for the illness to be treated. They literally prefer to risk death rather than face being told they have a medical problem.

People sometimes resist admitting they have a problem even when it is a minor one. Comedians like to poke fun at stereotypical men who are reluctant to admit being lost and who will drive considerable distances in search of a destination before finally giving in and asking for directions. Many people are reluctant to say, "I guess I'm lost, I'd better ask for help."

Refusing to admit being lost is not always a minor problem. For example, getting lost when hiking or camping in the wilderness can be a life-threatening situation, and this provides a dramatic example of how important it is to promptly recognize when you have a problem.

If you took a training course on how to survive when lost in the wilderness you would learn many important practical skills. You might learn to identify sources of drinking water in a desert environment, or how to make a fire and maintain body heat in a cold climate. But you would also learn the one thing you must do to survive getting lost in any environment: *you have to admit that you are lost*. Any wilderness expert will tell you that survival begins with saying the magic words, "I am lost." People who are unwilling to admit they are lost remain in a state of denial, and blunder along making things worse for themselves, getting even more thoroughly lost. Their unwillingness to admit the truth to themselves impairs their ability to think clearly and exercise sound judgment. This is because they are wasting their mental energy trying to convince themselves that they don't have a problem instead of focusing it on solving the problem. The poor decisions people make while in this state of denial can lead to tragic consequences.

However, simply confronting the fact of being lost – admitting to yourself that you have a problem – immediately frees your mind and allows you to focus on the question, "How will I survive?" It snaps you out of the denial mode and into the problem-solving mode. You can start thinking about the survival skills you have learned and deciding which ones are most useful in your circumstances. In fact, who lives and who dies when lost in the wilderness often comes down to this: those who live are those who are willing to promptly admit they have a problem.

This same powerful truth applies in your daily life. If things are not going well you can blunder along and hope for the best, or you can step back and say, "Wait a minute, I think I have a problem to solve." The moment you do that, you can start focusing on creating a great solution. **Recognizing that you have a problem is the first step in every successful problem-solving process.**

This is particularly important if, until now, you have felt that admitting you have a problem is a sign of weakness. The opposite is true. Ignoring or denying your problems is a Weak RESPONSE driven by emotions like fear, laziness, or insecurity. Confronting your problems without delay puts you in a position of strength and confidence.

This is where Weak emotions can give you valuable information by alerting you that a problem has arisen. Whenever you find yourself experiencing an unpleasant or uncomfortable emotion, realize that the feeling is being generated by a problem. Even a relatively unemotional problem such as a tough home improvement project or a technical issue at work can eat at you a bit, giving you a dissatisfied or restless sensation that goads you to find a solution.

So develop the habit of using Weak emotions as valuable cues, alerting you that you have a problem to solve. **Whenever you feel a Weak emotion, say to yourself, "I have a problem to solve."** Once you get in this habit, you will form a strong subconscious link between *having a problem* and *finding a solution*. In fact, you will find that saying, "I have a problem to solve" will immediately fill you with confidence, energy, and eager curiosity, because it will remind you of all the terrific problem-solving tools you will have learned to use. As soon as you consciously identify that you have a problem, you will start looking through your problem-solving toolbox for the best tool to solve it.

In time, you will begin to see all the difficulties you encounter in life as a series of *problems to be solved*. This is much better than seeing them as "disasters" or "failures." Your subconscious mind does *not* link concepts like "disaster" and "failure" with finding a solution. Instead, it links them with feeling bad and giving up.

Unfortunately, people often suffer with painful Weak emotions such as anxiety, sadness, frustration, or bitterness for months or years without ever coming to the clear realization, "I have a problem to solve." Instead, they think about their situations in dire terms like, "My career is a disaster" or, "My marriage is a failure." This kind of thinking is a dead end. They would get better results by viewing their challenges, mishaps, tasks, difficulties, and setbacks as *problems to solve* rather than as *misfortunes to endure*. Simply saying, "I have a problem to solve" would immediately help get them unstuck from feeling bad and on the way to finding a great solution.

So, you can use Weak emotions as cues alerting you that a problem has arisen. You can also use them as *motivation* to get it solved.

2. Use Weak Emotions as Motivation

Motivation can take the form of a *push* or a *pull*. You feel a motivational *push* to move *away* from something you dislike, and you feel a *pull* to move *toward* something you desire. Weak emotions provide motivational push because they feel unpleasant. You naturally want to "move away" from these feelings by finding a way to make them stop. Strong emotions provide motivational pull because they feel pleasant. You naturally want to "move toward" these feelings by finding a way to make them last, and to experience them again in the future.

Therefore, when a problem causes you to feel a Weak emotion, you naturally feel motivated to make that feeling stop. The force of this motivation is determined by the emotion's *intensity* and *frequency*. These characteristics determine how important the problem feels to you, and therefore how quickly and vigorously you will respond.

- If the Weak emotion has *low intensity* you will perceive a mild problem and feel a moderate level of motivation. You might choose to concentrate your resources on solving other, higher priority problems first. Or, you might choose to go ahead and solve it right away, especially if you can do so fairly easily and it will prevent the problem from getting bigger.
- If you are jolted by a Weak emotion that has *high intensity*, you will perceive an urgent problem. You will feel highly motivated to take immediate, vigorous action.

- If a Weak emotion pops up *repeatedly* under similar circumstances, then you will know that you have a chronic problem. These can be tricky. Even if the Weak emotion recurs at a low level of intensity, you should boost your motivation to a higher level in order to prevent the problem from continuing. It is easy to ignore low-level chronic problems for a long time, but it is better to solve them with prompt, decisive action as soon as you become aware of them.

While a Weak emotion gives you a motivational push to make the feeling stop, it does not tell you how to do so. It tells you how quickly and vigorously to respond, but it does not tell you *which* RESPONSE to use.

Unfortunately, people sometimes use a Weak RESPONSE in an attempt to escape from the unpleasantness of a Weak emotion. Some use a Weak & Still RESPONSE like avoidance. They try to make the bad feeling go away by pretending the problem does not exist, or by masking it with substance abuse or some other unhealthy coping mechanism. Or they may choose a Weak & Active RESPONSE. For example, they might lash out at others, venting their Weak emotions in the form of hostility. Unfortunately, these "solutions" do not resolve the underlying problem, and they often allow it to get worse. So the Weak emotions caused by the problem will inevitably return, and they will become more and more unpleasant.

This is particularly important because these behaviors can feed a debilitating cycle, in which Weak emotions trigger the behaviors, and the behaviors in turn reinforce the Weak emotions. Let's look at some techniques for spotting and avoiding this kind of Weak RESPONSE cycle.

3. Avoid a Weak Response

Earlier in this chapter we discussed the two-way link between where you focus your attention and what emotions you feel. There are many such links. For example, there is also a link between emotional feelings and physical behavior. When people feel tense or worried, they tend to tilt their heads down, curve their backs, tighten their facial muscles, and take short, shallow breaths. When people feel relaxed and happy, they tend to lift their heads, straighten their backs, relax their facial muscles, and take long, deep breaths.

Recall that these subconscious links work in both directions. Try this simple experiment: Drop your head, curve your back, clench your jaw, and take short, shallow breaths. Notice how you feel. Now, lift your head, straighten your back, relax your jaw, and take long, deep breaths. Remarkable, isn't it? Simply by making small changes in your physical posture and behavior, you can generate different emotional states.

This two-way link gives you a powerful tool for taking control of how you respond to problems. Because Weak emotions generate certain patterns of physical behavior, you can learn to recognize those behaviors as warning signs that you are beginning a Weak RESPONSE and then use specific physical behaviors to generate a Strong RESPONSE instead.

Weak & Active behaviors. Recall that the Weak & Active RESPONSE includes the "flee" reaction that is driven by fear, the "fight" reaction that is ignited by hostility, and the "throwing a fit" reaction that arises from agitation. Physical behaviors associated with this RESPONSE include:

- **Posture and movement.** Movements are likely to be abrupt and uncontrolled. A person might stomp around, stalk away, or slam a door. There can also be decreased fine motor control; for example a person's hands may

shake too much to perform small tasks. Someone may even quiver with anger or fear. There are often repetitive or jittery actions like fidgeting or nervous pacing.
- **Expression.** Facial muscles are often tight, including a clenched jaw and a furrowed brow. The eyes may be narrow with anger, or they may be wide with fury or fear.
- **Breathing.** Breathing tends to be rapid, shallow, and irregular. Agitation can induce a hurried breathing pattern that leads to hyperventilation, or a restricted breathing pattern that causes a lack of oxygen.
- **Speaking.** The voice is often high and tense, and originates from the throat rather than from the chest. The tone may be anxious and quavering, harsh and accusatory, or whiny and self-pitying. The person may speak louder than is necessary or appropriate.

Weak & Still behaviors. Recall that the Weak & Still RESPONSE includes the instinctive "freeze" reaction, the reaction of apathy and futility, and the reaction of timidity and submissiveness. Physical behaviors associated with this RESPONSE include:
- **Posture and movement.** People are likely to stand or sit with their backs bent forward and their shoulders slumped, as though pulled down by a heavy weight. The head often hangs down. Movements may be stiff and constrained, slow and listless, or nervous and hesitant.
- **Expression.** Eyes may be dull and downcast, or they may be furtive and darting. The face may be tense and fearful, blank and despondent, or timid and twitchy.
- **Breathing.** Breathing tends to be slow, shallow, and constricted, often leading to an energy-sapping oxygen deficit.
- **Speaking.** Again, the voice tends to originate from the throat. The tone may be tense and distressed, sluggish and

monotone, or placating and uncertain. Statements often end with rising inflection, so they sound like questions.

The easiest way to break a Weak RESPONSE cycle is to recognize Weak behaviors like these and stop them. This immediately interrupts the escalation of a Weak & Active RESPONSE, or the downward spiral of a Weak & Still RESPONSE. The best way to stop a Weak behavior is by replacing it with one of the Strong behaviors outlined below. You can use these Strong behaviors to help you generate any particular Strong RESPONSE you desire, turning the link between physical behavior and emotional feelings to your advantage.

4. CHOOSE A STRONG RESPONSE

You are free to choose whichever Strong RESPONSE is best suited to your personality type and to the particular problem at hand. This is a significant difference between *Solution Power* and other books or programs. The literature of personal improvement, problem-solving, and business success often advocates using *either* the Strong & Still *or* the Strong & Active approach. Some authors recommend a path of quiet contemplation and emotional tranquillity, whiles others advocate responding to every problem with supercharged drive and intensity. Both the meditative and motivational approaches are valid and powerful, *but not for every person, and not in every situation.* Some people, particularly Social Doers, feel that the serene approach is confining and ineffective. Others, especially Individual Thinkers, feel overwhelmed by the dynamic style.

In reality, most people are better off not choosing to follow just one path or the other. You will get the best results by employing whatever Strong RESPONSE is best suited to your personality type and to the particular problem you are facing. Recall that a problem exists when you want something that you don't have. So choose the RESPONSE that will best help you get what you want.

Here are some examples of the Strong RESPONSES you can use to solve different kinds of problems:

Strong & Active
- For getting a lot of problems solved quickly, tackling a particularly intimidating problem, or providing inspiration to others, use the **dynamic and forceful** RESPONSE based on passion, decisiveness, aspiration, and assertiveness.
- To make problem-solving more fun and to facilitate communication and teamwork, use the **exuberant and playful** RESPONSE based on enthusiasm, joy, and adventurousness.
- For problems requiring prolonged, energetic effort, use the **relentless and unswerving** RESPONSE based on desire, commitment, and tenacity.

Strong & Still
- For problems requiring careful analysis and thorough solution-finding, especially those of a technical or scientific nature, use the **intellectual and analytical** RESPONSE based on curiosity, patience, and perseverance.
- For problems that call for intuition, empathy, and communication, such as internal and interpersonal problems, use the **meditative and spiritual** RESPONSE based on serenity, gratitude, love, and thoughtfulness.
- For problems that demand prolonged attention, individual initiative, or resistance to criticism, like political or social advocacy, use the **firm and resolute** RESPONSE based on confidence, ambition, and perseverance.

5. GENERATE THE STRONG RESPONSE

Often, you can generate a Strong RESPONSE to a problem simply by choosing one and deciding to use it. In fact, as you absorb and use the ideas presented in *Solution Power* it will become increasingly natural and effortless to do so. But sometimes it is not so easy. Perhaps you have an ingrained habit of reacting with a Weak RESPONSE to a particular kind of problem, such as a confrontation with your supervisor, parent, or spouse. Or perhaps a problem comes along that seems particularly frightening, or that arises when you are a bit down in the dumps or have a low energy level. And sometimes you start out with a Strong RESPONSE, but solving the problem requires a sustained effort and you start to run out of steam. At times like these, you can use the link between behavior and emotion to give yourself a boost and strengthen your RESPONSE.

You can quickly achieve a Strong RESPONSE whenever you need one by *behaving as though* you are feeling Strong. The principle is simple: to *feel* strong, *act* strong. This creates a powerful cycle in which Strong behaviors trigger Strong emotions, which in turn generate additional Strong behavior.

One way to do this is to recall a time when you solved a problem in a particularly Strong manner. How did you stand and move? What kind of gestures did you make? How did your voice sound? What were your facial expressions? Visualize those behaviors and deliberately copy them one after another. Stand the way you stood then, gesture the way you gestured then, and so forth. It may feel artificial at first. However, by consciously replicating those behaviors, you will soon trigger the same Strong emotions you were feeling in that earlier situation and generate a Strong RESPONSE for solving your current problem.

A related approach is to use specific, proven physical techniques that reliably trigger and strengthen Strong RESPONSES.

There are two basic behaviors that are useful for generating any of the Strong RESPONSES:
- Breathing deeply
- Speaking from the chest rather than from the throat

Breathing. You have probably heard the phrase, "take a few deep breaths." This is excellent advice. Recall that both the Still and Active forms of the Weak RESPONSE are characterized by shallow breathing. In fact, many people have fallen into the habit of taking shallow, constricted breaths almost all the time, even when they are not facing a problem. Unfortunately, this pattern of breathing reinforces feelings of anxiety and reduces oxygen and energy levels. Breathing deeply and slowly immediately clears your mind, provides an energizing boost of oxygen, and relaxes your emotions. It's a great way to power up for an Active RESPONSE or cool down for a Still RESPONSE.

Here is a simple and effective breathing technique:
- Take a break for a moment from whatever you are doing. You may find it helpful to close your eyes.
- Empty your lungs by blowing gently from your mouth.
- Inhale slowly through your nose, drawing the air first into your belly and then expanding your chest outward and upward.
- Exhale gently through your mouth.
- Repeat this process, taking three or four deep, slow breaths.

(Note: You will find a more detailed version of this breathing technique in Appendix A.)

Speaking. Weak RESPONSES are also characterized by a constricted manner of speaking, in which speech is generated high in the throat. Make a conscious choice to let your voice originate at a deeper and stronger level by speaking from your diaphragm. Doing the deep breathing exercise makes this easier. This naturally makes your voice more resonant, causing it to sound more confident and relaxed. Just hearing yourself speak in this manner helps trigger a Strong RESPONSE, and it also creates a calming and inspiring effect on those around you.

There are additional behaviors you can use to generate any specific Strong RESPONSE. Here are some examples of techniques that many people find effective:

Generate a Strong & Active RESPONSE
- **Dynamic and Forceful**
  - **Posture and movement.** Stand up. Pull your shoulders back, lift your chin, and straighten your back. Move vigorously and expansively. Swing your arms freely, like you're getting ready for a game of tennis or golf. Pace rapidly with long steps. Act like you're warming up for a boxing match by running in place or bouncing on the balls of your feet and throwing some punches in the air. You can even do some calisthenics, like a few jumping jacks or twisting at the waist.
  - **Expression.** A dynamic state includes dynamic facial expressions that spontaneously reflect your confidence and enthusiasm. Activate your facial muscles by stretching them out and warming them up. Open your mouth as widely as you can and move your jaw back and forth. Scrunch your eyes tightly shut and them open them very wide. Raise and lower your eyebrows as far as they can go.
  - **Breathing.** Oxygenate with a few deep breaths, and turn the energy into action. If you ever feel your energy drop a notch, do it again.

- **Speaking.** Speak from your diaphragm with a full, expansive voice. Experiment with a variety of tones of voice to express your dynamic feelings. Use short, punchy phrases like "Okay!" "Let's go!" or "Show time!"

➢ **Exuberant and Playful**
- **Posture and movement.** Move! Dance! Wriggle and bend your body to get motion into your torso. Wave your arms above your head, and dance a little jig. Walk on your tiptoes, skip, hop, or waddle like a duck. Leap and twirl like a ballet dancer. Act just as silly as you want!
- **Expression.** Smile! Make outrageously funny faces at yourself in the mirror. Free your facial muscles to make expressions fully, readily, and enthusiastically.
- **Breathing.** Do the deep breathing exercise, but as you exhale sing some amusing lyrics, or a musical note like an opera singer.
- **Speaking.** Laugh! Sing! Talk with a silly voice. Recite some favorite funny lines from a movie or television show, imitating the character's voice. Hit high notes and low notes to loosen up your voice for expressiveness, like a singer warming up for a performance. Throw your head back and laugh out loud!

➢ **Relentless and Unswerving**
- **Posture and movement.** Stand tall but keep your body compact, with your shoulders and head slightly forward rather than pulled back. Place your feet at shoulder width, with one foot slightly

ahead of the other and your weight shifted a little ahead of center, ready to drive forward. Pace with controlled energy, taking strong, short strides. Make fists and bring them beside or in front of your chest.
- **Expression.** Look in the mirror and put on your "game face." Thrust your head forward and lower your chin a notch. Narrow your eyes slightly and maintain a steady gaze, focusing mentally on your goal with steely determination.
- **Breathing.** Breathe deeply and steadily, with control, like you are hiking rather than sprinting.
- **Speaking.** Speak with steady authority and certainty. Use short, motivating statements, like "Never surrender!" "I will succeed!" or "Nothing can stop me!"

Generate a Strong & Still RESPONSE
> **Intellectual and Analytical**
- **Posture and movement.** Stand up, stretch, relax. If you like to think on your feet, you may find it helpful to pace slowly. Try tilting your head down and cupping your chin with one hand, or clasping your hands together behind your back. When sitting, make yourself comfortable. Lean back in your chair, or lean forward with your elbows on your knees.
- **Expression.** Narrow your eyes slightly and gaze into the distance. If possible, look out a window. Relax your facial muscles by opening and stretching your jaw. Gently massage your temples. Purse your lips slightly, put your thumb under

your chin, and place your index finger across or next to your lips. Deliberately move your eyes up, down, and to each side to activate brain functions like memory, creativity, and analytical thinking.
- **Breathing.** Establish a steady, relaxed pace. Be sure not to hold your breath when trying to remember or analyze something. That is a common but counterproductive impulse. You need to feed a continuous supply of oxygen to your brain.
- **Speaking.** Reinforce your sense of reflection and insight by speaking in a calm, measured manner. Make comments like, "Let's get this figured out," and "Interesting."

➢ **Meditative and Spiritual**
- **Posture and movement.** Gently stretch your arms, body, and legs. Assume a comfortable position, either sitting or lying down. Progressively relax each part of your body, starting with the feet and working your way up to the top of your head. Lighten up, visualizing yourself as weightless and transparent. When it is time to rise, move with smooth, flowing, gentle motions.
- **Expression.** Close your eyes. As part of the progressive relaxation process, relax each muscle from your neck to the top of your head. It may help to rub your temples and around your eyes. Be sure to re-relax your arms and hands after doing so. Opening your eyes, choose an object and gaze on it, such as a candle, a tree moving in the breeze, or traffic going by on the street outside. Re-enter the world with a serene smile, capturing the feeling of calm focus and carrying it with you.

- **Breathing.** After the deep breathing exercise, continue to breathe slowly, with a relaxed center. Let the air flow in and out as a gentle breeze. Breathe attentively, focusing your attention on each breath without controlling or forcing it.
- **Speaking.** Your voice should be gentle and well-modulated, but also clear and assured. Speak with a smile, conveying warmth and understanding with your words.

➢ **Firm and Resolute**
- **Posture and movement.** Stand tall and steady, with your feet at shoulder width and your weight balanced evenly. Straighten your back, square your shoulders, lift your chin, and gaze ahead as though surveying the world from a height. Stand firmly, rooted and immovable.
- **Expression.** Go to a mirror and look yourself in the eye, seeing the immovable assurance within you. Generate a quiet, confident, knowing smile.
- **Breathing.** Breathe easily and regularly.
- **Speaking.** Express your assurance by speaking in a calm, direct, and confident tone.

Experiment with these exercises, and discover the ones that work best for you. Use them to generate a Strong RESPONSE anytime you have a challenging problem to solve.

CONCLUSION

Accepting responsibility for how you react to problems will allow you to solve them more successfully. Some people resist the idea that they can choose how to react to their problems. They continue to believe that their reactions are imposed on them by what other people say and do. This allows them to avoid accepting responsibility for their behavior. But by avoiding responsibility, they also surrender a large measure of control over their lives. Accepting that you are accountable for your RESPONSES puts you in charge of your life, and makes it more likely that you will create happiness and fulfillment for yourself and your loved ones.

When you start treating problems as promising opportunities or interesting challenges, you will react to them with Strong emotions like confidence, enthusiasm, or determination. You will experience Weak emotional reactions less often, and when you do they will seem easier to manage and will fade more quickly. The *Solution Power* approach not only *works* better, it also *feels* better.

RESPONSE: SUMMARY

- **Physical reactions.** Physical reactions to problems can be Active or Still. The problem-solving effectiveness of a physical reaction depends on the emotional reaction that accompanies it.
- **Emotional reactions.** Emotional reactions to problems can be Strong or Weak. "Strong" and "Weak" refer to how effective an emotion is for solving problems, not to how intense it may feel.

THE PROBLEM-SOLVING RESPONSES

- **Strong & Active.** Solves problems quickly and effectively through energetic, decisive action.
- **Strong & Still.** Solves problems thoroughly and efficiently through determined, measured effort.
- **Weak & Active.** Fails to solve problems, or solves them poorly, because actions are unproductive or even counterproductive.

- **Weak & Still.** Fails to solve problems, or solves them poorly, due to a lack of effective action.

Advantages of the Strong Responses
- **Focus.** Weak emotions keep you focused on having problems. Strong emotions help you focus on finding solutions.
- **Personal and professional growth.** People who use Weak emotions to solve problems limit their growth as problem-solvers. Strong emotions help you learn new problem-solving skills and ideas.
- **Ending procrastination.** Weak emotions feed a cycle of procrastination. Strong emotions break the cycle.
- **Self-control.** People who use Weak emotions are governed by outdated instinctive reactions. Strong emotions keep you in charge.
- **Using assertiveness instead of hostility.** Hostility sometimes solves problems, but it often creates new problems in the process. Assertiveness solves problems better and does so without creating new ones.

From Weak to Strong
- **Realize that you choose your Response.** If you do not choose your Response consciously, you allow the choice to be made subconsciously. Manage your Weak emotions, rather than trying to avoid them or allowing yourself to be governed by them.
- **Recognize that you have a problem.** It's the first step in every problem-solving process. When you feel a Weak emotion say, "I have a problem to solve." View difficulties as problems to solve rather than as misfortunes to endure.

SOLUTION POWER

- **Use Weak emotions as motivation.** They push you to solve problems so you can stop feeling bad.
- **Avoid a Weak RESPONSE.** Break the Weak RESPONSE cycle by recognizing and stopping Weak behaviors.
- **Choose a Strong RESPONSE.** Choose whichever Strong RESPONSE is best suited to your personality type and to the problem at hand.
- **Generate the Strong RESPONSE.** You can feel Strong by behaving as though you are in a Strong state. Use physical exercises that trigger and strengthen your RESPONSE.

THE THIRD TOOL

CLARITY

UNDERSTAND PROBLEMS
CLEARLY & COMPLETELY

The better you understand a problem, the more easily and effectively you can solve it. The CLARITY tool provides techniques for gaining an accurate and useful understanding of any problem you encounter.

There are two aspects to CLARITY: first, techniques you can use to gain *internal clarity* about a problem, and second, methods for effectively *analyzing* problems.

GAIN INTERNAL CLARITY

Internal clarity means clearing away unproductive habits of thought that interfere with your ability to perceive problems accurately, using methods for understanding problems more thoroughly and responding to them more constructively.

Define the Problem

How you define a problem has a big impact on how well you can understand it. Unfortunately, many people do not consciously decide how they will define the problems they encounter. As we saw in the previous chapter, any time you do not make a choice consciously, you allow the choice to be made subconsciously. So if you do not consciously decide how to define a problem, your subconscious will define it for you.

Your subconscious will base its definition on your existing habits of thought, on how you have reacted to similar problems in the past and how you react to problems generally. If you have had a "bad relationship" with problems, seeing them as frightening, irritating, or discouraging, then your subconscious will be conditioned to define problems in a negative manner. Even if you have a generally positive attitude toward problems, you will often experience a Weak emotion as your first reaction to a new problem, and this can cause your subconscious to quickly define the problem in negative terms.

For these reasons, the subconscious usually defines problems with short, forceful statements that focus on what is wrong. Some examples were presented in the Introduction:

- "I'm in terrible shape!"
- "My business is a failure!"
- "My marriage is miserable!"
- "I hate this lousy job!"
- "My yard looks awful!"

Many people simply accept these subconscious definitions, without ever really questioning them or reconsidering them. However, as we will see, viewing problems in such a negative light makes it harder to understand and solve them.

Identify your goal. As we discussed in the Introduction, a better approach to defining a problem is to shift from focusing on the undesirable situation that currently exists to focusing on the goal you want to achieve. This is done by using the format, "I want ____." So, "I'm in terrible shape" is replaced with, "I want good health and physical fitness," and, "My marriage is miserable" is replaced with, "I want a happy and loving marriage."

This method of defining problems helps you focus on what you *want* rather than on what you do *not want*. This is important, because *what you focus on is what you are most likely to get.*

If you are a golfer, you can confirm this principle through the following experiment: The next time you have to hit over a water hazard, close your eyes and say five times out loud, "I do not want to hit the ball into the water." While you say this, visualize what you do *not want*: the ball splashing into the water. Then open your eyes and hit the ball. More often than not, it will go straight into the water! Now drop another ball, close your eyes, and say five times out loud, "I want to hit the ball onto the green." While you say this, visualize what you *want*: the ball dropping onto the green and rolling to the hole. Open your eyes and hit the ball, without consciously thinking about how to swing the club. More often than not, you will hit a truly beautiful shot.

As another example, let's suppose that you are a parent, and one day you see your young son carrying a full glass of milk across the living room. You might respond by quickly saying, "Don't spill your milk!" If so, your child will be startled by your urgent tone of voice and at the same moment will visualize in his mind what your words are describing: milk being spilled. The combination of being startled and visualizing the milk spilling will often cause the child to spill the milk. It is better to calmly say, "Please carry the milk carefully." This will cause your son to visualize the outcome you want: the glass being carried steadily and not spilling. Your son will be much less likely to spill the milk.

Teachers know this technique well. The worst thing you can do in a hallway full of excited children heading outside for recess is to yell, "Don't run!" The kids hear an energetic voice and their minds automatically visualize the word they heard: "run." So that is exactly what many of them will do! It is more effective to firmly say, "Walk slowly please." This creates the image in the children's minds of the behavior the teacher wants, which makes it more likely that is what they will do. Techniques like this are important when you are managing a classroom full of children every day!

In fact, this approach works for all kinds of problems. If you say to yourself every day, "I shouldn't eat donuts on my break" you will become obsessed with eating donuts. Instead say, "I will eat fruit or a protein bar on my break." And instead of saying, "I shouldn't watch so much television," say, "I will spend more time reading good books and playing games with my kids." No matter what problem you are facing, it is more likely to get solved if the words you say out loud are focused on your desired outcome. That is why it is more effective to define your problems in terms of the goal you want to achieve.

We will now develop this approach further, and show how to gain an even better understanding of problems by expanding on the "I want _____" format.

Identify the obstacle. Recall from the Introduction that *a problem is when you want something you don't have.* If you think about this definition, you will realize that you are solving problems all the time. Every day there are many situations in which you want something you don't have and then you get it.

For example, if you are sitting on the couch at home and you think, "I'm thirsty," then you have a problem. Right at that moment you want something – a drink – that you don't have. The solution to this problem is simple: Get up off the couch, walk into the kitchen, take a glass out of the cupboard, open the refrigerator, take out a container of some refreshing beverage, pour it into the glass, and drink it.

This situation doesn't seem like much of a problem because you have a *pre-existing, habitual, and easy solution* for it. You go straight from realizing the problem exists to solving it, without needing to use CLARITY or any of the other problem-solving tools.

However, this same situation used to be a significant problem for you. When you were a small child you could not reach the glass in the cupboard, could not lift the container out of the refrigerator, could not pour the refreshing beverage without spilling it all over the counter, and could not drink from the glass without dribbling on your shirt. It took many years of practice for you to master all the actions required to achieve the solution. Being thirsty can seem like a very big problem to a small child!

And it would seem like a problem again if you were sitting on the couch feeling thirsty, and you had two broken legs! This is because a problem looks and feels like a problem when there is a significant *obstacle* that makes it difficult to reach your *goal*.

You can gain a clearer understanding of any problem by identifying the obstacle and the goal. This can be done by defining the problem using the following format, which expands on the previous one:

"I want _____, but _____."

This is what we call a *problem statement*. The first blank contains the goal you want and the second blank contains the obstacle you must overcome to achieve your goal. **Every problem consists of these two elements: a *goal* and an *obstacle*.** Whenever there is a goal that you want and an obstacle to getting it, you have a problem to solve.

This expanded definition can be illustrated by using the problems that were defined in the Introduction. In the Introduction, each problem was restated in terms of the goal. Now we will add the obstacle that exists in each problem:

Problem:	Goal:	Obstacle:
"I'm in terrible shape!"	Good health and physical fitness	Poor diet and lack of exercise
"My business is a failure!"	An increase in net profits	Flat sales and rising costs
"My marriage is miserable!"	A happy and loving marriage	Recurring nasty fights
"I hate this lousy job!"	A better job	A tight job market
"My yard looks awful!"	A beautiful lawn	Bare patches in the grass

Following this approach, the subconscious definition, "I'm in terrible shape" is replaced with the problem statement, "I want good health and physical fitness, but I eat poorly and don't exercise." "My marriage is miserable" becomes, "I want a happy and loving marriage, but my spouse and I keep having nasty fights."

Develop the habit of using, "I want *goal*, but *obstacle*" problem statements. Whenever you catch your subconscious mind defining a problem negatively, consciously create a problem statement identifying the goal and the obstacle. Over time, this will become a habit, and your subconscious will begin to automatically use this approach with each problem you encounter. This will naturally and effortlessly provide a clearer understanding of the problem, giving you a head start toward building a solution that will *overcome the obstacle* and *achieve your goal.*

Be Honest With Yourself

You can only define a problem accurately if you are honest with yourself about what goal you truly desire and what obstacle is truly blocking you from achieving it. This can be difficult, because self-honesty sometimes requires facing uncomfortable or even painful issues. Let's consider some situations in which there is a problem that can be defined in two very different ways. In each example, neither of the two problem statements is necessarily better than the other. Either one could be accurate. For a person facing one of these situations, deciding which definition of the problem is correct will require a high level of self-honesty.

Situation	Is this the problem…	…or is it this?
A father is worried about his eighteen-year-old daughter.	"I want my daughter to be happy, but she is making terrible choices in her life."	"I want my daughter to do exactly what I would do, but she needs to live life her own way."
A man sees that his wife is upset about his drinking.	"I want to enjoy a relaxing drink now and then, but when I drink my wife throws a fit."	"I want a successful marriage, but my drinking is causing problems and I can't control it."
A woman has learned she did not get a promotion at work.	"I want to get the promotion I deserve, but my boss has it in for me."	"I want to earn a promotion, but I'm not achieving the performance my boss is looking for."
A wife is concerned about her husband's increasingly extreme anger.	"I want my husband to be happy, but I keep doing things that upset him."	"I want a happy and loving marriage, but my husband is angry and abusive."

In the first example, the father is in a tough spot. On the one hand, his daughter may truly be heading for serious trouble. Even if she resists his help, she may actually need his guidance and be grateful in the long run that he provided it. If he does not intervene, she could make terrible mistakes with lasting consequences for the rest of her life. On the other hand, he knows that young adults need to be allowed to make their own mistakes and learn from them. He has seen other parents try to micromanage their children's lives, and how this created bitter conflicts between parent and child.

So which is the case for him? Is he a concerned parent whose child is headed for real trouble, or is he a controlling parent who is stifling his daughter's independence? Only by reflecting on the situation with an absolute commitment to self-honesty will he be able to perceive the situation clearly. If he deceives himself about either the seriousness of her problems, or his true motivations for wanting to intervene, he will not be able to define the problem accurately.

There is a lot at stake in these decisions. The man in the second example either has a drinking problem or an unreasonable and domineering spouse. If he defines the problem inaccurately, he will choose a solution that cannot succeed and may even make the problem worse. For example, if he decides the problem is that his wife is intolerant, when in fact he has a drinking problem, any "solution" he comes up with to change his wife's behavior will do nothing to stop his drinking and will probably harm their marriage even further. A support group or professional counselor could help him get the perspective he needs to look at the situation clearly and honestly.

In the third example, if the woman truly deserved the promotion and her boss really did deny it based only on personal dislike, then her most likely solution would be to look for a new position in a different department or company. However, if the real problem is poor work performance on her part, then that solution will not help her build a successful career, because she will need to improve her job skills to succeed wherever she goes.

With most serious problems, our self-deceptions eventually get swept away and we are forced to look reality in the face. For example, in the fourth example, the husband's chronic anger may finally escalate to the point that the woman cannot keep pretending that her behavior is the problem. She will have to admit that he will get angry and violent no matter how carefully she controls what she says and does. But by then she may have wasted years of her life, adopted harmful habits of submissive behavior, and endangered the safety of herself and her children.

Here are some phrases people often use when they have avoided being honest with themselves about a problem for a prolonged period of time, and then finally face up to it:

- "For a long time, I couldn't face the fact that..."
- "I kept telling myself..."
- "Eventually, it got so bad I couldn't avoid it any longer."
- "I had to stop kidding myself."
- "I couldn't go on ignoring it forever."
- "I had to stop making excuses."
- "One day I took a hard look in the mirror."
- "I finally admitted to myself..."

Imagine yourself in that position. A problem has caused you trouble and heartache for quite a long time. Now you realize that you have not been able to solve it because you have not been honest with yourself about it. But you are finally facing up to the problem. You know there are still difficult issues to deal with and hard work to be done, but you are confident you will now be able to get it solved. You already feel a sense of relief that you are dealing with it openly and honestly. You are pleasantly surprised to discover that confronting the problem is not quite as horrible as you had feared it would be. But you have one big regret: "I wish I had faced up to this a long time ago! I have wasted so much time avoiding dealing with this problem honestly. If only I had it to do over again!"

So when a difficult or unpleasant problem arises, skip past the part where you deceive yourself about it and go directly to the part where you level with yourself and see the problem as it really is. Often you will find that the most difficult part is simply making yourself confront it, and once you have done that it is surprisingly easy to go ahead and solve it. If you can do this consistently and make it into a habit, you will be able to understand and solve your problems while they are still relatively small and simple, and without putting yourself through prolonged emotional suffering.

Here is a technique you can use when facing a particularly difficult situation:

1. Make a firm commitment to look at the facts squarely, and to not make any excuses.

2. When deciding between different ways of defining the problem, pay attention to how each one makes you feel. Usually one will give you a sense of strength, responsibility, and understanding, even if it means facing up to something difficult. The other may give you a feeling of relief, but also an underlying sensation of weakness. Pay attention to your heart; it knows when you are being honest with yourself and when you are trying to avoid the truth. The true understanding of the problem is the one that helps you grow stronger as a person.

3. Ask yourself, "What goal do I *really* want?" and, "What obstacle is *really* blocking me from getting it?" Write these questions down and then start listing possible an-

swers. If you hold yourself to a high standard of integrity and look into your heart, just answering these simple but fundamental questions can generate powerful insights into the true nature of the problem.

TAKE RESPONSIBILITY RATHER THAN PLACE BLAME

Whenever you have a problem, you will understand it more clearly if you see it as *your problem to solve*.

Consider that:

1. If there is a goal that *you* want to achieve,
2. And there is an obstacle preventing *you* from achieving it,
3. Then y*ou* have a problem,
4. That y*ou* need to solve.

Since you are responsible for achieving your own goals, you are also responsible for solving your own problems, because a problem is just a goal that happens to have an obstacle in the way.

Of course, sometimes the obstacle has been caused by another person. Perhaps someone has made it harder for you to achieve a goal toward which you were working. Or perhaps you were in a good situation and someone screwed it up, so your goal is to get things back to the way they were. In situations like these, Weak emotions like irritation, frustration, or anger can cause you to focus on placing blame. This is an understandable reaction, but it is also a potential distraction. If you allow yourself to get so focused on whom to blame for creating the obstacle that you lose sight of achieving your goal, your ability to solve the problem will be greatly diminished.

Unfortunately, many people habitually respond to problems by focusing primarily on blame. The first question they ask is, "Whose fault is this?" Some direct the blame outward, while others turn it inward on themselves.

Outward-focused blamers are determined to see every problem as being someone else's fault. They blame others even when they actually caused the problem themselves, or when the problem isn't really anyone's fault. There are several types of outward-focused blamers:

- **The Victimized Blamer.** These blamers play the role of a powerless victim. They believe they are not responsible for solving their own problems because they are all someone else's fault. This is a Weak & Still RESPONSE arising from emotions like laziness, inadequacy, neediness, and anxiety. Their problem-solving strategy is to complain so much about the injustice and unfairness of the situation that others will solve their problems for them out of pity, guilt, or just to shut them up. If this strategy fails, and they are finally forced to solve the problem themselves, they do so resentfully and ineffectively, still hoping someone will step in at the last minute to finish solving it for them.

- **The Compensating Blamer.** These people deny responsibility for their mistakes and place blame on others because they are win/lose thinkers who believe that if they can make others look bad by blaming them, they can make themselves look better by comparison. This is a Weak RESPONSE generated by emotions like fear, shame, insecurity, and jealousy. They experience ongoing anxiety, because they believe everyone else is as eager to place blame as they are, and so they fear being blamed themselves. Since they see all problems in terms of blame, they associate *being responsible* with *being blamed*. For them, taking responsibility for a problem feels like an admission of guilt. When they are forced to take responsibility, they often react with a combination of embarrassment and irritation, saying things like, "I'll take care of it I have to, but I still say it's not my fault."

- **The Dominating Blamer.** These are also win/lose thinkers, but they see every problem situation as a power contest: someone will win by placing the blame, and someone will lose by getting stuck with the blame. This is a Weak & Active RESPONSE generated by emotions like aggression, hostility, suspicion, and selfishness. Their behavior often includes open belligerence, such as loud verbal confrontations and accusations. They are primarily interested in asserting their dominance, so when they are forced to accept responsibility they react with hostility, because they feel like someone else has dominated them. These people make terrible neighbors or coworkers, because they tend to escalate minor issues into major feuds. They often refuse to take simple steps to solve a problem themselves, because they are more interested in winning the feud than in achieving a positive outcome.

- **The Undermining Blamer.** These people engage in passive/aggressive behavior like sullen silence, constant complaining, and malicious gossiping. This is a Weak & Still RESPONSE motivated by emotions like bitterness, jealousy, ineffectiveness, or suspicion. In the workplace they often stir up resentment against management, and they tend to form cliques that pit some employees against others. They take problems, even minor ones, and turn them into weapons. If you have relatives like this, they are the ones who often spoil the fun of weddings or holidays by stirring up trouble.

All outward-focused blamers give away an important degree of control over their lives. Think of people you know who habitually try to make others solve their problems for them. They might expect their problems to be solved by their spouses, parents, friends, supervisors, or coworkers. Often these "others" have reinforced the habit by solving problems for the blamer in the past. This is not a healthy situation. As we saw in the discussion on procrastination in RESPONSE, giving away responsibility may feel like an advantage in the short term, but in the long run it is a losing proposition. Accepting personal responsibility is part of becoming a mature, capable adult. People who convince others to solve their problems for them end up trapped in a childlike state of dependence and immaturity. Taking responsibility for getting your own problems solved makes you stronger and more confident, and develops your problem-solving skills.

At the opposite end of the blame spectrum are the inward-focused *self-blamers*. These individuals feel compelled to blame themselves for problems even when it is obvious they are not at fault. This is a Weak & Still RESPONSE arising from emotions like submissiveness, guilt, shame, and timidity. It may appear preferable to outward-focused blaming because it is not an overt attack on others, but from a problem-solving perspective it is just as flawed. By focusing primarily on the concept of blame, and by inaccurately assigning the blame to themselves, they make it harder to clearly understand the true cause of the problem. *Taking blame* is different than *accepting responsibility*. Accepting responsibility arises from Strong emotions like confidence, serenity, and honor, and promotes clear understanding and action toward a solution.

Truly strong and confident people rarely focus on placing blame, just as they rarely focus on taking credit. They focus on *getting the problem solved*, and are therefore undistracted by the Weak emotions that arise from blame-focused thinking. Any time you suspect that you are not making good progress on a problem because you are focusing too much on whose fault it is, ask yourself, "What goal do *I want* to achieve?" and, "What is the obstacle *for me* to overcome?" Asking these questions with this extra emphasis will get you refocused on what *you* can do to achieve your desired outcome.

> **BE CAREFUL WITH BLAME: A TIP FOR MANAGERS**
>
> One of the key roles of a business leader is dealing with problems effectively. When a problem is brought to your attention, your job is to understand it, solve it, and ensure that it doesn't happen again. Sometimes part of this process is figuring out who, if anyone, caused the problem, so you can provide training, coaching, or discipline. But if your *primary* reaction to problems is to look for someone to blame, your staff will become fearful. No one wants to be the scapegoat, so they will become reluctant to inform you when a problem arises. They will focus more on avoiding blame than on producing results, stifling the healthy risk-taking that produces valuable innovation in any organization. This creates a "cover your rear" work environment in which employees seek to pass responsibility off on others rather than accept it themselves.
>
> Some managers even seem to believe that once they have figured out whom to blame, and have chewed out or punished the "guilty party," they have solved the problem. All they have actually done is ensure that the next time the problem happens (which it will, because it wasn't really solved), everyone will make sure it is kept secret from the manager. These managers end up not knowing what is really going on in their organization, diminishing their ability to lead.
>
> Don't make these mistakes. Instead, act as a role model for handling problems in an effective and positive manner. If you utilize a Strong RESPONSE focused primarily on helping to get the problem solved, you will encourage your staff to take responsibility for their actions and allow them to focus on producing results.
>
> *-Reagan*

Accepting responsibility for solving your problems helps you maintain your primary focus on *finding the best solution to achieve your goal*. But it does *not* mean you always have to do the work of overcoming an obstacle that someone else has caused. Sometimes your best solution will be to hold the person who created the obstacle accountable, and force that person to do the work of removing it. Other times you will be better off ignoring the question of fault and removing the obstacle yourself. By not getting sidetracked onto an obsession with blame, you will be able to evaluate the situation clearly and follow the strategy that gives you the best possible outcome.

LET OTHERS "OWN" THEIR OWN PROBLEMS

Almost as important as taking responsibility for *your* problems is *not* taking responsibility for *someone else's* problems. As you gain experience with the *Solution Power* tools, you will become an increasingly proficient problem-solver. In addition to solving your own problems more quickly and effectively, you will be better able to help your friends, family, and coworkers solve their problems. It's great to be willing and able to offer effective problem-solving assistance.

However, there is a fine line between being helpful and being a meddler. We all know how irritating it can be to have someone intrude into our problems in a manner that is not appropriate or welcome. So when a problem is primarily someone else's responsibility, *ask first* before helping. If you have something helpful to offer, and your assistance has not been requested, just ask, "May I help?" "Are you all right?" or, "I have an idea that might help, are you interested?" Then abide by the answer you receive.

There is also a difference between being helpful and being an enabler or rescuer. Don't end up being the kind of person we discussed earlier who makes others weak by always solving their problems for them. Allow others to gain strength and maturity by taking responsibility for their own problems, so they don't end up as problem-avoiders, procrastinators, or victims.

It can be difficult to distinguish between helpfulness and intrusiveness when you are in the role of a teacher, because *your* problem is how to help others learn how to solve *their* problems. For example:

- If you are a parent, you are responsible for ensuring that your child learns good behavior and useful skills. If you want to teach your child to fold the laundry, and the child does it slowly and sloppily at first, it would obviously be a mistake to take over folding all the laundry yourself.

- If you are a supervisor at work, you are responsible for ensuring that your employees learn to perform their jobs effectively. If an employee does poor work on a project, it would be a mistake for you to simply re-do all the work yourself, instead of having the employee correct the errors.

In these examples your goal as the "teacher" is not to get the laundry folded or to get the project done, but rather to help your "student" learn to perform the task successfully. Teaching well is your problem, but learning well is the student's problem. If you simply take over the task, you deprive the student of an opportunity to learn valuable skills.

If you have ever been in a situation like this, you know it is not always easy to handle it correctly. What if it is late in the evening, the children have homework to do, there is a huge pile of laundry, and you are just plain tired of nagging them to do the folding more neatly? What if your boss needs a project done ASAP and error-free, and the employee to whom you delegated it is a slow worker who will need a lot of coaching to get it done correctly? If you feel confused in situations like these, it is because you have *dual roles*. In the first example, you are both a parent *and* a head of household, so you are responsible for teaching your child how to fold the laundry and also responsible for ensuring that the folding gets done. In the second example, you are both a supervisor *and* a worker, so you are responsible for teaching your staff how to do projects and also responsible for ensuring that the projects get done.

In situations like these, you can use PRIORITY to help you decide which role should take precedence. If you decide that teaching is most important, have the student do the work. If, as a result, the family gets to bed late or you take some heat from your boss, point out these consequences to the student. If you decide to do the task yourself, or compromise and help the student do it, make it clear you are doing so only as a matter of short-term practicality.

USE CLARIFYING LANGUAGE

The words we use when we talk about our problems strongly influence how we perceive them. We actually do listen to ourselves talk, and we tend to believe what we hear ourselves say. In fact, the words we use can powerfully affect our thoughts, feelings, and beliefs on a subconscious level.

Avoid catastrophizing. Some people have developed the habit of using extreme words like "disaster" or "complete mess" to describe their problems, and words like "furious" or "driving me crazy" to describe how they feel about them. They talk about every problem as if it were a catastrophe, which is why this habit is called *catastrophizing*.

Catastrophizing makes it harder to perceive a problem clearly. If people describe routine problems as "absolute disasters" then how will they describe truly disastrous problems? Describing every problem in extreme terms makes it harder to distinguish ordinary problems from really serious ones. It also leads to the "crying wolf" effect: when they need help with a problem that actually is quite serious, others will be less likely to believe them and offer assistance.

People who habitually use extreme words also cause themselves to experience Weak emotions that hinder clear thinking.

Hearing themselves say that a situation is "hopeless" makes them feel discouraged. Describing it as an "absolute disaster" makes them feel anxious. Saying they are "absolutely furious" or "about to have a nervous breakdown" increases their stress level. These Weak emotions make it harder for them to think rationally and calmly, and therefore harder to gain a clear understanding of the problem. After all, if the situation is truly "hopeless" why make any effort to understand it?

Catastrophizing can even become a self-fulfilling prophecy. If someone feels a little angry and says, "I am absolutely furious," it can cause the anger to escalate into a state of fury. If someone is feeling a little discouraged and says, "I am devastated," she can talk herself into feeling truly depressed.

Avoid minimizing. There are also people on the other end of the language spectrum. They use phrases like, "It's nothing to worry about" or, "I've got it under control" to minimize problems that may actually be quite serious. This is a defense mechanism that allows them to avoid thinking about and dealing with situations that really need their attention, but that they find disturbing or frightening. Minimizing a problem, like refusing to admit having a problem, often causes a person to ignore it until it becomes a crisis. This is obviously not an effective problem-solving strategy.

MINIMIZING PROBLEMS: A TIP FOR MANAGERS

If you are in a supervisory or managerial position, be very sensitive to the phrase "Don't worry about it." It is a big red flag. If any member of my staff ever says that to me, I respond with "Well, if I wasn't worried about it before, I sure am now." And then I grill that person in detail until I know exactly what is going on. In my experience, the *only* time people say, "Don't worry about it" is when there is something you really *should* be worried about and they don't want you to know it!

-Reagan

Use words effectively. The goal when talking about a problem is to neither catastrophize nor minimize, but to instead use words *effectively*. What does it mean to use words effectively? It means using words that accurately describe the problem *and* help you generate a Strong RESPONSE to it.

For example, suppose a CEO discovers that 30% of his company's products contain significant defects and that as a consequence the company is rapidly losing its customers. In situations like this it is vitally important to use words effectively. The CEO might say to his staff, "This is a disaster! You're all a bunch of incompetent morons! The company is doomed!" Or he might choose to say, "This is a very serious situation. We're smart people, let's analyze the manufacturing process from the ground up. When we're done, we'll have the best quality control system in the industry!" It is hard to say which of these two statements is more *accurate*, but the second statement is certainly more *effective*. It will help the CEO and his staff understand and solve the problem by putting them in a positive, solution-oriented state of mind.

You can tell whether words are effective or ineffective by how they make you feel when you hear yourself or someone else say them:

Ineffective Words Make You Feel	*Effective Words Make You Feel*
Fearful	Courageous
Insecure	Confident
Pessimistic	Optimistic
Depressed	Energetic
Discouraged	Motivated
Frantic	Calm
Uninterested	Curious
Helpless	In Control

Think about some of the words and phrases you habitually use when faced with a problem. You may have become so accustomed to making certain comments that you hardly even realize you are saying them. Regularly using ineffective phrases can push you into Weak RESPONSES even if you just say them out of habit and "don't really mean it." See if any of the phrases on this list seem familiar:

- "This is just too much."
- "I don't care anymore."
- "Isn't that just typical."
- "What else do you expect from _____."
- "It's just killing me."
- "This is impossible."
- "It's hopeless."
- "Here we go again."
- "I am absolutely furious."

Phrases like these attach negative emotional "junk" to problems, which interferes with your ability to see them with clear eyes and a calm mind.

Some people who use such phrases say they are "just being realistic." Be cautious about "being realistic" when describing problems. On the one hand, as we discussed previously, it is important to face problems honestly and describe the problem as it truly is. On the other hand, you should carefully distinguish between *realism* and *pessimism* in your assessment of a problem. Often, people who say that they are "being realistic" when they describe a problem as "impossible" or "a disaster," are actually being pessimistic or defeatist. You can avoid doing this by adopting the habit of using effective, rather than ineffective, words to describe problems.

If you currently have a habit of using ineffective language to describe problems, it's time to get rid of it. The fastest and easiest way to eliminate a bad habit is to replace it with a new and better habit, so choose some effective words and consciously use them whenever a problem arises. To start with, we recommend choosing a few effective words from the following list:

- "Interesting"
- "Exciting"
- "Challenging"
- "Inconvenient"
- "Concerned"
- "Unpleasant"
- "Unfortunate"
- "Serious"
- "Critical"

"Interesting" is quite possibly the best all-purpose word to use when you don't know what else to say about a problem. For one thing, every significant problem really is interesting on some level. Plus, "interesting" is a neutral word that keeps your options open while you decide how you ought to feel about the problem. Finally, it stimulates your sense of curiosity, and curiosity is a powerful problem-solving emotion.

Notice that we do not recommend reacting to difficult problems with phony cheerfulness, or by pretending there is nothing wrong. It is useful and healthy to describe the seriousness of a problem accurately, and in a way that strengthens your confidence. You can use words like "concerned," "unfortunate," and "serious" to recognize the magnitude of a problem instead of using catastrophizing words like "terrified," "awful," or "disastrous." If someone says he is "terrified" by a problem, he makes himself sound weak, and probably makes himself *feel* weak. Saying you are "concerned" shows that you are aware of the seriousness of the problem, but that you are confident you can handle it. And in many circumstances you can use words like "exciting" and "challenging" to cast a positive light on the situation.

Don't limit yourself to our list of suggested effective words. Explore the almost endless variety of words that can help you describe problems more precisely and effectively. Listen to, and read about, people who are effective problem-solvers. When they use a word or phrase that seems especially useful, make a note of it and try using it yourself. The richer your vocabulary becomes, the better you can describe the wide variety of problems you encounter. When you find words that put you in a Strong state, start using them regularly when problems arise.

DESCRIBING PROBLEMS EFFECTIVELY

I was once given the opportunity to create a new claims management operation, but it had to be up and running in less than two months. That was a tough challenge! I needed to hire people who could perform well under difficult circumstances, and I also needed to put them in the right frame of mind.

When I interviewed applicants, I described the challenge frankly but with carefully chosen words. I told them it would be "a wild ride" like being "on a roller coaster." At times it would seem "pretty intense" but it would also be "fun and exciting." I assured them "no one will be flying solo" and that we would "support each other and succeed as a team."

I hired the applicants who responded to these phrases with excitement rather than trepidation. We worked long, hard hours, and we succeeded. When we talked about the experience later, several of them said it had been an exciting, challenging, and positive experience, but that *if I had not told them up front what to expect and how to feel about it, it would have been a miserable ordeal.* This shows how important it is to describe a problem accurately and effectively to the team that is responsible for solving it. It gives them a mental framework for how think and feel about the experience in a positive manner.

-Reagan

GET PERSPECTIVE

How big do your problems appear to you? If you perceive your problems as being bigger or stronger than you are, you will likely feel discouraged or overwhelmed. Seeing a problem as a huge fearsome monster towering over you, or as a vast swamp in which you are lost, will make it difficult for you to think clearly about it and take action to solve it. It is easier to understand a problem if you shrink your perception of it down to a manageable size.

One technique for putting a problem in perspective is to mentally view the situation from a distance, as though you are an outside observer. Imagine yourself in an airplane or balloon high above the problem, or in a tower on a distant hilltop, observing the problem through binoculars. From these vantage points any problem will look smaller and more manageable. It will also seem less threatening, because you are observing it from a safe distance. You can say to yourself, "Look at that person down there with that problem. How would I solve that problem if I were in that situation?" Problems always look simpler to those viewing them from the outside than to those caught up in the midst of them, so give yourself the benefit of that perspective.

You can also get perspective by imagining that you are watching a video of the problem on your TV set. You can use your remote control to replay the problem any way you want. For example, if your problem is that your boss is hostile and intimidating, try replaying a recent encounter on your imaginary television set. If you start to feel intimidated, just turn off the sound and watch the old SOB rant and rave without making any noise! Or play it on fast forward so his voice sounds like a squeaky chipmunk! Or pause in the middle of one of his criticisms and say to yourself, "Wait a minute, that's just not true! I am *not* going to feel bad about that!" You can even edit the scene, changing how you felt, what you said, and how you acted during the experience. This allows you to mentally practice a better way of handling the problem the next time it occurs.

You can use imagery in another way by visualizing the problem as an object of some kind, which you can then manipulate and control. For example, suppose you had the problem of being in debt. You might already have a vague image of that debt as an enormous wave threatening to crash down and drown you, or as a huge mountain that you cannot hope to climb, or as a monster that will consume you. Allowing this kind of imagery to get planted in your mind makes it harder to find solutions, and often ends up making the problem worse. If you are afraid of your debt, you are more likely to avoid paying the bills and balancing the bank statement, because those activities make you think about the frightening debt. In order to solve the problem effectively, you first need to cut your perception of it down to size.

Let's use the "monster" image as an example. Start by imagining your debt as a huge, fearsome, fire-breathing dragon. It is taller than a house. The flames it shoots from its mouth could burn you to a cinder. Its roar is loud enough to shake the earth. Its glistening scales make it invincible to attack. You are powerless before it!

Now imagine that you have a hidden weapon the dragon does not know about: a magic wand. The wand has the power to shrink anything, including scary dragons. So take out your wand and shrink that nasty debt dragon down to size! Shrink him down to the size of cow, than to the size of a dog, and finally to the size of a tiny mouse. Poor little thing, he hardly knows what to do. Scoop him up and set him on your kitchen table. Put your finger in front of his snout and tease him a little bit. Oh look, he's so mad he's shooting his tiny flame at you! That's fine, all it does is make your finger tip pleasantly warm. Now he's trying to roar, but it just sounds like a little kitten mewing. You have absolutely nothing to fear from this little debt dragon. If he gives you any trouble, just flick him across the room!

Now you have created a state of mind in which you can analyze your debt situation calmly, without your thoughts getting jumbled by fear and anxiety. Similarly, you can turn the image of a giant wave into a little puddle, shrink a mountain to the size of an anthill, or change a vast swamp into a little weed patch. This technique of using visual imagery is a great way to gain a calmer and clearer understanding of any problem.

USING HUMOR TO GAIN PERSPECTIVE

Looking for the bright side (or at least the amusing side) of a problem is a good way to get perspective. If nothing else, you can always laugh at yourself for getting into such a predicament! Sharing humor with others when times are tough is also a good way to build teamwork, to create a sense of facing the challenge together.

I worked for a printing company during the years when the industry was changing from manual paste-up to computerized graphics. Needless to say, there were many occasions when the new equipment failed, in ways that caused everything from mild irritation to jaw-dropping dismay.

One of my coworkers during that period was a sharp young guy with a great attitude. He habitually reacted to these difficulties with an amused smile and a wry comment like, "Why, that's crazy!" By pretending to be surprised when the software crashed or the hardware malfunctioned, even though it had been happening regularly for quite some time, he defused the frustration and tension, instantly replacing it with a positive and lighthearted mood. Then he would dig right into solving the problem.

One time, upon observing a particularly spectacular failure, he said, "That's so crazy, it's almost ... *wacky!*" Everyone laughed along. His attitude and his choice of words were an important part of what made him an effective solution-finder. His ability to laugh at a problem established that he was bigger than the problem, that he saw it as a little bump in the road rather than as an overwhelming catastrophe. And he helped the rest of us feel the same way.

-Kevin

Analyze the Problem

In this section we will discuss techniques for analyzing problems in order to understand them more fully. These are not the kind of specialized analytical techniques that apply only to one particular kind of problem, such as a doctor diagnosing a medical condition or an auto mechanic identifying the malfunctioning part of an engine. These are broader techniques that can be applied to problems of any kind.

Put it in Writing

In order to analyze any kind of problem, you must first *stop and think about it*. This seems obvious, but it is surprisingly easy to skip this fundamental step. It is one thing to *worry about* a problem as you go about your busy life, but how can you make yourself take a step back and really think about it?

One good method is to sit down with a pad of paper, or at a keyboard, and write. The process of writing automatically concentrates your attention, creating a mental space that is dedicated to understanding the problem. Writing also naturally clarifies your thinking. Thoughts are often vague and undefined when they are floating around inside your head. Putting them in writing immediately makes them more detailed and specific. Plus, when you write something you also *read* it. You will often be pleasantly surprised by the insights that appear on the page.

There are many useful ways to analyze a problem by putting it in writing. Use whatever approach works best for you and for the particular problem at hand. For example:

- Create a problem statement using the "I want *goal*, but *obstacle*" format. Make a list of possible goals and obstacles, and identify the ones that best define the problem.
- Make a list of possible causes of the problem.

- Develop a chronology listing the events relating to the problem in the order they occurred. When did the problem start, and how has it progressed?
- List the people who are involved in the problem, and what role they each play.
- Draw diagrams, doodles, graphs, pictures, charts, or any other method you can use for expressing the problem visually.
- Write down what you know about the problem, and what you still need to learn about it.
- As you think about the problem jot down whatever words occur to you, such as names, physical characteristics, risks, rewards, emotions, and visual images.
- If the problem involves making a difficult choice, create two columns listing the pros and cons, or the possible outcomes of both choices.
- Compose a poem about the problem, or write about the problem as a mystery story or a fairy tale.
- Create a journal by jotting down ideas and insights about the problem as they occur to you, or at a set time each day or each week.
- List the solutions you have already tried, and the results each one produced.

Putting your thoughts in writing will make many of the other *Solution Power* techniques even more effective. For example, later in this chapter we will recommend turning complex problems into problem-solving projects. Putting a problem-solving project in writing will make each stage of the project clearer, give you a written game plan to keep you organized, and allow you to track your progress more easily.

> **THINKING IN WRITING**
>
> My Freshman English class at Haverford College was taught by Professor Paul, a tough teacher with strong opinions and high standards. One of his maxims was, "You have not truly had an idea until you have put it in writing." I was inclined to dismiss this as an exaggeration at the time, but experience has taught me its essential truth.
>
> The act of writing, of committing an idea to words, is itself an exercise in CLARITY. I frequently use the discipline of writing when tackling a tough problem at work. After gathering and analyzing the facts, I sit down at the computer and draft a detailed memo on the problem and my proposed solution. Putting it in writing helps me identify gaps or flaws I had previously overlooked, leading me to gather additional information or reconsider my assumptions. It is amazing how often the act of writing causes me to fundamentally alter my thinking, leading to a very different and much better solution. It also provides a sense of progress, because by putting my ideas on paper I am already taking action toward finding a solution.
>
> Most of the time I don't actually send these memos to anyone; I write them mainly to clarify my own understanding of the problem.
>
> *-Reagan*

GATHER THE FACTS

When analyzing a problem, first collect and record as much objective information about the problem as possible and then use your experience, intuition, and judgment to determine what those facts mean. A common problem-solving error is trying to understand a problem based only on impressions, rather than on reliable information. Trust your gut instincts, but base your problem-solving on solid facts whenever possible.

Gathering facts helps overcome false or limiting assumptions. Life teaches us again and again that our understanding of a situation is often inaccurate even when we are "absolutely sure" we know what the problem is. Impressions can be wrong, and sometimes *very* wrong, even among knowledgeable people who are close to the situation. More than anything else, confronting yourself with undeniable facts can help you, or even compel you, to get rid of inaccurate assumptions. When the plain facts reveal that your previous understanding was not correct, you have no choice but to open your mind to fundamentally different possibilities.

For example, gathering information can:

- Help you better understand the true cause and nature of the problem
- Show you that the cause or nature of the problem is fundamentally different than you had thought
- Reveal that there actually is no problem

Getting complete and accurate data is obviously important when analyzing scientific or financial problems, or problems involving business processes. However, it is also important for problems of the heart. You can probably think of a relationship problem that arose because one person misunderstood what the other person actually said, did, or intended. It is easier to understand and work through interpersonal conflicts when those involved share an accurate understanding of the facts.

THE VALUE OF FACTS

While working for an insurance organization, I organized a task force of high-level employees to solve a long-standing claims management issue. We held several lengthy meetings discussing the many difficult aspects of the issue without arriving at a good solution.

We finally delegated one member of the team to conduct detailed factual research. His report at the next meeting stunned us. The issue had always loomed large in our minds because it was so complicated and time-consuming to address when it arose in a claim. However, the data revealed that it actually affected very few claims and had minimal financial impact. Even the worst possible outcome would have no appreciable impact on the financial health of the company.

We quickly created a streamlined process for handling the claims affected by issue, and then disbanded the task force.

-Reagan

Find the Root Problem

Consider these problems:

- A business is receiving a high volume of calls from angry, dissatisfied customers.
- A child brings home a report card with low grades.
- A man is reprimanded by his boss for being repeatedly late for work.
- A woman's car makes a disturbing noise whenever she turns the steering wheel.

In these examples the phone calls, report card, reprimand, and noise are *secondary problems*. They are actually just symptoms of an underlying problem, which we call the *root problem*. If someone spends significant time and energy trying to solve a secondary problem, but does not solve the root problem that is causing it, the secondary problem will quickly crop up again. For example, some parents try to "solve" a bad report card by pressuring their child's teachers into raising the grades. However, the child's low grades might be caused by a learning disability, poor study habits, undiagnosed nearsightedness, lack of sleep, or just plain laziness. Even if the parents convince the teachers to change the grades this time, none of these possible root causes will be solved and the secondary problem of low grades will occur again.

Of course, in order to solve a root problem, you first need to identify it. One good way to do so is to *follow the symptoms to the source*. In other words, you can use secondary problems as clues or trail markers, and follow them back to the root problem.

This is not always easy to do. Often, people mistakenly think that a secondary problem *is* the root problem, and waste time and effort trying to solve it. This happens because secondary problems are usually more conspicuous than root problems, so they are likely to attract people's attention. In each of the four examples above, the secondary problem is something that can be easily seen or heard, while the root problem is more difficult to discern.

Here is a dramatic illustration of the difference between a secondary problem and a root problem: Imagine that a man is in his living room when a candle falls over and sets a couch cushion on fire. He gets a fire extinguisher from the kitchen and rushes back into the living room. What will capture his attention? Most likely it will be the flames. They are bright, constantly in motion, and dangerous. Because his attention is focused on the flames, he is likely to aim the fire extinguisher at them, and spray the contents of the extinguisher *through* the flames onto the back of the couch. Unfortunately, that will not put out the fire. The flames themselves are only symptoms of the root problem, which is the chemical reaction occurring in the overheated couch cushion. What he needs to do is aim the extinguisher lower, at the *source* of the fire. If he sprays the couch cushion that is burning, he will put out the fire.

Visualize that image of the fire and the extinguisher, and store it in your memory. In the future, if you find yourself wrestling unsuccessfully with a problem, bring the image back to mind and ask yourself, "Am I aiming the fire extinguisher at the flames or at the fuel?" Meaning, are you wasting your efforts on a secondary problem rather than attacking the problem at its root? If the answer is yes, then "aim your fire extinguisher lower" by seeking to discover and address the source of the problem.

If you prefer a more serene image, think of a problem as being like a dandelion growing in your lawn. The flower and leaves are the visible symptoms of the problem, but plucking them off is will not get rid of the weed. It will soon grow back again. You have to dig the dandelion up by the root, just as you have to "dig up" the root cause of any problem to solve it effectively.

> **SOLVING PROBLEMS AT THE ROOT**
>
> A friend of mine built a very successful career as an effective problem-solver. He traveled widely in the employment of a Fortune 100 company, keeping a number of difficult projects on track and turning around the ones that were struggling. The company-wide awards he won in his position as Director of Quality reflected his strong solution-finding skills.
>
> The following story provides insight into a fundamental strategy he used to solve problems of all kinds:
>
> One summer his wife was frustrated with their nine-year-old son, because the boy's shoes were always untied and his hair was never combed. However much she reminded or disciplined him, the problems continued. One Saturday morning the man and his son got in the car and were gone for a few hours. When they returned, the boy had a crew cut and was wearing slip-on shoes. Problems solved! Can't keep the hair combed? Cut off the hair! Can't keep the shoes tied? Get rid of the shoelaces! Everyone was pleased to have the issues resolved with no need for further dispute.
>
> What problems could you eliminate in this way? Is there something in your life – a possession, a relationship, or even a way of thinking – that you could simply get rid of once and for all, rather than having to continually deal with the secondary problems that it generates?
>
> *-Kevin*

You can follow secondary problems to their root by asking questions. Asking questions is one of the most fundamental and powerful problem-solving techniques. Consider the incredible ability of young children to solve problems. *Everything* is new and confusing to them. At every turn they confront problems with which they have no experience. "What is inside this box?" "Where did Mom hide the candy?" "Who took my favorite toy?" "How can I button my shirt?" Relentless curiosity is their problem-solving method of choice, and they end up mastering some of the biggest problems they will face in their entire lives, like learning to walk, talk, and read.

However, despite the tremendous problem-solving success we experience as children, many of us lose the habit of asking questions when we become adults. This is quite a loss, because people who continue to ask questions throughout life have a tremendous solution-finding advantage. Curiosity has extraordinary power to help you understand yourself and the world you live in, and to create the greatest number of opportunities for enlightenment, growth, success, and fulfillment.

There is a simple and effective technique for using curiosity to discover root problems. If you have been wrestling unsuccessfully with a problem, just take a look at the problem and ask, "Why?" Then, like a curious child, ask it again and again until you discover the root.

Let's consider the example mentioned previously of the man who has been reprimanded by his boss for repeatedly showing up late for work. He has known for some time that he has a problem: "I want to succeed in my job, but being late so often is hurting my reputation and affecting my performance evaluations." So he starts asking himself "why":

Q: "Why am I late for work?"

A: "Because I leave the house too late."

Q: "Why do I leave the house too late?"

A: "Because I don't get out of bed on time. I'm so tired I just keep hitting the snooze button."

Q: "Why am I too tired to get out of bed on time?"

A: "Because I stay up too late at night, so I don't get enough sleep."

Q: "Why don't I go to bed on time?"

A: "Because almost every evening I turn on the TV and then I stay up late watching it. I don't turn it off and go to sleep when I should."

Q: "Why do I stay up watching TV?"

A: "I don't know. I don't even enjoy it very much. There are hardly any really good shows on. I just channel surf, watching five minutes of one show and then ten minutes of another show. I get tired, but I keep on changing channels looking for something worth watching. It's just a habit."

Q: "How will I break this lousy habit and replace it with a better habit that will help me regularly get to bed on time?"

Notice that the man had to dig through several layers of symptoms – several secondary problems – before he got to the root. His previous problem-solving efforts had concentrated on what he should do differently in the morning in order to leave for work on time. He had made sincere and determined resolutions to get out of bed as soon as his alarm clock went off. These resolutions did not last, because his willpower could not consistently overcome his chronic lack of sleep. By the time his alarm clock went off it was too late for him to effectively solve the problem, because the problem had started when he turned on his television set the previous evening. Problems are rarely solved effectively at the symptom level.

Now that he has identified the root problem he can look for ways to break this pattern of behavior. Perhaps he could move the TV out of his bedroom into the living room, place an alarm clock on top of it set to go off 30 minutes before his bedtime, and put the remote control away so he can't channel surf. Even better, he could replace his current routine altogether. Instead of sitting passively in front of a TV set each evening, he could pursue more satisfying hobbies that reflect his interests and abilities, or that include more interaction with his friends and family.

The technique of following symptoms to the source can be used for problems that are emotional in nature. As we discussed earlier, people sometimes experience Weak emotions like anxiety, sadness, or anger without clearly identifying the problem that is causing it. They could do so by mentally following the Weak emotion back to its source.

For example, suppose you are in the middle of a workday and realize you are feeling anxious. Rather than just trying to ignore the feeling, take a few moments and look within yourself. Don't try to stifle the anxiety. Instead, view it with curiosity: "Where did this start? Why am I feeling this?" Allow your thoughts to follow the emotion back to its source. It helps to close your eyes, and it usually takes just a minute or two. You will be surprised how often you can track the feeling right back to the event that caused it. Perhaps it arose from some little remark a coworker made several hours earlier about your work or your appearance.

Now that you know where the feeling began you can do something about it. You can analyze the remark, and say to yourself, "What nonsense! That's just not true, and I'm certainly not going to feel bad about it any longer!" It is a good idea to identify and deal with the causes of Weak emotions promptly. Otherwise they can pile up over a period of days, weeks, and months until they seriously interfere with your enjoyment of life.

They can also cause problems in relationships. When people experience Weak emotions and don't know what caused them, they often end up redirecting those emotions at their loved ones. For example, if a woman comes home from work feeling angry without knowing why, she may end up taking it out on her husband or her children. Identifying the true source of a Weak emotion and taking steps to deal with the root problem promptly would help her to prevent this from occurring.

CREATE A PROBLEM-SOLVING PROJECT

A useful technique for analyzing a complex or challenging problem is to treat it as a series of smaller problems. Instead of trying to find a single grand solution that will solve the problem all at once, it may feel less daunting and be more efficient to turn it into a project, in which you systematically solve the problem one piece at a time.

For example, starting your own business can be quite a challenge. The process can include conducting market research, securing various licenses and registrations, obtaining financing, renting office or shop space, purchasing supplies, generating publicity, and a hundred and one other things. It works better to concentrate on one task at a time, because thinking about the whole process at once can be intimidating.

To turn the problem of starting your own business into a project, your first step would be to create a list of all of these tasks, arranged in the order in which they should be completed. Creating the list is a task in itself! Obtaining information from your local Small Business Administration and seeking advice from others who have successfully founded companies can help. Then start with the first item on the list and tackle one after another until you have them all checked off.

As much as possible, concentrate on the tasks one at a time. If you find yourself peeking ahead and getting discouraged by an item that you don't need to be working on yet, just tell yourself, "I will cross that bridge when I get to it" and put it out of your mind. You will make faster progress if you keep your attention and energy focused on the task at hand.

Almost any significant problem in the workplace can be handled as a project, and it also works well for complex problems in your personal life. Here is a system for creating problem-solving projects:

1. Write down your problem statement: "I want *goal* but *obstacle*." State the goal as positively and vividly as possible, in a way that will inspire and motivate you to achieve it. Describe the obstacle as accurately as possible.
2. Divide the problem into three to five main pieces, and list them in the order they will be addressed.
3. If necessary, you can subdivide those pieces into even smaller tasks.
4. Set a deadline for solving the entire problem, one that seems possible but will require you to work quickly and efficiently. The right deadline will provide your project with a positive, energizing sense of urgency.
5. Working backward from the final deadline, set interim deadlines for solving each piece of the problem. If doing so reveals that the final deadline is truly impossible to meet, you can push it back, but just enough to make it possible.
6. For each step of the project, state in writing what must be accomplished by the interim deadline and by whom. Assigning responsibility, to yourself or someone else, is vital. Don't leave anything up in the air.
7. Monitor your progress. Be open to modifying the plan as you go; it is rare that a plan is executed exactly as planned. However, only revise deadlines if truly necessary. Repeatedly extending deadlines will diminish your energy level and sense of urgency.
8. Acknowledge and celebrate each successful interim solution. Remember that you get more of what you focus on, so if you focus on success you will become more successful.

Conclusion

On one hand, problems *are what they are*. Problems involve hard facts, inescapable deadlines, plain words, and real people. So it is important to see problems as they really are. Ask questions, dig down to the root, honestly define your goals, and take responsibility for reaching them.

On the other hand, problems *are what you make them*. You can often choose to treat a problem as a minor irritation, a major trauma, or a great opportunity. So it is important to define problems by what you want rather than by what you lack, and to choose perspectives that give you the most control over how you see them and feel about them.

These are not contradictory ideas. In reality, they are a one-two punch that you can throw at any problem. Develop the habit of defining problems clearly, then giving yourself all the leverage you need to get them solved quickly and effectively.

Clarity: Summary

Gain Internal Clarity

- **Define the problem.** Change an initial, negative definition of a problem into a positive one by creating a problem statement in the "I want *goal* but *obstacle*" format.
- **Be honest with yourself.** Make a firm commitment to look at the situation squarely and not make any excuses. Face problems sooner, rather than later.
- **Take responsibility rather than place blame.** You are responsible for reaching your own goals, even when someone else has created the obstacle. Focusing too much on blame can distract you from finding a solution.

- **Let others "own" their own problems.** Don't irritate others by meddling, or weaken their problem-solving abilities by rescuing. In a teaching situation you must handle dual roles and shared responsibility.
- **Use clarifying language.** Do not catastrophize or minimize. Rather, use effective words that accurately describe the problem and support a Strong RESPONSE.
- **Get perspective.** Change your mental viewpoint or your image of the problem in order to make it less threatening and more manageable.

ANALYZE THE PROBLEM

- **Put it in writing.** Clarify your understanding of a problem by writing about it.
- **Gather the facts.** Collect as much objective information about the problem as possible and then use your experience, intuition, and judgment to determine what the facts mean.
- **Find the root problem.** Finding and solving the root problem is more effective than dealing with secondary problems. Asking "why" repeatedly is an effective way to find the root problem.
- **Create a problem-solving project.** Turn a complex problem into a series of tasks, and set deadlines for completing them.

The Fourth Tool

Focus

Keep Moving In the Right Direction

There are four levels of Focus:
1. Focus on **Having a Problem**
2. Focus on **Overcoming Obstacles**
3. Focus on **Achieving Your Goal**
4. Focus on **Attaining Fulfillment**

Each of these levels of Focus can be powerful and helpful if used properly, but each can also become a trap. Getting stuck in any of the levels makes it very difficult to solve a problem. Therefore, the Focus tool includes learning to use each level in the most effective manner, and also learning to move quickly and easily between them while working on a problem. It means developing the ability to shift into the level of Focus that is most useful at each stage of the problem-solving process.

When you learned how to drive a car, you had to develop the skill of shifting your focus effortlessly and effectively. Driving is difficult at first because you must consciously remember to pay attention to many different things: the speedometer, the mirrors, the fuel gauge, road signs, traffic lights, and, of course, the road in front of you. With experience, the conscious effort of checking each of these items became habitual, and now your attention shifts automatically and effortlessly from one item to another, allowing you to easily keep track of everything that is happening around you. Likewise, you can develop the habit of shifting your attention among the different levels of FOCUS as you work on solving a problem.

FOCUS ON HAVING A PROBLEM

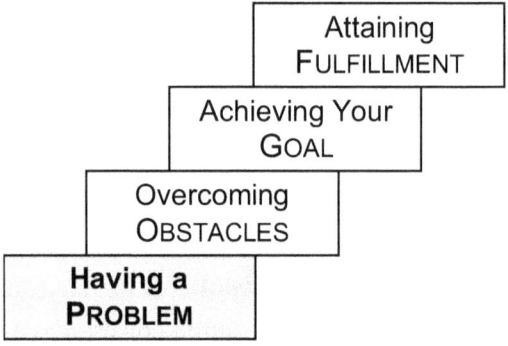

FOCUS EFFECTIVELY ON HAVING A PROBLEM

Focusing effectively on having a problem means recognizing it, understanding it, and reacting positively to it. You can do so by using problem-solving techniques we have already discussed:

- RESPONSE. Promptly recognize that a problem has arisen by saying, "I have a problem to solve," and use the techniques for generating motivation and a Strong RESPONSE.

- CLARITY. Define the problem as, "I want *goal*, but *obstacle*," which helps you think positively about what outcome you want to achieve and what you will have to overcome in order to produce that outcome.

This will put you in an excellent position to shift your focus to overcoming the obstacles and achieving your goal.

DON'T GET STUCK AT THE PROBLEM LEVEL

Getting stuck at the problem level is one of the most common problem-solving mistakes. You should focus on a problem just long enough to gain CLARITY and generate a strong RESPONSE. Then it's time to move up to the overcoming obstacles level. Allowing yourself to continue focusing on a problem any longer than that is unproductive.

Every time you focus on something, you send a message to your subconscious: "This is important to me." The more often you choose to focus on the same thing, the more your subconscious learns that it is important to you, and it will then be on the lookout for it. Whenever it arises your subconscious will remind you: "This is something that is important to you, so you had better focus your attention on it." A self-reinforcing cycle is created.

This ability to train the subconscious to focus on what is important is a valuable survival mechanism. For example, in ancient times it helped primitive humans focus their attention while hunting. Their subconscious minds became keenly attuned to focus on any sound or movement – a tuft of hair, a movement in the brush, the sound of a twig snapping – that might indicate the presence of an animal that could become food for their families.

This trait continues to serve a useful purpose in the modern world. For example, parents train their children to focus on certain things to help keep them safe. When a child is about to cross a street, the parent will say something like, "Look both ways before crossing the street!" By repeatedly directing the child to focus her attention on looking for oncoming traffic before stepping off the curb, the parent trains the child's subconscious mind that this is important. At some point the child's subconscious "gets it" and the child reflexively looks both ways every time she comes to a street without needing to be reminded.

Once established, these habits are powerful. As an experiment, try walking across a street without looking both ways. (To ensure safety, have someone watch for traffic for you.) Even in a quiet, low-traffic neighborhood you will find it is surprisingly difficult to resist this subconscious patterning. Even if you don't turn your head, you will notice that your ears are automatically on high alert for the sound of an approaching car.

Your problem-solving identity. The same process is at work in the development of problem-solving habits. If you focus on having problems just long enough to be motivated by them and understand them, and then shift your focus to getting them solved, you send a message to your subconscious that *solving problems* is what is important to you. If you do this consistently, your subconscious will eventually conclude that *you are someone who solves problems*. That message now becomes a part of your self-identity, a part of *who you are* on a fundamental level.

Your subconscious automatically acts in accordance with any characteristic that has become a part of your self-identity. So once your subconscious has concluded that you are someone who solves problems, whenever you encounter a problem your subconscious will automatically do everything it can to help you find a solution.

The problem-suffering identity. Unfortunately, many people fall into the opposite habit and become permanently stuck in the problem level. Even though this is an unproductive and disagreeable way to live, it is hard for them to escape because habits of belief and behavior are difficult to change once they have become embedded in the subconscious.

Suppose someone focuses on the negative aspects of problems when they arise, rather than on getting them solved:

- "This is so unfair, and it's not my fault!"
- "What a disaster, I'm doomed!"
- "I am so humiliated."
- "There is no way out of this mess!"
- "Someone is going to pay for this!"

When a person focuses on thoughts like these, he sends a message to his subconscious that *suffering from problems* is what is important to him. If he does this consistently, his subconscious will conclude that *he is someone who suffers from problems.* That appalling message now becomes a part of his self-identity.

As we have seen, the subconscious automatically acts in accordance with self-identity. Because his subconscious knows that he is someone who suffers from problems, if one of his problems ever happens to get solved, his subconscious will immediately go looking for a new problem he can suffer over!

Although it may seem strange that someone would actually go looking for trouble in this way, just think about it: *you know people like this*. Maybe you work with one. Maybe you are married to one. Maybe you were raised by one. We all know at least one of these *problem-suffering people*, and dealing with them can be quite a challenge. These individuals would be truly, deeply uncomfortable if all of their problems somehow went away. They simply would not know what to say or how to behave, because their basic self-identities, and their habits of thought, conversation, and behavior, all revolve around suffering from their problems.

Problem-suffering people lead difficult and unhappy lives. They experience almost constant anxiety, and their pessimistic patterns of thought make it hard for them to solve even relatively simple problems. Of course, they don't think they have badly-programmed subconscious minds; they just think they have a lot of lousy problems. However, even if they don't know who they are, the rest of us can quickly identify them because their characteristic behaviors are easy to spot. See if you can think of people who exhibit one or more of these behaviors:

- They complain *a lot*, to anyone who will listen. They hunt for sympathy by "playing the martyr," making frequent reference to how difficult, exhausting, and full of sacrifice their lives are. They seem addicted to suffering, cherishing their problems as though they were precious possessions.

- They use catastrophizing words to describe their problems, and often foresee terrible consequences arising from simple problems: "My car won't start so I'm going to be late for work again and I bet they'll fire me this time and then I'll have to declare bankruptcy which will make my wife so disgusted she'll finally just take the kids and leave and I'll be alone and miserable all the rest of my life!" Or, "I can't believe the kids left this huge mess on the floor again they obviously don't really love me or they wouldn't treat me this way so now I'll have to clean the house all day and I'll be bored and miserable and the house will never look neat and my mother never let her house get this messy so I'm a failure as a mom."

- They try to prove that they have the worst problems. You think *you* have a problem? Oh my goodness, your problem is just a sorry little thing compared their huge, complicated, gosh-awful problems! And they will be happy to explain why. This frequently leads them to exaggerate the severity of their problems.

- They deny responsibility for their problems, claiming that others are at fault. They talk about how unfair it is that they have been stuck with these awful problems.
- They reject suggested solutions out of hand, or go to great lengths to prove that the solutions won't work. They make it clear that their problems will be difficult or even impossible to solve.
- They suffer from the same problems for a long time, or find themselves dealing with problems that occur over and over again. If one problem actually gets permanently solved, they soon acquire a new one (or two or three) to take its place.

Not an attractive picture, is it? And although some of these behaviors may generate short-term sympathy or pity, they are certainly not the most effective methods for solving problems, or for living a happy and satisfying life.

Changing self-identity. Now it is time to ask yourself a difficult but important question:

"Am I a problem-suffering person?"

Of course, a person who has a strongly-embedded problem-suffering identity would immediately answer, "No, not me!" because problem-suffering people have a hard time recognizing their own behavior patterns. So take your time, and consider the question with some care. Try to be objective about it, neither seeking to avoid responsibility nor being too hard on yourself.

The fact that you are reading a book about improving your problem-solving skills indicates that you are probably not a full-blown problem-sufferer. But check to see if you have unknowingly adopted one or more problem-suffering habits. For example, you may have fallen into a routine of indulging in a little complaining party whenever you get together with certain friends. Maybe you have developed a quick temper regarding specific kinds of problems, perhaps relating to your children, spouse, or a particular co-worker. Or perhaps you have been dwelling on a perceived injustice, or nursing a grudge.

If you have a problem-suffering habit that you would like to break, you can do so by consciously re-training your subconscious about what is important to you. Make the cycle of identifying and focusing on what is important work *for* you rather than *against* you. As we mentioned previously, the fastest and easiest way to eliminate a bad habit is to replace it with a new and better habit. You will almost certainly get better results by consciously adopting a new problem-solving habit than by simply trying to stop the old problem-suffering habit. For example:

- *Analyze* and *discuss* your problems rather than complain about them. Bear your burdens with strength and grace rather than with self-pity or self-recrimination.
- Use *effective* language instead of catastrophizing language when you think about and talk about problems.
- Accept *responsibility* for reaching your own goals. Make issues of fault or fairness secondary.
- Remind yourself that you are more likely to find fulfillment by building great *solutions* and reaching worthy *goals* than by proving that you have the worst problems.
- Be *receptive* to, and *appreciative* of, suggested solutions. Evaluate them on their merits rather than rejecting them reflexively.

This reprogramming requires consistent, conscious effort at first, but it quickly becomes easier and more natural. It will help if you remember (from RESPONSE) that there is a link between where you focus your attention and what emotions you feel. Focusing on the negative aspects of having a problem tends to generate Weak emotions, so you may have become accustomed to living with feelings like anger, frustration, or anxiety. However, as you shift your focus from *having the problem* to *getting it solved*, the Weak emotions fade and are replaced with Strong ones like confidence, enthusiasm, and happiness. These Strong feelings will help reinforce your new way of thinking, and eventually you will reprogram your subconscious to replace your problem-suffering habit with a problem-solving one.

Even if you do not have problem-suffering habits, you can probably think of occasions when you wasted time dwelling on a problem rather than taking action to get it solved. The key is promptly recognizing when you are stuck at the problem level.

When you catch yourself engaging in any "stuck" behaviors, that is your cue that it is time to move out of the problem level. Use the RESPONSE and CLARITY tools to focus on the problem in a positive and productive manner, and then immediately shift your focus to the *overcoming obstacles* level. Taking action to overcome obstacles is a great way to escape from the trap of dwelling on the problem

FOCUS ON OVERCOMING OBSTACLES

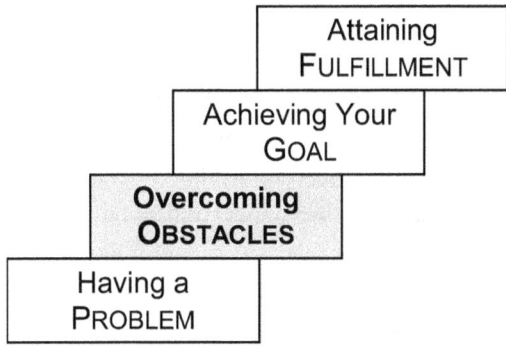

Focus Effectively on Overcoming Obstacles

Recall from CLARITY that the basic problem statement is, "I want *goal*, but *obstacle*." You can shift your focus from the problem level to the obstacle level simply by asking the question, "How will I *overcome this obstacle*?" This is what we call an *obstacle question*. Obstacle questions always begin with, "How will I..." Using these three specific words gives you several powerful advantages:

- Asking "How" indicates that you have already decided that the obstacle *can* be overcome; it is now only a question of finding the best way to do so. This is more powerful than asking questions that imply doubt or a lack of commitment, such as, "Can I overcome this obstacle?" or, "Will this obstacle ever go away?"

- The word "will" indicates that you have already decided that the obstacle is going to be overcome, and that you are now tackling it with confidence and determination. This is more powerful than questions like, "How might I overcome the obstacle?" or, "How should I overcome the obstacle?"

- "I" is the most important of the three words because it makes it clear that you are taking personal responsibility for overcoming the obstacle. This is more powerful than questions that shift responsibility to someone else, such as, "When will my spouse start treating me better?" or, "Why can't my staff be more competent?"

Asking, "How will I overcome this obstacle" focuses the power of your subconscious on generating solutions that will answer the question. So, a problem statement like, "I want good health and physical fitness, but I eat an unhealthy diet and I rarely get exercise," would generate an obstacle question like, "How will I improve my diet and increase my exercise?" You can increase the effectiveness of an obstacle question by saying it out loud or writing it down, or by developing a *problem-solving project*, as we saw in CLARITY.

Consistently asking obstacle questions communicates a positive message to your subconscious. In time, your subconscious will understand that you are *someone who overcomes obstacles*, reinforcing your identity as a problem-solver. Every time you encounter a problem, your subconscious will immediately begin scanning your knowledge and experiences for possible solutions. Because your subconscious mind has access to much more of the information stored in your memory than does your conscious mind, you will be amazed at the great solutions that you will produce.

Instead of wasting time suffering, you will respond to any obstacle you encounter by automatically seeking a way to overcome it. For example, suppose you have decided to improve your diet, but you find that you are continuing to eat unhealthy food. Instead of sinking into shame or indulging in excuse-making, you might think something like this:

> "Well, I decided a month ago to eat healthy food instead of unhealthy food, but here I am halfway through a carton of chocolate chip ice cream. This is the third time this week I have done something like this. How will I replace this old habit of eating so much unhealthy food with a new habit of eating healthy food?"

A problem-solving mindset naturally generates this kind of objective, achievement-oriented approach. It helps you view setbacks with strength and curiosity rather than with anger and despair. This allows you to think clearly about what has been triggering the undesirable habit of behavior, and how you can replace it with a new and better habit.

SOLUTION POWER

> **FOCUSING ON OVERCOMING OBSTACLES AT WORK**
>
> Organizing a meeting to analyze and solve a problem can be very effective if done properly. One danger, however, is that meetings can get stuck at the *having a problem* level. You have probably attended meetings at which one or two participants continued complaining about the problem at great length, preventing the group from effectively focusing on possible solutions.
>
> Several years ago I came up with a simple technique for handling this situation. After the problem has been defined and the meeting participants have had a chance to get their complaints off their chests, say, "I believe we have defined the problem thoroughly. The problem is..." Then in three or four sentences describe the problem and its effects, including who is being impacted by it. This lets all participants know that their concerns have been heard and understood. Then go on to say, "We are now all done talking about the problem. The rest of this meeting will be about how we will solve it."
>
> After that, if anyone starts complaining about the problem again, you politely interrupt, saying, "Remember, we are all done talking about the problem. What ideas do you have for how we will solve it?" This moves the meeting to the *overcoming obstacles* level of FOCUS.
>
> *-Reagan*

Look for obstacle-level opportunity. If you simply overcome the obstacle or obstacles that stand between you and your goal, you will solve your problem. In most situations that will be a satisfactory outcome. But now let's recall (from INSIGHT) that a problem becomes an opportunity the moment you decide to turn it to your advantage. So, how can you turn the obstacle level of FOCUS to your advantage? Simply this: **enjoy the journey.**

For example, instead of asking, "How will I improve my diet and increase my exercise?" try, "How will I *enjoy* eating healthy food and *have fun* exercising?" Instead of, "How will I deal with flat sales and rising costs?" try, "How will I *inspire* myself and my staff to boost sales and reduce costs?"

Finding an opportunity to enjoy the process of solving a problem is inherently motivating and empowering. Wouldn't you be more likely to stick with a healthy diet that you truly enjoyed? Experiment with new foods until you find the ones that are good for you *and* that you love to eat. Wouldn't you exercise more regularly if you found a way to make it fun? After all, you don't have to be grim and determined in order to do something that's good for you. Make exercise into a game, or into a method of introspection and meditation. Wouldn't you find greater sales success if you viewed it as an exciting challenge? And don't you think your staff would be more inspired if you were leading them with joy and enthusiasm? An *opportunity mindset* is a wonderful ally in your quest to overcome obstacles.

Don't Get Stuck at the Obstacle Level

There are two ways people get stuck at the obstacle level:

Becoming a fly on a window. Think about a fly buzzing against a window. It butts its head against the glass again and again trying to get to the other side, but it will never break through. It needs to find some other path in order to reach its goal. If it stopped pounding itself against the window for a few minutes and looked around, it might find an open window just a few feet away.

Similarly, it is easy for people to get so focused on overcoming a particular obstacle that they lose sight of the goal they started out seeking to achieve. Sometimes they even begin to think that overcoming this particular obstacle *is* their goal. If that obstacle simply cannot be overcome, or would take a very long time to overcome, they become stuck beating their heads against it, just like that poor fly.

It's great to be determined, to feel that nothing can stand in your way. But be alert for that frustrating feeling that comes from working hard without making much progress. Watch for a sensation of weariness in dealing with the problem, a feeling that you are at your wit's end. When you get the sense that your best effort is not getting you very far, that is your cue to stop for a moment and say, "Wait a minute, I'd better make sure I'm not acting like a fly on a window."

Veering off course. The other way of getting stuck in the obstacle level is to veer off course, solving obstacle after obstacle without actually making progress toward your original goal. This can be harder to detect than the "fly on a window" trap, because it often creates the illusion that you are making progress.

Become alert for a feeling that you are getting a lot done but not making real progress. If you repeatedly have the sensation at the end of the day that you kept busy and worked hard but that you don't have much to show for it, that is your cue to examine whether you have veered off course.

If you realize that you are stuck in the obstacle level, whether as a fly on a window or by veering off course, what should you do? There are two basic techniques for getting unstuck:

Shift your focus down. One antidote is to shift your focus back to the problem level. The CLARITY tool is particularly useful in this situation. Take a step back and get some perspective on the situation; give yourself a mental fresh start. This may also be a good time to develop a written problem-solving plan. Or you may discover that you have been working to overcome obstacles that are just symptoms of the problem when you really need to identify and tackle the root cause.

Shift your focus up. The other way to get unstuck is to shift your focus up to the *achieving your goal* level. After all, being stuck at the obstacle level means that you are working hard but not making progress toward your goal. Let's take a look at how focusing on your goal can help you to get your problem-solving back on track.

Focus on Achieving Your Goal

Focus Effectively on Achieving Your Goal

Create a goal question. At this level you focus on what you *want* rather than on what is preventing you from getting it. If we look again at the basic problem statement, "I want *goal,* but *obstacle,*" your new question is, "How will I *achieve my goal?*" This *goal question* concentrates your attention on the outcome you desire in solving the problem.

If you have veered off course, reminding yourself of the goal you are working toward will help you get back on track. Reconnecting with your goal is also a great way to stop butting your head against an immovable obstacle. As we mentioned earlier, people who are stuck in the fly-on-a-window trap often come to believe that overcoming that particular obstacle *is* their goal, that they *must* find a way to break through it. Refocusing on your true goal will often reveal that you do not need to get *through* that obstacle in order to reach your goal, because there is another path to your goal that allows you to simply go *around* it. Like the fly who would see an open window just a few feet away if he would back up and look around, you will often discover that you can achieve your goal without having to overcome the stubborn obstacle you have been pounding on.

Let's consider the example of a young man who is dating a young woman. Her birthday is coming up, but they are both college students and neither of them has a job. He defines his problem as, "I want to give my girlfriend a wonderful birthday present, but I don't have much money." So his goal question is, "How will I give my girlfriend a wonderful birthday present?"

He knows there is a beautiful necklace that she admires, and he thinks it would look wonderful on her. He wants to buy it for her, but it costs more than he can afford. He can't qualify to buy it on credit, and he doesn't want to ask his parents for a loan because they've already contributed so much to his education. He considers getting a part-time job, but his course load is too heavy. He feels stuck, as he simply can't come up with any promising ideas for how he could buy the necklace.

Eventually he realizes that he has fallen into the fly-on-a-window trap. He has gotten so focused on overcoming the obstacle of getting enough money for the necklace that he has forgotten what his actual goal is.

He refocuses on his goal: giving his girlfriend a "wonderful birthday present." Now he has a little more room to maneuver. He starts shopping around for a different gift that he can afford, and that will make the kind of impression he wants. But he still comes up dry. He has so little money that any gift within his budget does not seem adequate to the occasion.

He refocuses on his goal once again: "How will I give my girlfriend a wonderful birthday present?" He finally realizes that "giving a wonderful present" does not necessarily require purchasing a gift, and that in focusing only on purchasing a gift he had veered off course. What is it he really wants to accomplish? He wants to show her how much he cares about her, to impress her, and to make her feel delighted and happy. Now he can see that he has many options available.

For example, one of the most precious experiences in modern life is simply spending time "in the moment" – truly enjoying what we are doing and appreciating the people who are with us – rather than having our thoughts caught up in what we ought to be doing or what we will be doing tomorrow. He realizes that he could make *the day itself* a wonderful present by doing things with her that he knows she enjoys. He could also invest his time in creating a personalized gift, for instance by writing a poem, making a bouquet of wildflowers, or making a birthday card.

LOVE ON A BUDGET

My wife and I have a tradition of exchanging gift baskets at Easter. One year money was very tight, to the extent that I wondered how I could afford to fill her basket. After spending some time trying to come up with ideas for an inexpensive gift, I thought, "I just want her to know how much I appreciate her and care for her." That thought was immediately followed by, "Well, why don't I just tell her?"

I spent a dollar or so on a bag of plastic eggs. Then I cut a piece of paper into small strips and wrote a "thank you" on each one, such as: "Thank you for having a radiant smile," "Thank you for making great pizza," "Thank you for turning our garden into a thing of beauty every year," and "Thank you for taking such good care of yourself." I rolled the slips, put them inside the eggs, and filled her basket with them.

That basket and those eggs are on display in our home to this day, while the more expensive gifts I have given her since then, while appreciated, have come and gone.

-Kevin

We can see that refocusing on your goal produces several advantages:

- It opens a wider range of possible solutions, and provides an opportunity to use the CREATIVITY tool to develop a clever or innovative solution.

- It may reveal that a seemingly insurmountable barrier was actually only an *apparent* obstacle. Refocusing on your goal causes it to disappear or allows you to easily bypass it.
- It could result in a much better solution. In the example above, buying the necklace or doing the usual "dozen roses and a meal in a fancy restaurant" would have been okay solutions. But if the relationship has real promise, a special time together and a personalized gift will be more memorable.

If you make a habit of focusing on and achieving goals, your subconscious will add *someone who achieves goals* to your problem-solving identity. This will boost your confidence and effectiveness as a problem-solver.

You can further reinforce your identity by taking notice when you achieve a goal and giving yourself credit for doing so. Whether your goal was, successfully completing an evening college course, painting the living room, or lowering your handicap by a stroke, pause for a moment to say to yourself, "I did it. I set a goal for myself and I achieved it. Good job!"

Look for goal-level opportunity. Recall again that a problem becomes an opportunity the moment you decide to turn it to your advantage. Another way of phrasing this is that you create an opportunity when you seek to end up better off than you were before the problem arose.

Let's consider the example of a person who is in debt. Perhaps she is a young woman who applied for a few credit cards when she got her first real job and then quickly accumulated some large balances. Suppose she identifies "becoming debt-free" as her goal. She might achieve that outcome by consolidating her credit card balances at a lower interest rate and getting her spending under control by following a written weekly budget. This is a classic example of a break-even solution.

This result is certainly a good one, but she could do even better. She could turn the problem of having to deal with debt into an opportunity to develop good financial management and investment skills. She could decide to set goals for earning, spending, saving, and investing money in ways that would take her far beyond being "debt free."

Whatever problem-solving goal she sets will define her maximum outcome. Solutions generally either achieve a goal or fall short of doing so; they rarely achieve something more. So she would do better by aiming high. Suppose she sets an ambitious goal of having one million dollars in savings and investments ten years from now. If she falls short of her goal and ends up with "only" $500,000, she would still be a half-million dollars richer than if she had set a goal of becoming debt-free. Pursuing the goal of becoming debt-free might end up eliminating or reducing her debt, but her debt-reduction solutions would probably not make her wealthy.

Here are some additional examples of turning a problem into an opportunity by setting a more ambitious goal:

Goal question:	*Goal-level opportunity:*
How will I lose ten pounds?	How will I attain my maximum level of strength, health, energy, and fitness?
How will I attend church more regularly?	How will I build a life of deep faith and devotion?
How will I spend more time with my kids?	How will I become the best parent I can be?

Don't Get Stuck at the Goal Level

There are two ways to get stuck at the goal level, and there is a method for quickly getting unstuck from each of them:

Dreaming without action. One common mistake is for people to focus on a goal by hoping for it and wishing for it, but never taking action to achieve it. This is a particular danger for Thinker personality types, especially Intuitive Thinkers. They often have a crystal-clear image and deep understanding of what they want to achieve, but may lack a natural impulse to start working toward it.

If you feel stuck in this way, shift your focus down to the *overcoming obstacles* level. This action-oriented level of FOCUS helps you take short-term action toward your long-term objective. You may discover that your reluctance to get started has been the biggest obstacle all along, and that "well begun is half done."

Thinkers who are dreaming without taking action may be tempted to shift their focus further down to the problem level and create a written problem-solving project. Creating projects can be useful, but be careful! Thinkers love to plan (and plan, and plan, and…) so set a time limit when you will stop planning and start working to overcome obstacles.

Pursuing the wrong goal. The second potential pitfall at the goal level is pursuing a goal that will not actually give you a true sense of satisfaction. Perhaps you are unknowingly working toward a goal that is not really *your* goal, because it was chosen for you by someone else. Or it could be a goal that you chose for yourself without fully considering whether or how it will contribute to your fundamental happiness.

If so, achieving a major goal after years of careful planning and hard work can leave you feeling frustrated and dissatisfied. Without a clear understanding of what you really want out of life, your goal-setting, strategic planning, and hard work may be fundamentally misdirected.

If you suspect that you are spending time and energy trying to reach a goal that is not right for you, it is time to raise your focus to the level of *attaining fulfillment*. This is a step that, unfortunately, few people ever take. But if you do so, you will gain the ability to identify the goals that will fulfill your deepest beliefs and desires.

FOCUS ON ATTAINING FULFILLMENT

DISCOVER YOUR FUNDAMENTAL BELIEFS

The first step in attaining fulfillment is discovering your *fundamental beliefs*. We have talked about the important role your self-identity plays in determining how effectively you can solve problems. At the core of your self-identity are your *fundamental beliefs*. These beliefs are the vital principles that define who you are and the kind of life you are meant to lead. They may evolve and grow as you mature, but they are unlikely to change frequently, suddenly, or radically. **You attain fulfillment by acting in accordance with your fundamental beliefs.** The best way to lead a fulfilling life is to gain a clear understanding of your fundamental beliefs and then pursue goals that put those beliefs into action.

Keep in mind that you are *discovering* or *clarifying* your fundamental beliefs rather than *creating* them. Ask yourself, "What *do* I believe" rather than, "What do I *want* to believe" or, "What *should* I believe." Do not base your life strategy on wishful thinking. Only your own authentic beliefs will lead you to true fulfillment.

An easy way to begin identifying your fundamental beliefs is to complete the statements below in ways that most accurately describe you. Approach this as a brainstorming exercise. Use RESPONSE to put yourself in a Strong emotional state of enthusiasm and insight, and generate a number of different words or phrases to fill in the blank in each statement. Write them down to create a list of the roles, adjectives, values, and ideals that matter the most to you. Don't evaluate or judge your answers; don't worry about whether they seem "important" enough or "deep" enough. Just write them down as they occur to you.

- **"No matter what, I must _____."**

    What actions or characteristics define your path in life? Are you meant to create new things, express yourself, create, inspire others, enjoy life, attain victory, grow in your faith, or search for truth? Do you seek to contribute, acquire, clarify, nurture, lead boldly, follow loyally, or live morally? Is it your quest to do your best, live in luxury, make new discoveries, look great, persevere through adversity, take risks, or seek enlightenment?

- **"No matter what, I must be _____."**

    What roles define you? Were you born to be an artist, a leader, a teacher, an entrepreneur, an adventurer, or a scientist? What adjectives best describe you? Is it vitally important for you to be sympathetic, wealthy, optimistic, inquisitive, honest, decisive, spontaneous, relaxed, famous, or generous? (To assist you, a list of adjectives is included in Appendix B.)

- **"No matter what, I believe _____."**

  What values and ideals are most important to you? Do you deeply believe that the rule of law must be maintained, that science is the path to true knowledge, that a person has to work hard to get ahead? Do you have faith that people are basically good, that family comes first, that God has a plan for you, that there is a cycle of death and rebirth? Is it evident to you that life is a great adventure, that people should make the most of their gifts, that real happiness comes from giving?

Once your list is complete, examine each word or phrase to determine whether it is truly fundamental to you, using the following process:

1. Organize the list by grouping similar ideas. For example, you could put entries like: "I must explore," "I must be adventurous," and "I believe life is a voyage of discovery" together in one group.

2. Looking at each group, choose the one word or phrase that resonates most deeply, that seems to best capture the belief, and set the others aside. You can also combine words and phrases into a single statement, such as: "I believe that life is an adventure."

3. Compare each belief with the others. Ask yourself which ones you believe more strongly, which ones are more central to your identity. Set aside those that do not pass this test, even if they seem worthy and valuable. For example, suppose the list includes, "I must be polite," and "I must help others." You might conclude that it is more fundamentally important to you to help others than it is to be polite. That does not mean you have to stop being polite,

or give up believing that being polite is important. But through this process of comparison, you can home in on the beliefs that truly define you.

4. For each remaining item on the list, ask the following questions. Retain the beliefs for which your answers are "yes."

- Would you still act in accordance with the belief if all your needs were provided for and you had all the money you wanted? For example, would you still believe in the value of hard work if you won a multi-million dollar lottery?
- Would you continue following the belief if you were offered great wealth, fame, or some other tempting reward in exchange for abandoning it or acting contrary to it?
- Would you continue following the belief even if you were *not* rewarded for it? Would you continue to be generous even if you were never thanked? Would you continue to be adventurous even if no one would ever know about it?
- Would you continue to follow the belief even if doing so caused serious trouble for you? If you were punished for holding the belief, would you still act in accordance with it?

5. At this point, most people will have identified three to six beliefs. Now you can take each of those beliefs and drill down to its deepest and most fundamental level. Consider each belief and ask, "Why?" or, "Why is that important?" For example, starting with, "I must be a teacher":

Q: Why?

A: Because I like helping others learn and grow.

Q: Why?

A: Because it makes me feel good to help others discover their potential.

Q: Why?

A: Because nothing feels as good to me as helping others follow their unique path in life.

Q: Why?

A: Because my own greatest fulfillment comes from helping others find their fulfillment.

Q: Why?

A: Well, that's just who I am.

When you reach an answer like "That's who I am," or "If I didn't believe that, I wouldn't be me," when you just can't ask "why" anymore no matter how hard you try, then you have reached the level of fundamental belief. In this example, one of this person's fundamental beliefs is, "My own greatest fulfillment comes helping others find their fulfillment."

It is possible that you will ask "why" only once for a particular belief, that you will not need to dig deeper than your initial statement. But challenge yourself not to give up too easily. If you find that each time you ask "why" you quickly answer "just because," then go back and consider the question more carefully, and see if you can discover a deeper level of belief.

It is possible to have a fundamental belief that exists deep within you but that has been neglected or suppressed and therefore has not made itself apparent in how you have acted in the past. If you find that there is a belief on your list that has not been consistently reflected in your behavior, but you are strongly reluctant to discard it, you may want to keep it. It may be that learning to act in accordance with this latent belief will be a key to attaining fulfillment.

Once you have discovered your fundamental beliefs you will always carry them with you. They will provide guidance in all your problem-solving, like a compass pointing toward fulfillment. You will not have to rediscover them every time you use FOCUS. Using your fundamental beliefs as the basis for your goal-setting and problem-solving will quickly become a natural and effortless habit.

FOCUS EFFECTIVELY ON ATTAINING FULFILLMENT

Recall that *you attain fulfillment by acting in accordance with your fundamental beliefs.* You will find that life is most satisfying and productive when your decisions are guided by your fundamental beliefs. This creates a powerful alignment of your conscious and your subconscious, allowing you to achieve more with less effort. The more your behavior is aligned with what you deeply believe, the more you will perceive problems as opportunities.

Your subconscious already understands that your fundamental beliefs are a vital part of your self-identity. By consistently *acting on* those beliefs, you send your subconscious the message that you are *someone who leads a fulfilling life*. Eventually, that powerful message will also become part of your self-identity.

It will now become much easier for you to determine whether, and to what extent, solving a particular problem will contribute to your fulfillment. Fulfillment is the highest level of FOCUS, and FOCUS is all about getting what you really want when you solve a problem. By focusing on the fulfillment level, you can determine the importance of achieving any particular goal. Pause and ask, "Why am I trying to solve this problem? Why am I seeking to achieve this goal? How important is this to me in light of my fundamental beliefs? How will solving this problem contribute to the fulfillment of those beliefs?"

Based on how you answer those questions, you can make decisions about how to best allocate your problem-solving resources.

- **If you determine that the goal is vital to your fulfillment, pursue it vigorously.** Concentrate your solution-finding efforts on those goals that are most in alignment with your beliefs. Never surrender a "want" that is essential to your fulfillment even if it is difficult to get.
- **Consider whether there is an even more fulfilling version of the goal.** Raising your focus from the goal level to the fulfillment level can help you to identify the best possible outcome in solving any given problem.
- **If the goal is unfulfilling, drop it.** After you have considered and clarified your fundamental beliefs, you may be surprised to discover that some of the major goals you have been pursuing are not worth further effort. Stop wasting resources on those unfulfilling goals. Don't keep pursuing a goal just because other people think it is important, or because you previously assumed it was important to you. If you can't drop it entirely, reduce the amount of time and effort you dedicate to it in accordance with its true priority.

Don't Get Stuck at the Fulfillment Level

Some people get stuck at the fulfillment level of Focus because they know what their fundamental beliefs are, but they don't dedicate their resources to solving the high-priority problems that would best advance those beliefs. To be fulfilled, you must translate your beliefs into action. If you conclude that solving a particular problem is necessary to your fulfillment, commit yourself to reaching it and then shift down through the levels of Focus as necessary to make progress toward it.

Other people have a general sense of who they want to become, or a heartfelt wish for a life that would fulfill them, but they lack an effective plan for making their dreams a reality. They long to contribute to the world and to savor the good things that life offers, but they don't have a clear vision of how they can fulfill those longings. If you find yourself adrift in this way, wondering what to do in order to live your version of a successful and satisfying life, it is time to use the next tool, PRIORITY. Creating and using a PRIORITY *fulfillment action plan* is a powerful way to get unstuck and translate your fundamental beliefs into lasting, satisfying success.

CONCLUSION

Effective problem-solving requires concentrated effort in a positive direction. The FOCUS tool allows you to apply your resources efficiently by shifting your attention to where it is needed most at each stage of the solution-finding process.

The FOCUS tool:

- Helps Thinkers *keep moving* in the right direction, and
- Helps Doers keep moving *in the right direction.*

FOCUS: SUMMARY

FOCUS ON HAVING A PROBLEM

- **Focus effectively on having a problem.** Use RESPONSE and CLARITY to recognize, understand, and react positively to the problem.
- **Don't get stuck at the problem level.** Establish your self-identity as someone who solves problems, rather than as

someone who suffers from problems. As soon as you understand a problem, shift your focus to overcoming obstacles.

Focus on Overcoming Obstacles

- **Focus effectively on overcoming obstacles.** Create an obstacle question using the format: "How will I overcome this obstacle?" Create obstacle-level opportunity by enjoying the journey.
- **Don't get stuck at the obstacle level.** Beware of becoming a fly on a window or veering off course. Shift your focus down to the problem level to get a fresh start, or shift up to the goal level to help you move in the right direction.

Focus on Achieving Your Goal

- **Focus effectively on achieving your goal.** Create a goal question using the format "How will I achieve my goal?" Create goal-level opportunity by turning problems to your advantage.
- **Don't get stuck at the goal level.** If you are dreaming without action, shift your focus down to the obstacle level. If you suspect that you are pursuing the wrong goal, shift your focus up to the fulfillment level.

Focus on Attaining Fulfillment

- **Discover the beliefs that define your fulfillment.** You attain fulfillment by acting in accordance with your fundamental beliefs. Make a list of your beliefs, then identify the ones that are truly fundamental.
- **Focus effectively on attaining fulfillment.** Put your fundamental beliefs into action. Pursue or abandon goals according to how much they will contribute to your fulfillment.

- **Don't get stuck at the fulfillment level.** Commit yourself to achieving any vital goal, and shift your focus as necessary to achieve it. If you feel adrift, it is time to make use of the PRIORITY tool.

THE FIFTH TOOL

PRIORITY

CHOOSE THE RIGHT PROBLEMS

Although you may not be aware of it, you are continually making choices about which problems are most deserving of your time and energy. It is easy to assume that problems "just happen" and that you have no choice but to deal with them as they arise. In reality, you either *choose* to allow random problems to absorb your time and energy, or *choose* to focus your efforts on the truly important problems that lead to a fulfilling life.

Of course, you will always need to deal with some problems that arise uninvited, such as a leaky faucet, a traffic jam, or the unexpected departure of a valuable employee. The *Solution Power* tools will enable you to solve problems like these more efficiently. But if you use your problem-solving skills only to do a better job of handling whatever problems happen to arise from day to day, you leave your future to chance. Although you will certainly be a more effective problem-solver, your efforts may not advance you in a direction that you will ultimately find fulfilling.

People whose lives are dominated by the chance occurance of problems are usually not aware that a fundamentally better strategy exists, that it is possible to take a more self-directed and rewarding path through life. In reality, you *can* learn to choose your problems consciously, rather than letting life choose them for you, and by doing so you gain control of your personal destiny.

The PRIORITY too is a guide for making the best use of your *problem-solving resources*: the time, money, physical effort, mental effort, knowledge, skills, relationships, and experience that you can bring to bear on solving problems. The best way to make progress toward fulfillment is to apply more of those resources to solving the problems that will make the greatest difference in your life. Solving a large number of unimportant problems is no substitute for solving a small number of truly crucial ones. **Choosing to dedicate your resources to the problems that contribute the most to your fulfillment helps you build a better life.**

Consciously choosing your problems also produces *cumulative progress*. Rather than just solving one isolated, unrelated problem after another, your efforts will add up to something. Solving random problems is like dashing around aimlessly, expending energy without advancing very far in any particular direction. But when you choose your problems strategically, each solution takes you further in a consistent direction, carrying you further along your path of fulfillment.

To aid in this process, we have developed the PRIORITY pyramid. The pyramid is a system for choosing the problems you *want* to solve, the ones that will help you build the most successful and satisfying life possible.

The *Solution Power* Priority Pyramid

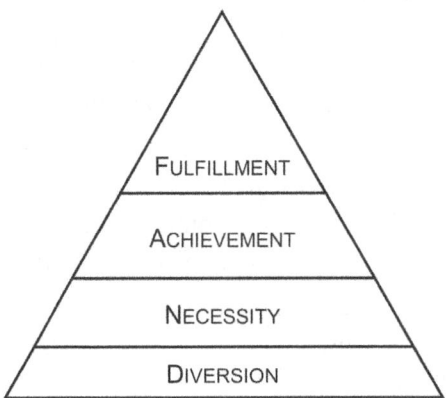

The PRIORITY pyramid is, in its simplest form, a method for categorizing the wide range of problems that exist in the world. The problems found in each level of the pyramid are defined by a *primary goal question*. Let's look at what kinds of problems are found in each level:

Diversion-Level Problems

The primary goal question at the diversion level is, *"How will I have fun and feel good?"*

There are many kinds of problems within this level. Some are beneficial while others are inherently harmful. Some are important while others are trivial. Some will seem appealing to you while others will appear quite unattractive. We all choose to pursue different diversion-level problems because each of us finds different kinds of activities and experiences to be enjoyable. We each have our own ways of having fun and feeling good.

Here are some examples of diversion-level problems:

- **Entertainment** (watching television or movies, attending concerts or sporting events, playing computer or video games, gambling): "How will I find the time to watch all my favorite TV shows?" "How will I get good tickets to the concert?" "How will I beat my new video game?" "How will I hit it big and win back my losses?"
- **Hobbies** (gardening, collecting, doing crafts): "How will I create a beautiful bed of flowers?" "How will I find the missing piece that will complete my collection?" "How will I make the trees in my paintings more realistic?"
- **Physical recreation** (playing sports, engaging in outdoor activities): "How will I lower my golf score?" "How will I find the best fishing spot?"
- **Chemical Use** (drinking, smoking, using drugs): "How will I choose the best wine for this meal?" "How will I find time for a cigarette between flights?" "How will I keep getting this great high without getting caught?"
- **Recreational versions of necessary activities** (snacking, reading, napping, shopping): "How will I make my melted-cheese nachos tastier?" "How will I find time to read the latest book by my favorite author?" "How will I take a nap when my neighbor is running his leaf blower?" "How will I be able to afford this terrific bargain?"

This is the level of life's "extras." In some objective sense these problems don't *need* to be solved. If you decided to stop solving any diversion-level problems your life would probably become less fun or interesting, but it would go on.

NECESSITY-LEVEL PROBLEMS

The primary goal question at the necessity level is, *"How will I satisfy my basic needs and complete my routine tasks?"*

Here are some examples of necessity-level problems:
- **Basic needs** (buying food and clothing, obtaining shelter and transportation, attending to personal maintenance): "How will I pick out groceries that will satisfy my whole family?" "How will I find time to take my car in to the shop?" "How will I identify the best medication for my condition?"
- **Routine tasks and responsibilities** (going to work, attending class, paying bills, doing household chores, running errands): "How will I work an extra shift and still get my homework done?" "How will I set up a better system for getting my bills paid each month?" "How will I find time to get the lawn mowed?" "How will I get to the bank and the dry cleaner during my lunch hour?"

This is the level of the to-do list, of solving the problems of daily life. While many of these problems are relatively minor, as a group they need to get solved in order to keep life running smoothly. Neglecting necessity-level problems often causes them to become more serious and more numerous.

Achievement-Level Problems

The primary goal question at the achievement level is, *"How will I achieve my long-term objectives?"*

Here are some examples of achievement-level problems:
- **Career** (creating a business or product, earning promotions, increasing earnings). "How will I get the financing to start my business?" "How will I make vice-president by next year?" "How will I qualify for a higher bonus?"
- **Education** (earning a diploma or degree, acquiring new knowledge or skills): "How will I succeed in college after

being out of school so long?" "How will I become a true expert on the history of the Civil War?"
- **Finance** (reaching savings or investment objectives): "How will I save enough money to pay for my children's college education?" "How will I become independently wealthy?"
- **Well-being** (attaining objectives relating to personal appearance, health, and fitness): "How will I quit smoking?" "How will I lower my cholesterol and blood pressure?" "How will I get in good enough shape to go hiking with my grandchildren?"
- **Relationships** (establishing and supporting friendships, family relationships, and romance): "How will I make friends in my new school?" "How will I help my daughter experience a happy adolescence?" "How will I find the right person to marry?"

This is a broad level, encompassing problems that range from building a house to running a 10K race. Ignoring achievement-level problems may not have a noticeable impact in the short term, but in the long term it will greatly diminish your chances for happiness and success.

Fulfillment-Level Problems

The primary goal question at the fulfillment level is, *"How will I put my fundamental beliefs into action?"*

The problems at this level arise from the fundamental beliefs that you discovered in Focus. For example, your fulfillment-level problems will be quite different depending on whether you fundamentally believe in being adventurous and spontaneous or in seeking serenity and acceptance.

Here are some examples of fulfillment-level problems:

- **Personal development** (strengthening your character, reaching your potential, building faith or spirituality): "How will I become more generous and accepting?" "How will I fully develop myself as a leader?" "How will I truly embody my faith?"
- **Experience** (enjoying the richness of life, exploring the world around you): "How will I discover and appreciate the finest music and art?" "How will I meet and make friends with fascinating people?"
- **Contribution** (building a legacy, helping others, giving back to the world): "How will I have a lasting, positive impact?" "How will I be the best parent I can be?" "How will I pass along to others the blessings I have received?"

If you neglect this level, as many people do, you may only sense it in a vague way, as a nagging feeling that you have not led a fully satisfying life. Many people have this sense that "something is missing," but that their day-to-day lives are too busy for them to stop and figure out what it is.

Building the Pyramid

People who choose to spend most of their resources on problems from the lower levels of the PRIORITY pyramid rarely experience as much success and satisfaction as they would like. The happiest and most successful people are those who concentrate on tackling problems at the higher levels of the pyramid. This is what allows them to build great careers and rewarding personal lives. You can use the PRIORITY pyramid to consciously improve your problem-choosing habits, to make wise choices about how you spend your problem-solving resources.

Let's take a closer look at each level of the pyramid and see what happens if you make the problems in that level your highest priority. We will start from the bottom and work up, because there is a powerful "building" effect that occurs as you prioritize problems at higher levels. You do not *move from* one level to a higher one; instead you *add* each higher level to the ones below it. Doing so greatly enriches those lower levels. When you have completed your own individual version of the pyramid by making fulfillment-level problems your top priority, you will automatically choose and solve problems at *all* levels of the pyramid more easily and effectively. After all, achieving goals, completing necessary tasks, and having fun are all vital to a truly fulfilling life.

PRIORITIZING DIVERSION-LEVEL PROBLEMS

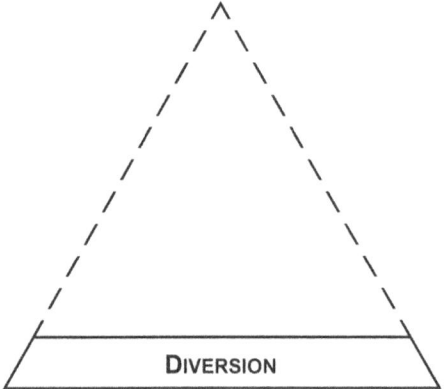

Life at the diversion level. People who make diversion-level problems their highest priority are pursuing a self-defeating strategy, because in the long run they will *not* have fun and they will *not* feel good. They often neglect necessity-level problems like paying their bills, maintaining their homes, or getting to work on time. This causes these everyday problems to multiply and to worsen into serious crises. These individuals find it almost impossible to set and achieve meaningful goals, or to define and attain true fulfillment. Their thoughts ultimately become dominated by fear, transforming their pursuit of fun into unhealthy escapism.

This does not mean that solving diversion-level problems is inherently bad. Solving problems like, "How will I make my barbecued ribs even tastier?" or, "How will I find the ultimate vacation getaway spot?" can greatly enrich your life by adding pleasure and enjoyment. What matters is *why* you choose to solve diversion-level problems and *how much* of your problem-solving resources you dedicate to them.

Many people who make diversion-level problems their top priority are seeking to hide from the responsibilities and pressures of life. They mask their anxieties by distracting themselves with avoidance activities. People who spend most of their time doing things like watching television, shopping, and drinking are often doing so in an attempt to numb their awareness and their feelings. Although they may succeed in temporarily forgetting their pressing, higher-priority problems, this approach cannot provide lasting peace of mind.

The lure of escapism is strong because it repeatedly provides a temporary sense of relief. For some people, shopping, smoking, gambling, or even going to the movies provides them with a few moments of blissful escape from their worries. People who get trapped in this cycle of fleeting gratification allow themselves to be fooled by the sensation that, "my needs are being met," "my problems are going away," or, "my life feels good." They mistake a temporary absence of emotional suffering for true happiness. This is the cycle of avoidance, and ultimately of addiction.

Building the pyramid. If you desire real long-term happiness and success, or even just a sense of basic stability in life, you will not get it by making diversion-level problems your highest priority. Let's look at what can be accomplished by prioritizing necessity-level problems instead.

Prioritizing Necessity-Level Problems

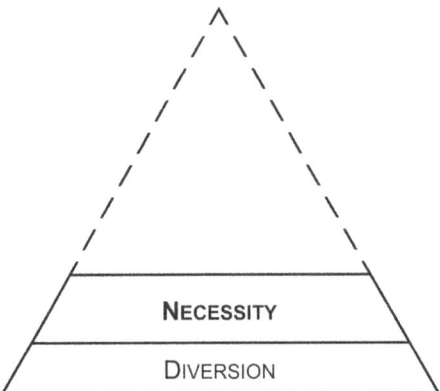

Life at the necessity level. Compared to a life centered on diversion-level problems, a life based in necessity is a noticeable improvement. People who make the problems at this level their top priority are able to establish a solid, stable foundation of competence. They tend to deal with the difficulties of daily life as they arise, rather than seeking to avoid them. They consistently work through the items in their planners or calendars.

Still, although they may move competently through one day after another, they do not achieve much real progress. No matter how many problems they solve at this level they rarely get beyond even; they rarely end up better off than they were before the problem arose. Their lives are dominated by their to-do lists. They often end up feeling like they are running on a treadmill, that they are working hard but not really getting anywhere.

Choosing to live this way is not the best use of your problem-solving resources. It is reactive rather than proactive because it allows the world to choose your problems for you. You end up spending most of your time on short-term, minor, recurring problems rather than on making long-term progress toward important goals that could give you real feeling of accomplishment.

Building the pyramid. Prioritizing the necessity level actually makes diversion-level activities more enjoyable. You can take time off from your daily routine to pursue recreational activities without being distracted by the nagging sensation that you are neglecting the basic requirements of life. But if you are not content with a life of repetitive tasks and occasional entertainment, you need to prioritize achievement-level problems.

PRIORITIZING ACHIEVEMENT-LEVEL PROBLEMS

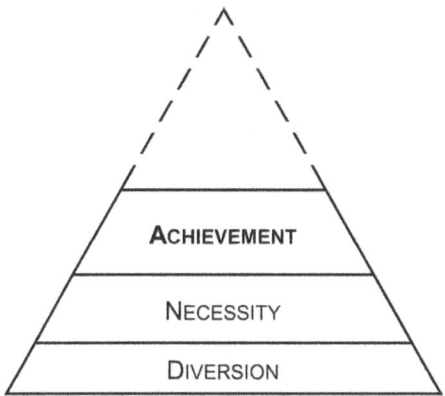

Life at the achievement level. This is where a dynamic, rewarding life becomes possible. Many people have built successful careers and enjoyable personal lives by making achievement-level problems their top priority.

Dedicating more of your resources to solving problems that lead to the achievement of long-term objectives greatly increases your ability to attain success in areas like better health, greater wealth, and more prestigious awards or recognition. Because this is a proactive, future-oriented strategy you will tend to anticipate and resolve major challenges before they become crises, and often find ways to turn them into opportunities.

Humans are most happy when they are seeking to achieve clear goals that are important to them. In fact, research has shown that people are happier when they are working toward a goal than when they are experiencing leisure and pleasure. This explains why financially successful individuals often observe that they enjoyed the process of making their money more than they enjoy having it and spending it. So setting the achievement level as your top priority rather than the diversion level will actually make your life happier and more enjoyable in the short run, as well as producing greater success in the long run. You will immediately begin to experience the deep sense of satisfaction that comes from pursuing exciting long-term goals.

Building the pyramid. Achievement-level problems usually cannot be solved in a single step. For example, solving a problem like, "How will I run a 10K race in 40 minutes next year?" requires you to define and solve a series of short-term problems:

- "How will I find running shoes that are comfortable and will help prevent injury?"
- "How will I fit training time into my weekly schedule?"
- "How will I build up my distances so I peak on the day of the race?"

The best way to turn an achievement-level problem into a series of short-term problems is by developing a written problem-solving project, using the process presented in CLARITY.

As you begin creating and implementing these projects, you will automatically start making different choices about how you spend your resources on problems at the necessity and diversion levels. For example, suppose you were tackling the achievement-level problem, "How will I become independently wealthy?" As you develop a project to achieve this goal you begin to re-prioritize your short-term problems, deciding which are most deserving of your time and energy. You might realize that while you can save a little money in the short run by mowing your own lawn, you could use that time to earn much more money in the long run by tackling the next problem in your "becoming wealthy" project. So you pay a neighborhood teenager to do the mowing for you and spend that time researching sound investment strategies.

Or suppose your achievement-level problem was, "How will I write a great novel?" As you create your problem-solving project you realize that a great deal of your evening and weekend time is occupied by doing the family laundry. You have always done the laundry yourself to ensure that the washing and folding would meet your high standards. Now you realize that achieving your goal as a writer is a higher priority, so you delegate the laundry to your children, accepting that they might not do it perfectly.

However, while the achievement level has great advantages over the necessity level, it does have its limits. All too often when people have reached what they expected to be the pinnacle of success – great fame, luxurious belongings, prestigious awards – they still feel fundamentally unfulfilled. They achieve their long-term goals after many years of effort, only to end up asking, "Is this all there is?" Looking back, they may realize that they were traveling the wrong road, and solving the wrong problems, all along.

It is certainly easy to move through life without pausing to consider the problems that lie beyond the achievement level. The consequences of this can only be guessed at because they are "what-might-have-beens." They are the experiences that were missed, the opportunities that were overlooked, and the relationships that were not nurtured. The hidden danger in making the achievement level your top priority is that you may spend your life pursuing objectives that will not contribute to your personal fulfillment. You can avoid this trap by adding the fulfillment level to your PRIORITY pyramid.

PRIORITIZING FULFILLMENT-LEVEL PROBLEMS

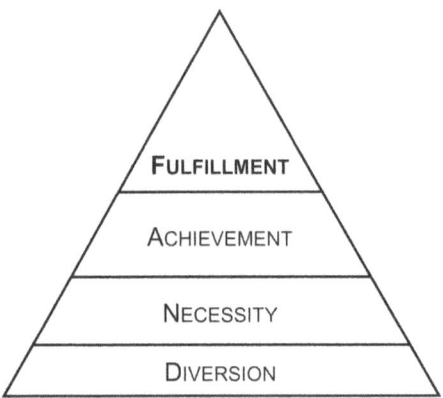

Life at the fulfillment level. This highest level of PRIORITY allows you to lead a life that reflects who you really are and what you most deeply believe. When you prioritize fulfillment, you seek out, and even create, the challenging problems that will help you fulfill your fundamental beliefs. You can then move forward with the confidence that you are dedicating your resources toward your highest dreams and ambitions.

Building the pyramid. Adding the fulfillment level makes your PRIORITY pyramid complete. You now have open access to the best that each level has to offer:

- Setting and attaining high-priority goals at the achievement level

- Accomplishing important, practical tasks at the necessity level
- Enjoying satisfying recreation at the diversion level

All of these are now enriched by being brought into alignment with your true fulfillment. In turn, they support the attainment of that fulfillment. You can put this powerful leverage to work in your life by creating a *fulfillment action plan*.

CREATE YOUR FULFILLMENT ACTION PLAN

Creating a fulfillment action plan consists of five steps, one for each level of the PRIORITY pyramid plus one more step that gives you the motivation to make the plan a reality:

1. Identify your fundamental beliefs (fulfillment level)
2. Create compelling goals (achievement level)
3. Create problem-solving projects (necessity level)
4. Include fun (diversion level)
5. Envision fulfillment

As you follow these five steps, be sure to put them in writing. Idle daydreams and vague intentions will not take you far toward fulfillment. The more specific you can be in defining your aspirations and the steps you will take to attain them, the more likely you will be to make them a reality. Putting your thoughts in writing will help you make them detailed and clear.

Keep in mind, though, that developing a fulfillment plan is not primarily a drafting exercise. Concentrate first on what truly encourages and inspires you. You can take care of getting the words just right later. The plan is for your own motivation and direction, not for a scrapbook or a wall hanging. What ends up on paper only needs to serve as a record and reminder for your later use.

Create your fulfillment plan with the assumption that you will never show it to anyone else. That way you will not feel self-conscious or inhibited by how others might react to it or judge it. Worrying about what your friends and family might say about the plan could lead you to play it safe, preventing you from really thinking big and pushing the limits. At some later time, perhaps after you have already made a good start toward making your plan a reality, you might choose to share it with others to gain their assistance and support. But to begin with, create it for your eyes only.

1. Identify Your Fundamental Beliefs

Recall (from FOCUS) that your fundamental beliefs are the positive keys to your self-identity, the vital principles that define and motivate you. If you have already used FOCUS to identify your beliefs, then the first part of your fulfillment action plan is already complete. If not, now is the time to go back and do so.

2. Create Compelling Goals

The second step is to create a set of *compelling goals* that are based on your fundamental beliefs. It is by pursuing these goals that you will put your beliefs into action.

Be sure to focus on what *you want* rather than on what *others have*; this will help you to avoid the Weak emotion of jealousy. Acting on jealousy substitutes another person's desires and priorities for your own. You end up thinking, "I want what they have" instead of, "I want what will fulfill me." Set goals to define your own path through life, not to copy the path taken by someone else.

You will be the one pursuing the goals, so set them for yourself, not for your parents, your spouse, or your peer group. They should come from within you, rather than mimicking some image or lifestyle that is promoted by movies, television, or popular music. These media messages may have slipped into your subconscious without your noticing them, giving you the impression that fulfillment absolutely must include things like:

- Living the big life of wealth, celebrity, sex, beauty, and glamour
- Seeking enlightenment through rigorous self-denial, seclusion, and meditation, renouncing earthly attachments and desires
- Living on the edge as an athletic danger-seeker who climbs cliffs, skydives, runs with the bulls, and goes whitewater rafting

If one of these truly embodies your deepest inner values, then go for it. But don't be too quick to choose one of the pre-packaged standard versions of "the good life." Your true individuality will be better expressed through your own unique blend of dreams and ambitions.

You can use the brainstorming techniques that are presented in CREATIVITY to identify your compelling goals. Review your fundamental beliefs, generate a Strong state of energy and insight, and then just start writing down as many potential goals as possible.

If you prefer, you can make the brainstorming process more structured by creating a series of *compelling goal statements* based on your fundamental beliefs. Do this by completing the statement, "Because I believe _____, I will _____."

For example:

"Because I believe in sharing my blessings with those who are less fortunate, I will...

- Lead the creation of a program to teach homeless children in my community how to read."

- Find a way to make a $100,000 contribution to a worthy charity."

Another example:

"Because I believe in savoring the full richness of life, I will...

- Make a lifetime travel list of ten fascinating places that I will see and appreciate in person."
- Treat myself to a new sensory indulgence each year on my birthday."

Completing several statements like these for each of your fundamental beliefs will leave you with a good list of potential goals. Then compare and combine these goals until you arrive at a short set that is truly compelling. As you do so, consider whether each potential goal on your brainstorming list actually arises from your own fundamental beliefs. What *must* you accomplish to feel complete? Concentrate on identifying *achievement* that will lead to *fulfillment*. As you review each potential goal, ask yourself how strongly you desire to reach it. Is it truly *vital* that you solve this problem? If your answer is, "Well, kinda..." then cross it off the list.

Also eliminate goals that are only on the list because you think you *should* want them, or because they might impress someone else. Focus only on the goals that powerfully draw you toward them, that charge you with enthusiasm. Be sure that your compelling goals are *really compelling for you*, not just "that would be nice" wishes.

Make your goals as challenging and motivating as possible. A compelling goal should make you feel excited and a little intimidated at the same time. It should inspire you and give you butterflies in the stomach. It should be right at the upper limit of what you believe you can accomplish.

- You will know that you have aimed too low if the goal leaves you emotionally flat because you know can accomplish it fairly easily.
- You will know that you have aimed too high if a goal seems so daunting that reading it makes you feel pessimistic and de-motivated.
- You will know you have it just right if you find yourself thinking something like, "Wow, could I really do that? Maybe I can. And if I do, it would feel great!"

Be guided by fulfillment rather than fear. As you develop your compelling goals, be aware of the influence of fear. Previously, you may have been using fear as one of your primary guides when deciding whether or not to tackle a tough problem. If a problem seemed like an exciting challenge, you would move forward, reassured by the absence of fear. On the other hand, if a problem seemed frightening, you would steer clear, warned off by the presence of fear.

Certainly, fear can play a useful role in warning you away from unnecessary risks. However, now you have a new standard for deciding whether an achievement-level problem is worth pursuing: will it lead to fulfillment or not? This allows you to consciously choose whether and when to override the message of fear. You may find yourself considering a goal that seems necessary to your fulfillment but that also scares the dickens out of you. Examine your feelings carefully: is your subconscious generating fear to warn you away from a genuine and serious danger, or are you just feeling anxious because tackling this problem would require you to move beyond your current comfort zone? You may conclude that reaching the goal *in spite of the fear* is a necessary step toward your fulfillment. If so, you must overcome the fear and set your sights firmly on achieving the goal. (See DETERMINATION for techniques that will help you move forward in the face of fear.)

Question all limiting assumptions. Don't allow past setbacks or disappointments to prevent you from setting ambitious goals for your future. View any previous unsuccessful efforts as experiments and scouting expeditions rather than as failures. They do not define the boundaries of what is possible for you; instead they are guideposts that will help you find a better path to your future success.

Be wary of telling yourself, "I know who I am and I just have to accept it." While it is healthy to accept the central essence of who you are, that does not mean you must be satisfied with how you have behaved and what you have achieved in the past. It does not mean you must continue to be limited by your previous assumptions about the extent of your abilities. Aim to become the highest and best possible version of your true self. To settle for anything less is to sell yourself short. Aspects of yourself that you thought were permanent can actually be changed, improved, or replaced. Many people have found fulfillment precisely by achieving the one thing they had been programmed to believe they could never do.

Make your goals specific. Once you have created a list of compelling goals, you can clarify them by setting a specific date for the achievement of each goal. This provides motivation and organization, and gives the goal a sense of reality and inevitability.

For example, **"By the end of 20__:**

- **I will experience ____."** (What would you love to see and do, to hear, touch, or taste?)
- **I will be able to ____."** (What skills or abilities would you like to master?)
- **I will create, build, contribute, or invent ____."** (What do you want to give to the world?)

- **I will own ____."** (What possessions are you motivated to acquire?)
- **I will feel ____."** (What physical and emotional states do you long to experience?)
- **I will receive ____."** (What award, academic degree, or professional certification do you seek?)
- **I will earn, or be worth, at least $____."** (What financial goals do you find compelling?).

Once you have developed your list of compelling goals, you must determine what concrete steps you will take to reach them. As we discussed in the achievement level, you can do this by using the process presented in CLARITY to turn each goal into a problem-solving project.

3. CREATE PROBLEM-SOLVING PROJECTS

These projects lay out the series of short-term tasks you will perform in order to achieve your long-term goal. The achievement date you have set for a goal serves as the starting point for the problem-solving project. Working back from that date, identify the tasks you will tackle this year, this month, and this week in order to achieve the goal on time. If you can, take one small step *today* that will advance you toward each goal.

Shift your resources. Consider what objectives you have been treating as your top priorities until now. Think about the goals that have actually been occupying most of your time, money, and effort. You may be surprised to discover that you have been expending most of your resources on goals that are not on your list, and that will not contribute significantly to your long-term fulfillment.

What share of your resources are you currently dedicating to goals like:

- Watching every episode of all your favorite television shows
- Keeping your car perfectly clean, inside and out
- Getting your hair or makeup just right every morning
- Reading every page of the Sunday newspaper
- Hitting all the sales early in the morning each weekend, before the best deals are gone
- Doing all your own home maintenance and repair
- Buying and decorating a showcase home
- Beating all the levels in your new video game

Many people discover that they have been allocating more of their time, energy, and money to lower-priority activities than to reaching the objectives that will really matter the most to them in the long run. **Reallocating your resources toward achieving fulfilling goals is one of the most crucial steps in the action plan process.** We saw two examples of this in the achievement level:

- Hiring a neighborhood teenager to mow your lawn, so you can reallocate your time toward the goal of building wealth
- Delegating doing the laundry to your children, so you can reallocate your time toward the goal of writing a book

Think about how you have spent your time, money, and effort during the past week. You will probably see many opportunities to shift your resources away from lower-priority activities. You may be able to make some quick and easy changes, like resolving to limit your television viewing. You could also make a list of the lower-priority activities that have been consuming your resources. Then identify specific ways you will reallocate those resources to pursuing your compelling goals. Set an appointment with yourself in four weeks to check your progress and to congratulate yourself for the positive results you have achieved.

4. Include Fun

Fulfillment includes having fun. Remember that you do not move from one level to a higher one, instead you add each higher level to the ones below it. So making fulfillment your top priority does not mean you have to give up pleasurable diversion-level activities. In fact, pursuing fulfillment will help you select diversionary activities that enhance your life and reject those that are a waste of your resources. Once you are in touch with who you are and what you believe, you will naturally be drawn toward activities that give you the greatest pleasure and enjoyment, and that are in alignment with your fundamental beliefs.

The diversion-level activities that you have previously enjoyed will become even more fun, because you will not be distracted by any background anxiety about whether you are on the right path in life. You will live much more "in the moment." You will find that fun is *more* fun because you are living life to the fullest, rather than seeking to escape from it. In fact, you will find that pursuing your compelling goals is so rewarding that using diversionary activities as escapism will lose whatever appeal it once had.

5. Envision Fulfillment

The final step in creating your fulfillment action plan is to give yourself a big motivational boost by clearly envisioning what it will be like when you have achieved your compelling goals. What feelings of accomplishment will you enjoy? In what ways will your life be easier, happier, more fun? How will your relationships improve? What will you be contributing to the world? These images should stimulate you, inspire you, and bring a smile to your face.

Here are some examples of what you might write down as part of your envisioned future:

"When I achieve my goal of becoming a certified scuba instructor by the end of next year, I will…
- …experience the unique pleasure of being paid to do the activity I most enjoy."
- …help others in times of crisis by volunteering for search and rescue missions."
- …travel to the Bahamas and write it off as a business expense."
- …reward myself by buying the high quality diving gear I have always wanted."

"When I achieve my goal of having a net worth of ten million dollars by the end of 20__, I will…
- …experience the confidence and peace of mind that comes with financial security."
- …be able to provide assistance to my parents and my children in their times of need."
- … have the freedom to travel to [the place you have always wanted to visit]."
- …reward myself by buying [the luxury car you would love to own]."

Vividly imagine how your life will look and feel when you are consistently putting your fundamental beliefs into action. Put your vision in writing and use it to provide a lift anytime you need one. Whenever you need a boost of enthusiasm, you will always have the touchstone of your vision to reinvigorate you.

THE BENEFITS OF LIFE AT THE FULFILLMENT LEVEL

Flow. As you put your fulfillment plan into action you will begin to experience *flow*, which is the experience of effortless achievement. Recall times in your life when you mastered a new skill, like riding a bicycle. When you finally got it right, awkwardness and wasted effort were replaced in an instant by smooth efficiency. That is the feeling of flow.

At the fulfillment level, more and more of life has that same wonderful feeling. Problems seem to melt away before you, or are transformed into enjoyable opportunities. In the flow state, you:

- Create more, produce more, and solve more than ever before, but it feels like recreation rather than like work
- Surprise yourself by reaching goals that formerly seemed very difficult or impossible
- Feel naturally pulled toward success rather than fearful of failure
- Find that what you *want to do* is usually the same as what you *should be doing*
- Realize that the your biggest problems are not catastrophes that have befallen you, but rather are opportunities that you have sought out or created for yourself

Flow is an experience to watch for and enjoy rather than a skill for which to strive. It is a manifestation of fulfillment-level living, a delightful benefit of acting in accordance with your fundamental beliefs.

Career advancement. Let's assume you work in a typical medium-to-large-size organization and that you want to build a career by earning promotions and pay increases. The following scenarios illustrate the impact that your level of PRIORITY will have on your ability to build a successful career:

If you consistently choose diversionary problems like, "How will I take a nap while appearing to work?" or, "How will I do my online shopping without getting caught?" you will probably end up getting fired. If you are spending most of your time playing computer games, shuffling papers, and visiting with coworkers, you are not worth much to the organization because you are not solving the organization's problems. In fact, *you are* a problem. Your potential to earn any kind of livelihood is at risk.

If you focus on solving problems at the necessity level you can work effectively in a staff-level position. You have value to the company as a worker bee because you can solve the day-to-day problems that are necessary to get your work done. You generally solve problems directly through your own effort rather than through leadership or delegation. These will primarily be short-term problems that are solved within a day or two, rather than ones that require long-term planning or analysis. However, your promotion opportunities are limited. You might earn a promotion into a team leader or foreman position, but if you cannot consistently focus on setting and accomplishing achievement-level goals you will probably never rise into management.

If you function consistently at the achievement level you can become an effective manager. This is in recognition of your ability to set challenging goals and achieve them through the organized efforts of your staff. At this level problems and solutions become more abstract, harder to quantify, and longer-term. Success is often not determined for weeks or months. Success is also more dependent on the actions of others, which makes leadership and team building essential. Setting annual goals and budgets are included in the achievement level. You have high value to your organization because you can prevent and solve major problems, and turn problems into opportunities. However, while you can succeed as a manager, you may never attain an executive position. You can achieve financial security and success, but you will likely not cross that fine line that makes virtually unlimited rewards possible.

If you consistently operate at the fulfillment level you have limitless potential for success. You can be promoted to the top executive positions in the organization. Crossing the line from achievement to fulfillment increases your earning potential a hundred-fold. You have ultimate value to the organization because you help create its culture, its envisioned future, and its compelling goals. Your character shapes the company and your ambition drives it. Companies with fulfillment-level leaders are the ones that achieve breakthrough innovations and long-term success.

Conclusion

Great problem-solvers direct more of their efforts toward solving the right problems, the ones that will give them the biggest advantage and produce the most desirable results. Dedicating your resources to high-priority, fulfillment-level problems creates incredible leverage; small actions on your part will now produce great outcomes. Getting your thoughts, feelings, and actions into alignment with your fundamental beliefs generates a flow of solutions that carries you toward fulfillment.

Priority: Summary

- **Choose your problems.** Choosing your problems consciously, rather than letting life choose them for you, puts you in control of your personal destiny.

The Priority Pyramid

- **Diversion-level problems.** "How will I have fun and feel good?"
- **Necessity-level problems.** "How will I satisfy my basic needs and complete my routine tasks?"
- **Achievement-level problems.** "How will I achieve my long-term objectives?"

- **Fulfillment-level problems.** "How will I put my fundamental beliefs into action?"

BUILDING THE PYRAMID
- **Aim for the top.** You will be more successful if you choose to tackle higher-level problems. There is a powerful "building" effect that occurs as you add higher levels of PRIORITY.
- **Prioritizing diversion-level problems.** This is self-defeating, as it leads to *not* having fun and *not* feeling good. Daily problems multiply, and it is almost impossible to achieve meaningful goals or true fulfillment. Avoidance may lead to addiction.
- **Prioritizing necessity-level problems.** This creates a stable base of competence, dealing with daily difficulties rather than avoiding them, but it is reactive rather than proactive. You are more likely to stay even than to make real progress.
- **Prioritizing achievement-level problems.** Success and enjoyment is much more likely. You often resolve challenges before they become crises, and tend to treat problems as opportunities. However, you may end up fundamentally unfulfilled.
- **Prioritizing fulfillment-level problems.** This allows you to build a life that reflects who you really are and what you most deeply believe. You seek out, and even create, challenging problems that help you fulfill your fundamental beliefs.

CREATE YOUR FULFILLMENT ACTION PLAN
- **Identify your fundamental beliefs.** Use the process in FOCUS to discover your fundamental beliefs.
- **Create compelling goals.** Focus on what you want, rather than on what others want or on media messages. Question all limiting assumptions, and be guided by fulfillment rather than fear. Create specific, motivating goal statements.

- **Create problem-solving projects.** Use the process in CLARITY to create projects with interim and final deadlines. Shift your resources in order to reach your new goals.
- **Include fun.** Include plenty of diversion-level fun in your plan. Seek experiences that give you the greatest pleasure and enjoyment, that are in alignment with your fundamental beliefs.
- **Envision fulfillment.** Give yourself a motivational boost by vividly imagining how it will feel when you achieve your compelling goals. Put it in writing for future motivation.
- **The benefits of life at the fulfillment level.** At the fulfillment level you will experience *flow* – the sensation of achievement without effort – and enhance your ability to earn promotions and raises.

THE SIXTH TOOL

DISCOVERY

FIND & USE EXISTING SOLUTIONS

Let's suppose you have a problem to solve, either one you have chosen for yourself through PRIORITY or one that has simply arisen by chance. What solution-finding technique should you use first? The phrase "creative problem-solving" is so commonly used that you might automatically think, "I have a problem, so I guess I need to come up with a creative solution." It is especially easy to assume that you need to create a new and innovative solution when you are encountering a particular kind of problem for the first time.

Be uncreative. In reality, you don't have to *create* solutions for the vast majority of your problems; you just need to *find* one of the proven solutions that already exist. Other people have encountered similar problems in the past, and they figured out great ways to solve them. Some of these people shared their solutions with others, some wrote about them, and others even turned their solutions into products or services. You just need to find them.

Of course, it is true that creating a brand-new, innovative solution to a problem can generate several benefits. Doing so gives you a chance to exercise your "creativity muscles" and helps you develop confidence in your abilities as an innovative problem-solver. Plus, you might come up with a solution that is better than the solutions used in the past. CREATIVITY can indeed be a useful and powerful problem-solving tool.

However, if you plunge into creating new solutions for every problem you encounter, you will waste a lot of time and effort re-inventing the wheel. The DISCOVERY tool is essentially one simple idea: the most efficient way to solve most problems is to look for existing, proven solutions rather than creating brand-new ones of your own. This means adopting the habit of seeking ready-made, off-the-shelf solutions first, and saving your creative energy for the fewer, tougher problems that truly need custom-made solutions.

Bear in mind that a solution does not always come labeled as a solution. What you are seeking is any fact, service, idea, strategy, product, method, or insight that can help you reach your goal. So an important aspect of DISCOVERY is not just looking for solutions that are pre-packaged and complete, but being open to any idea or piece of information that solves your problem.

Also keep in mind that although it would be great to find *the* solution, you will often be better off accepting *a* solution. For many problems the ideal, polished solution is not required. Instead, all you need is a workable solution that gets the job done well enough. Realizing that you don't have to find the one perfect needle in the haystack can be liberating. There may be thousands of needles in the haystack, but perhaps the first one you discover will work well enough to repair the hole in your shirt. Consider using the first sufficient solution you find, particularly in cases where you are working under budget or time constraints, or where the stakes are not very high.

SHARE SOLUTIONS

We humans are good at passing along ideas and information. For example, scientists are able to solve increasingly complex problems because they learn from, and build on, the solutions created by previous generations of scientists. People have a natural desire to share their solutions, a built-in impulse to tell others about their discoveries. Think of how many times you have heard a child shout, "Look what I did!" or, "Look what I made!" The child feels the excitement of accomplishment and immediately wants to share it with others. In adults, this experience takes the form of "eureka moments" of insight and invention.

People feel pleasurable Strong emotions when they share their solutions. You can encourage others to assist you by helping them experience these positive feelings:

- **A feeling of *friendship* or *affection*.** It's as simple as this: People who like you are more likely to help you. If you are friendly and appreciative to those around you, you will build up a reservoir of goodwill you can tap into when you need problem-solving assistance.

- **A feeling of *generosity*,** the pure pleasure of helping others. In many cases all that the giver desires in return for providing problem-solving help is a word of thanks. People who have a genuine calling to be teachers, for instance, are illuminated by this spark: "I've learned something really interesting! Let me tell you about it!" You should express appreciation for such generosity whenever possible: "Hey, thanks for the directions! I really appreciate it!" or, "That advice you gave me helped a lot!"

- **A feeling of *camaraderie*.** This is what helps make teams work: the positive feeling that comes from tackling a problem together, and the knowledge that each member of the team can benefit by helping the team succeed as a group. You can encourage this feeling by pitching in as a positive, productive teammate, and by talking in terms of "we" and "our" instead of "I" and "my."

- **A feeling of *wisdom* or *pride*.** People often experience a pleasurable sense of being knowledgeable and capable when they help solve a problem. So when you ask others to share their expertise, present your request as a compliment: "I am coming to you because I respect your ability, experience, and judgment." When you receive assistance, acknowledge the giver's skill or knowledge: "Wow, you really know a lot about this!"
- **The desire to create or pay back a *solution debt*.** People may wish to help you with the expectation that you will return the favor, or because you have helped them in the past. So, the more help you give, the more you will get in return. Keep the cycle going!

Since most people have a reason for wanting to help you, feel free to ask for their assistance. Here are some guidelines for asking effectively:

Stay Strong. Do you know people who readily offer advice and assistance to others, but rarely accept it in return? People who behave this way mistakenly believe that giving help makes them look strong, while asking for help would make them look weak. Because of this perception they are reluctant to seek assistance, and they may even feel resentful toward anyone who tries to offer them information or advice.

Reject this approach. If you are a dedicated problem-solver, your main focus will be on finding a great solution. It won't matter much to you whether you find it on your own or get it from someone else. There are people all around you whose knowledge, experience, and skills could give you better and faster solutions to your problems than you can invent on your own. The best way to tap into these solutions is by building problem-solving partnerships in which helpful tips and techniques are freely exchanged. People are usually most comfortable in relationships in which they both accept *and* provide problem-solving help, so make a habit of both giving and getting solutions graciously and with self-assurance.

Seeking assistance is certainly not a sign of weakness. In fact, the opposite is true: the more confident you are, the more comfortable you will be reaching out for suggestions and information. Asking someone for solutions in a confident manner is easy. People are more willing to help if you are positive and upbeat, so approach them with friendliness, self-assurance, and enthusiasm. Request assistance sincerely and directly, using questions and statements like:

- "Do you have any information on...?"
- "I'm hoping you can help me with..."
- "I've heard you know a lot about..."
- "I'd really appreciate it if you could..."
- "I'm having a problem with..."

It often helps to briefly explain the goal you are trying to achieve and what you already know about the obstacle and potential solutions. This makes it easier for the other person to provide you with a solution well-suited your needs.

Communicate clearly. When you are seeking problem-solving ideas and advice, it is important to communicate clearly and precisely. Communication is most effective when you see it as a cycle, a back-and-forth process in which you build clarity and understanding by alternately *sending information to* and *receiving information from* the other person.

When you are sending a message, express yourself in a way that is not only accurate, but is also likely to be understood by the particular person to whom you are speaking. For instance, while it may seem to you that using the jargon of your trade or profession is the most accurate way to express an idea, the listener will probably receive your message more clearly if you use ordinary words instead. You can make your message even clearer by providing examples, using analogies, or literally drawing a picture such as a graph, chart, or illustration.

When you are receiving a message, be alert to the real meaning of what you are hearing. Actively interpret what is being said, rather than just passively listening. Put yourself in the shoes of the person who is speaking: pay attention to the message he or she is trying to convey instead of what that message may sound like to you. Don't let your individual preconceptions or prejudices interfere with your ability to receive valuable information.

All too often people miss out on valuable information because they wrap up a conversation too quickly, before they have a clear and complete understanding of the potential solutions. Keep the cycle of communication going by continuing to ask questions and clarify answers until you have a full understanding of all the information the other person has to offer. This is another example of the problem-solving power of curiosity. Here are some useful methods:

- **Restate.** Make sure that you correctly understand the substance of what someone has said by saying it back to them in your own words. For example, use this technique when the other person employs unfamiliar jargon or technical terms and you are unsure of their meaning.
- **Repeat.** Make sure that you have heard the message correctly by repeating back exactly what you think was said. This is especially useful when you are in a noisy or distracting location or when the other person is speaking very rapidly.

- **Specify.** When someone speaks vaguely or imprecisely, seek agreement on more specific language. For example, if someone says, "You have to turn in the application soon," you could say, "So, if I get it to you by five p.m. on Friday, will that be soon enough?"
- **Question.** Gather useful details and keep the conversation moving by asking probing follow-up questions. For example, if someone says, "Keep going until you get to Willow Street," you might ask, "About how far is that?" or, "Is there a landmark I can watch for?"
- **Summarize.** To make sure you haven't missed anything, recap what you believe are the most important points of the conversation so far. This is useful when the solution requires you to take several steps, and you want to make sure you have all of them.
- **Express ignorance.** If you don't understand what the other person is telling you, just say so. For example, say, "I'm not sure what you mean by that" or, "I don't understand what you just said." This works better than pretending that you understand and hoping you can figure it out later.

Always remember: you may be one question away from a great solution!

Pass the help along. In many cases, you will use the solutions you discover as is. But sometimes you will see a way to improve a solution by making it faster, cheaper, easier, or more effective. And sometimes gathering information about existing solutions will inspire you to create a completely new and better one. In either case, be sure to share the wealth by passing along your improvements and innovations, making life better for those who encounter the same problem in the future.

> **BORROW IT, IMPROVE IT, AND PASS IT ALONG**
>
> When I was helping turn around a struggling insurance organization, one of our most successful strategies was to identify other companies in the industry who were achieving good results in a particular area and ask them how they did it. Everyone we asked was happy to share information with us. We would then take their basic idea or process and improve on it a bit before implementing it ourselves. We found that while it is pretty difficult to come up with an entirely new and innovative idea from scratch, it is usually pretty easy to take someone else's innovative idea and make it ten or twenty percent better.
>
> We were grateful for the help we had received from others, so we were willing to provide assistance to anyone who asked us for help in turn. But it's a funny thing, even after we pulled the organization back from the brink of disaster and started achieving some of the best results in the country, people seldom bothered to ask us how we had done so. It is amazing how few people follow the simple strategy of asking others to share their proven problem-solving ideas.
>
> -Reagan

USE DISCOVERY RESOURCES

These are individuals, organizations, reference tools, and other resources that can provide you with ready-made solutions to most of your problems.

HUMAN RESOURCES

- **Friends.** Have you fully considered what your circle of friends has to offer in the way of problem-solving experience, knowledge, and advice? There are probably many people in your life you like and trust, but from whom you have never sought advice or information. One of the hallmarks of a true friendship is the willingness to offer and accept help.

- **Family.** As with your friends, it is worthwhile to consider the pool of experience that may lie untapped in your family. Become better-acquainted with your family members, and discover what they know a lot about and what they are good at doing. Even if you have not had a great relationship with a particular relative, it is still possible that he or she might give you the solution you are looking for. Leave your emotional baggage at home and stay focused on the task at hand. "I know we've had our differences, but I could really use your help right now." Sometimes, asking for help is a great way to break the ice and start building a better relationship.

- **Coworkers.** Consult a long-term employee who remembers what did and did not work the last time the problem arose. See if the new guy has a fresh perspective or outside experience that could help you overcome a long-standing obstacle. Go to the shop floor and ask, "Is this design going to work?" Ask a sales rep, "Why do we get so many complaints about this product?" Ask your supervisor for help, or get permission to take the problem further up the chain of command.

- **Business staff.** Knowledgeable customer service, sales, repair, and technical support staff are great solution resources. They can give you guidance toward purchasing a tool or service that will solve the problem, and they often provide free advice that helps you solve the problem and without making a purchase.

- **Government and social workers.** Employees at all levels of government are potential solution sources, as are the staffs of public and private social service agencies. Call or visit and see what information or assistance they can provide. They can often provide free publications relating to your problem.

- **Organizations.** There are organizations formed around a wide variety of common interests, such as business, charity, health, hobbies, athletics, professions, religion, and self-help. They share ideas through regular meetings, conventions, seminars, presentations, trade shows, newsgroups, and newsletters. By their very nature, these organizations are likely to provide a high concentration of people interested in solving specific kinds of problems.

- **Networking.** Networking means always "having your line in the water" or "keeping your antenna up" as you go through life. There is potential for learning from every person you encounter. Make the most of opportunities to talk with *interesting* people by becoming an *interested* person. Whenever you meet someone new, ask questions rather than make statements. Listen with genuine interest while others discuss their areas of expertise, rather than just waiting for your turn to talk.

- **Role models.** These are people who are currently doing what you aspire to do, such as building a successful career, being a good parent, or performing skillfully at a sport. You can learn from them by asking them to mentor you or simply by observing them. Be inspired by your role models and learn from them, but do not seek to become them. Adapt what you learn from them to suit your own personality, strengths, and goals. The way to excel is to be the finest version of yourself.

YOU GOTTA BE YOU!

Shortly after I joined a law firm as a young, very inexperienced lawyer, one of the senior partners sat me down in his office and gave me some advice:

"There is only one way to be a good lawyer, and that is *your* way. There are many excellent attorneys in this firm and in this city, and if you are smart you will observe them and learn from them. But do not seek to imitate or become 'just like' another lawyer, no matter how talented he is. You will never be as good at being him as he is, and you will never become a great lawyer in your own right if you pretend to be someone you are not. Every individual has to find his own way to being the best attorney he or she can be."

This was excellent advice, not just for practicing law but for everything else we do in life. There is only one way to be a great manager, teacher, spouse, athlete, artist, or parent and that is *your* way.

-Reagan

Media Resources

- **Bookstores and libraries.** These contain a wealth of information and ideas for solving all kinds of problems, including how-to projects, self-help issues, business challenges, and religious or spiritual matters. Good bookstores and libraries have helpful staff who can help guide you through the vast array of books, magazines, and other sources of solution-rich information.

- **Newspapers and magazines.** Reading periodicals regularly is a good way to stimulate your thinking and keep informed about new and better solutions as they become available. In addition to your local newspaper, consider subscribing to a national newspaper and to several magazines covering your areas of interest.

- **Business and government listings.** Use printed or online yellow pages to identify a business or government agency that can help you solve a problem. We suggest keeping a phone book in your car. One phone call can save you a lot of drive time.

- **Radio and television.** You can gain problem-solving ideas from programs addressing topics like business, gardening, and home improvement. You can also seek specific advice regarding issues like personal finance, car repair, and relationship issues through radio call-in shows. Be sure to check out the informational programming on your local public radio station.

- **Internet.** Many sources of information that were previously difficult or impossible to locate are now available online. Find them using search engines, experimenting with various word combinations that describe your obstacle, goal, or potential solutions.

> **A Spectacular Find on the Internet**
>
> Reagan and I have had a lifelong interest in fireworks. A number of years ago, we decided to create a "grand finale" to top off our Fourth of July festivities, a fireworks extravaganza that would thrill our friends and families. We fastened a bunch of fireworks to a wooden frame and attempted to ignite them with a homemade fuse consisting of strips of cotton cloth soaked in lighter fluid. The result was basically a bonfire with explosions, which was short-lived but well-remembered by all who were present.
>
> Over the years the finale has grown more sophisticated and elaborate, with large numbers of fireworks affixed to a series of frames, connected with hundreds of feet of cannon fuse. Of course, each year we face the challenge of making the show even bigger and better than the previous one.
>
> Several years ago I used the DISCOVERY process and searched the Web for fireworks information. That is how I discovered a marvelous device known as the "creamer bomb." It's fairly simple to create, using a metal can, black powder, and a specific brand of powdered coffee creamer. It produces a spectacular fireball of the kind you might see in an action movie. We immediately set to work experimenting with the idea: what size cans to use, what ratio of gunpowder to creamer, and so forth. We've incorporated the effect into our last two finales, and it has been a real crowd-pleaser.
>
> -Kevin
>
> Warning: Do *not* attempt to create a creamer bomb without first obtaining complete instructions!

Educational Resources

- **Classes.** Could you benefit from taking a course in personal finance, parenting, or computer skills? There are evening, community outreach, and adult education programs in most areas. Check the course listings at your local university, community college, or trade school. You can also enroll in courses and even earn degrees online.

- **Tutorials.** Training courses covering many subjects are available online and in the form of software tutorials.

Conclusion

Solutions to your problems are all around you, everywhere you go. Everyone you meet is a potential problem-solving resource, a living repository of solutions. You need only learn to seek out these solutions and recognize them when you find them. You will begin to find solutions in unexpected places, and will discover ideas and techniques for solving problem in ways you never imagined.

When you make DISCOVERY a habit, you will start scanning for possible solutions as soon as a problem arises. Opening your eyes and ears to the world's wealth of information allows you to experience *synchronicity*, in which the solution to a problem appears like magic just when you need it. The saying goes: "When the student is ready, the master appears." In this case, when the problem-solver is ready, the solution appears.

Discovery: Summary

- **Be uncreative.** Most problems you encounter have previously been solved by others, so seek first to find a solution rather than create a solution. Be open to imperfect solutions.

Share Solutions

- **The rewards of sharing.** There are many reasons why others want to share their solutions with you, including generosity, friendship, camaraderie, demonstrating prowess, and creating or paying back a solution debt.
- **Ask for help.** Ask for assistance confidently and enthusiastically. Communicate clearly by repeating, restating, specifying, questioning, summarizing, and expressing ignorance. Pass along your great discoveries.

USE DISCOVERY RESOURCES

- **Human resources.** Make full use of the solutions available in your circle of friends, family members, and coworkers. Consult customer service representatives, government employees, and organizations. Engage in networking, and use role models.
- **Media resources.** Visit bookstores and libraries, read periodicals, consult business and government listings, tune in helpful radio and television programs, and go online to find solutions.
- **Educational resources.** Enroll in classes or use tutorials to find problem-solving information.

The Seventh Tool

Teamwork

Delegate & Partner

Teamwork, like Discovery, involves getting help from other people. The difference is in the kind of help you receive. Discovery is used to gather information and advice about existing solutions that you can use to solve a problem. Teamwork is for obtaining active assistance, getting others to work *for* you or *with* you to help solve a problem.

Life is a Team Effort

Humans are social, meaning that we are most successful when we act cooperatively rather than individually. The fundamental reason for this success is the problem-solving efficiency of *shared effort* and *shared rewards*.

Think about the extraordinary chain of coordinated work that goes into designing and building a car, growing crops and processing them into food, or gathering and broadcasting news stories. Consider how you benefit from the coordinated work of thousands of individuals every time you turn on the lights, or open a faucet for a cool glass of water. Their efforts provide you with solutions that you could not hope to achieve on your own, and you make a contribution in return by doing work that helps other people solve their problems more efficiently.

You are a member of many teams. A team is any group of people working together to achieve a common goal, such as a sports team or a community service organization. In a broader sense you are a member of many groups that have the potential to act as teams: your family, your friends, your neighbors, the people with whom you work, other members of your trade or profession, your community, and even your nation. Ultimately, people all around the world can be seen as potential problem-solving teammates.

Many people do not think of these groups as teams that can help them solve problems. In particular, strongly Individual problem-solvers do not utilize TEAMWORK as often as they might. Therefore, people are often passive members of the groups to which they belong, neither contributing nor benefiting as much as they could. Becoming more aware of the potential problem-solving TEAMWORK that is available allows you to:

- Use teams more often in solving your problems
- Get more out of the teams to which you already belong
- Decide to join a new team, leave a current team, or create and lead a team of your own
- Choose new members who will enhance the performance of your teams, or identify existing members that your teams would be better off without

Forms of TEAMWORK. There are two types of TEAMWORK: *delegation* and *partnership*.

Delegation means giving a problem-solving task to someone else. You can delegate by assigning a task to someone over whom you have authority, for example to one of your children or to an employee you supervise. You can also delegate by hiring someone to solve the problem for you, or by asking someone to do it as a favor.

Partnership means working with others to solve a problem. This can include anything from getting on-the-spot help for solving a single problem to establishing an ongoing group for tackling a series of problems.

DELEGATION TEAMWORK

Delegation offers many advantages:

- As we saw in PRIORITY, delegating low-priority tasks allows you to re-allocate your resources to the problems that matter the most. This increases your ability to pursue fulfillment. For example, delegating household tasks to your children could allow you to pursue a compelling goal of performing onstage in a community theater production.
- Delegating tasks you find unpleasant allows you to spend more time doing the things you enjoy. This makes your life more pleasurable. For example, hiring someone to repaint your house rather than doing it yourself could allow you to spend the weekend enjoying time with your family.
- Delegating tasks that you don't have time for allows you to finish other necessary work. This makes your life run more smoothly. For example, asking your spouse to take over putting the kids to bed for two weeks so you can work on installing a bathroom in the basement.
- Delegating tasks that you don't do particularly well allows you to concentrate your efforts on the things you do best.

This allows you to be more successful. For example, delegating the bookkeeping tasks for your small business to an employee who is better at detail work could free up your time to develop a new marketing campaign.

Overcoming Reluctance to Delegate

Despite its many advantages, people often resist using delegation. Let's evaluate some of the most common excuses for not delegating:

- **"I've always done it, and it would make me uncomfortable to give it up."** Don't assume that you have to keep doing something just because you have been doing it for a long time. Habits can be hard to break, and a sense of familiarity can be pleasant and comfortable. However, if those are the only reasons you are continuing to do something that is not advancing you toward fulfillment, hand it off to someone else.

- **"People will think I'm lazy."** It's true that some people delegate just because they are too lazy to do the work themselves. However, since you are reading *Solution Power* you are probably the kind of positive-thinking person who uses delegation for more constructive reasons. So don't worry about how other people choose to perceive your motives. As you work toward your vision of fulfillment you will silence the criticisms of some and will grow less concerned about the criticisms of others.

- **"If I try to make someone else do it, they might get angry."** As long as you delegate in a polite and fair manner, recognize that other people are responsible for dealing with their own Weak RESPONSES. If you are truly committed to tackling your fulfillment-level problems, go ahead and delegate lower-priority problems despite the emotional reactions others may choose. There are tips later in this chapter on how to delegate in a positive manner.

- **"I'm the only one who knows how to do it."** Performing a particular task may be your specialty, and it may make you feel more secure in your job or more important in your position. However, you might be better off risking this feeling of security in order to pursue growth and fulfillment. Rather than seeking to keep others dependent on your expertise, make yourself even more valuable by becoming a great teacher as well as a skilled specialist. Don't tie yourself to a low-priority problem-solving task by being the only one who can do it.

- **"No one else will do it as well as I do."** Maybe you're right. Maybe the problem won't be solved quite as neatly or thoroughly by someone else. But being the best at performing a low-value activity, like mowing the lawn, is not a sufficient reason to keep devoting your resources to it. Would you be willing to lower your standards a little if delegating the problem would allow you to refocus your resources on more important problems? If hiring a neighborhood teenager to mow the lawn allowed you to work toward a college degree on the weekends, could you put up with some missed spots or ragged edges? Additionally, someone may surprise you by doing the task as well or better than you did. Be self-assured enough to welcome, rather than fear, that possibility.

People who are focused on achieving fulfillment delegate easily and frequently. So if there is a problem you do not need to personally solve in order to advance on your path to fulfillment, look for a way to delegate it. There are three ways to do so: downward delegation, sideways delegation, and paid delegation.

Downward Delegation

You can use downward delegation whenever you are in a position of authority that allows you to assign a problem-solving task to someone else, such as when you are a parent or a supervisor.

Take responsibility. If you have the authority to delegate, then you bear the responsibilities of leadership that come with that authority. This includes the responsibility for ensuring that the problems you delegate actually get solved. Delegation is not a method for decreasing your responsibility. In fact, it allows you take on greater and greater levels of responsibility by focusing your personal effort on higher-level problems while delegating lower-level problems to others.

Therefore, whenever you delegate a problem downward, bear in mind that you must ensure that it gets solved, even though you are not personally performing the work of solving it. For example, a manager who delegates a project to a subordinate must accept responsibility if the project does not get done, or gets done poorly. The manager can't very well say to his boss, "It's not my fault that I delegated the project to the wrong person and then failed to monitor his work."

Since you are still responsible for ensuring the problem gets solved, you should periodically check to see how things are going. This helps prevent communication breakdowns from turning into crises. Plus, even if all is going well, the fact that you checked will reinforce your status as a thorough and attentive leader.

Welcome suggestions. Invite delegatees to let you know if they find a better way to solve the problem. Thank them for their suggestions, and either use them or explain briefly why they will not be implemented. Be wary of the impulse to reject an idea just because it is unfamiliar or is coming from a relatively inexperienced person. There can be great value in fresh eyes. If you want people to keep giving you innovative ideas, make them feel appreciated and rewarded when they do so.

> **A Tip for Managers: Reward Communication**
>
> One day, when I was Chief Operating Officer of an insurance organization, a young entry-level employee walked into my office. She informed me that she, and a number of other employees, thought that I had recently made a very foolish decision regarding company policy. Her tone of voice was angry and sarcastic, and she used phrases like "stupidest thing I have ever heard" and "unbelievably dumb." Her behavior was, to put it mildly, rude and inappropriate.
>
> I rapidly began to feel angry, particularly because her understanding of the situation was mistaken. The decision she was so upset about had never been made. So not only was she behaving badly, she hadn't even bothered to get her facts straight.
>
> I was about to deliver a stern reprimand when my intuition told me to look at the situation from another perspective. After all, I had consistently invited employees to stop by my office and share their thoughts with me. Even though she had the facts wrong and her behavior was inappropriate, she was still providing me with valuable information. Thanks to her, I now knew that a number of employees were upset about an issue, and I could address their concerns.
>
> I realized that while her communication skills needed improvement, she was trying to do what I had asked my employees to do, which was to share their concerns with me. If I made her feel punished for doing so, the next time a problem arose no one would tell me about it. I would become one of those managers who don't know what is really going on because they punish people who bring them bad news. I had to reward the behavior that I wanted to encourage.
>
> So when she finished speaking, the first thing I said was, "Thank you very much for telling me about this. I am so glad you took the initiative to give me this important news." Then I explained what the actual decision had been. Within a few minutes she was quite satisfied, and her anger abated. Only then did I say, "Now, let's talk about how to communicate effectively in the workplace."
>
> *-Reagan*

Speak effectively. While out shopping at the grocery store or the mall, you have probably seen parents who try to make their children behave by pleading with them, bribing them with goodies, threatening them with punishment, or barking nasty commands at them. You may also have known business managers who use delegating as an opportunity to inflict cruelty, indulge in rudeness, or lord it over their staff. Other managers are so meek that they ask their employees to do work as a favor, and actually allow them to reject the requests. These are not effective delegation methods. In fact, these parents and managers are actually undermining their own authority through their poor behavior. Their ineffective management techniques will make it even harder for them to delegate effectively in the future.

Learn from these mistakes. You can delegate most effectively by being *politely assertive*. You may recall from RESPONSE the important differences between being assertive and being aggressive. Being assertive means using a voice and manner that are friendly and respectful, but also firm and decisive. You will gain more willing participation if you use this approach instead of issuing a harsh command or a weak plea.

Explain the benefits. While you should never present downward delegation as pleading for help or requesting a favor, there is nothing wrong with showing how the assignment could benefit the delegatee. You will get better results if you can convince the individual that accepting the assignment is a good idea.

Whenever possible, present delegation assignments as a reward, as a way of recognizing outstanding performance. Whether delegating to staff or to children, let them know that the assignment shows your confidence in their growing abilities, that it marks a step up in their development. Point out that this is an opportunity to grow, to earn advancement, or to learn a new skill. Using this technique depends on the reality of the workload and the nature of task, but you can present delegated tasks in a positive light more often than you might think.

It can also help to explain how their performance of the task will help the family or organization reach its goals. This helps the delegatee feel that he or she is making an important contribution to the achievement of shared goals, and is therefore a valuable member of the team.

Define the assignment. Have you ever had someone explain an assignment to you so poorly that you were not really sure what you were supposed to do? Unpleasant, wasn't it? Don't put your delegatees in that uncomfortable position. When delegating, clearly explain the essential elements of the assignment:

- **Goal.** What is the outcome you desire? How important is it that the goal is achieved?
- **Method.** Is there a particular approach to solving the problem that must be followed, or is the delegatee free to innovate?
- **Effort.** How much effort will be needed? What level of quality is required?
- **Resources.** How much money can be spent? What equipment will be provided? Is training available? Who else can be brought in to help?
- **Timetable.** When should work begin? Is this a temporary or permanent assignment? What is the deadline? Is it a firm deadline, or just a target?

Ensure that the assignment has been clearly understood by having the delegatee briefly restate the essential elements you have just explained. This technique may seem awkward at first, but with a little practice it will begin to feel natural and it is a very effective way to prevent miscommunication and fumbled handoffs.

Give credit. Always give credit where it is due. If someone else compliments you on the success of a delegated task, be sure to credit the efforts of the delegatee, and pass the compliment along to him or her. Never take credit for doing the work; take credit only as the person who was clever enough to delegate and mentor so effectively.

SIDEWAYS DELEGATION

Sideways delegation means handing a problem over to someone else when you are not the other person's "boss," for example to your spouse or a coworker. Because you do not have the authority to require the other person to solve the problem, there must be mutual agreement regarding the handoff.

Make a case for the delegation. The delegatee must perceive some benefit from accepting the hand-off. After all, you are asking for an investment of solution-finding resources – time, money, or effort – that could be used to solve the delegatee's own problems. Fortunately, the same motives that were discussed in DISCOVERY ("Share Solutions") can motivate others to solve a problem for you. For example:

- **Wisdom or Pride.** Present your request as a compliment: "I am asking for your help because I respect your knowledge, experience, and judgment. You can solve this problem better than anyone else I know." This is a great way to initiate on ongoing problem-solving partnership.
- Creating or repaying a **solution debt.** People may take over tasks for you because you have helped them in the past, or with the expectation that you will do so in the future. Acknowledge your willingness to repay the favor with a comment like, "Thanks buddy, I owe you one." Then be sure to honor that commitment by giving help when it is needed.
- **Generosity.** Some people seem born to be helpful, and all you need to do is convince them that accepting the task

would be a nice thing to do. Treat these people as treasures in your life. Thank them sincerely for their help, and never take unfair advantage of their open-hearted spirit. Find ways to repay them even if they insist that you don't need to do so.

- **Friendship or Affection.** Those who truly care for you will be there to provide help when you need it. Surround yourself with a network of problem-solving supporters by building a healthy *life team*, as is explained later in this chapter.

Speak effectively. Use the same effective communication skills that you would use in downward delegation to ensure that the other person understands when the transfer will take place and what his or her new responsibilities will be. In the workplace, you may need to get approval for the transfer of responsibility. Of course, in daily life, most handoffs are quick, informal exchanges: "Could you please help that customer? I'd like to take my break now," or "Do you have time to help the kids with their homework? I need to work on a presentation for tomorrow."

PAID DELEGATION

Paid delegation means solving a problem by paying someone else to solve it for you. We have become so accustomed to using paid delegation that we don't really notice how often we do so. However, consider how impractical it would be – in fact how absurd it would be – to try to solve most of our daily problems without using paid delegation:

- "How will I raise cows, milk them every morning, pasteurize the milk, and maintain a fresh supply in my refrigerator for my family to drink?"

- "How will I locate an aquifer, dig a well down to it, pump up water, treat it for safety, and generate enough pressure to make it flow steadily when I open a faucet in my house?"
- "How will I grow cotton, harvest it, mill it, spin it into thread, weave it into cloth, dye it, cut it, and sew it into a pair of jeans in the latest style for my teenage daughter?"

People used to solve problems like these through their own individual effort. Each family raised its own food, dug its own well, and made its own clothing. Now we delegate these problem-solving tasks to others who specialize in doing this work, which provides us with highly efficient solutions. This process of interdependent problem-solving has turned the global economy into one huge problem-solving team.

Weigh the benefits as well as the cost. You may be reluctant to pay someone else to solve a problem that you are capable of solving yourself. However, as was discussed in PRIORITY, you should consider paying for a solution whenever your time could be better spent solving a higher-priority problem. What this boils down to is balancing the value of money against the value of an opportunity. "Buying" a day's worth of time by taking your car in to the shop instead of working on it yourself could allow you to study for a professional licensing exam, apply for a business permit, outline a novel, or spend a perfect summer day with your children.

There are plenty of contractors, service providers, professionals, and manufacturers who are ready and willing to solve your problems for a fee. Allow them to do what they do best so you can devote more of your resources to doing what you do best, or what is most important to your fulfillment. Use your fulfillment action plan to help you make decisions about which problems to delegate and which problems to solve yourself.

Of course, no one has unlimited financial resources, and few people can afford to hire out *all* of their lower-priority problems. But if you are firm in your desire to achieve your compelling goals, be willing to re-prioritize your spending. Spend your money strategically, balancing your healthy desire for short-term enjoyment against your deeper need for long-term fulfillment. In many cases, spending less money on diversionary activities will help you afford paid delegation, freeing up more of your time to tackle fulfillment-level problems.

INSIST ON GREAT SOLUTIONS

Be open to hiring experts to solve your problems, but monitor their work and insist that they provide a solution that truly meets your standards and your needs.

When I was Chief Operating Officer of an insurance organization, we contracted with a number of companies to provide services to us and to our customers. During a lunch meeting with executives from one of these companies, I took them to task for their lack of innovation. I pointed at that all the creative improvements in their services during the past several years had been our ideas, even though we presumably knew less about their specialized line of work than they did. I said we should be able to count on our hired experts to continually develop new and better ways to perform their work, rather than having to force innovation upon them.

The top executive couldn't disagree with my facts, but commented that he never heard this complaint from his other clients. Those clients often tried to negotiate lower prices, but they never demanded innovation. He said, "Reagan, we only get beat up like this when we visit you folks." He implied that our expectations were too high.

At that moment it became clear to me that hiring "leading experts" does not guarantee a great solution. They encounter little pressure to innovate, and it is easy for them to become complacent, applying a one-size-fits-all solution that is ill-suited to your specific needs. In fact, when you suggest a new approach some will tell you "that will never work." But again and again, people and organizations have found ways of doing what the "experts" said could never be done.

-Reagan

Partnership Teamwork

Partnership TEAMWORK means working with others to solve a problem. Partnership has a variety of problem-solving benefits:

- Partners can help you solve problems that would be impossible to solve on your own. For example, you might ask your neighbors to help push your car out of a snowdrift, or get some coworkers to work through the lunch hour in order to complete an important project.
- You can work with others to achieve a shared goal, as when your family pitches in to get the dishes done quickly so you can all get to a movie on time, or when neighbors share the effort and expense of throwing a block party that everyone can enjoy.
- It is easier to turn problem-solving work into enjoyable recreation when you tackle a tough or boring problem with partners you like. You can turn a chore into a game, or keep one another's spirits up while working on a dull task.
- It is usually true that "two heads are better than one." People thinking together can create solutions that none of them could have thought of alone. Partners can brainstorm, improve each other's suggestions, and pool their knowledge and experience.
- Solving problems with partners is a great way to make friends and allies. Facing and overcoming adversity as a team is a powerful way to forge strong bonds and build a sense of loyalty and group identity. You really get to know and trust people when you share setbacks and triumphs with them. This sense of camaraderie will naturally motivate your teammates to help you solve your problems, and you can gain valuable experience by helping them solve their problems in return.

Everyday Partnership

The potential for partnership is around you at all times. This will not be news if you are a Social problem-solver, since it is natural for you to ask for advice, information, or an extra pair of hands whenever a problem arises. However, if you are an Individual, you can benefit from consciously considering the problem-solving assistance that you can tap into on a daily basis.

Who's on hand? Often, TEAMWORK requires nothing more than an informal, spur-of-the-moment request for help from someone in a position to provide immediate assistance. For example, asking your spouse to come upstairs and help you hang a picture, calling your sister to discuss ideas for your mother's birthday gift, seeking advice from the person at the next workstation on a document you are writing, or asking a passerby for directions. It is remarkable how much more quickly, or more thoroughly, a problem can be solved with just a few minutes of assistance. So develop the habit of reaching out for help whenever a problem arises, using simple phrases like:

- "Could you give me a hand with…"
- "Would you please have a look at…"
- "What do you think about…"

Sharing. Sometimes just talking to someone about your problem can be a great help. Confiding your emotional, mental, or spiritual distress can give you relief from anxiety, uncertainty, or regret. Sincerely asking for forgiveness can be an important step toward repairing a relationship or making amends for behavior that you regret.

Constructive confrontation. If someone else's behavior is causing your problem, address that person directly. Gossiping or griping with others about the individual's actions rarely solves the problem, and often makes the situation worse. Take a positive, constructive approach. Use "straight talk," which simply means laying out the problem as calmly and objectively as possible. Discuss the situation confidently rather than in a placating or aggressive manner. Look the person in the eye and say what is on your mind without any attempt at manipulation or attack. You can certainly be blunt, and you can make it clear that you are not pleased with the person's behavior or with the situation, but you do not need to be hostile, accusatory, or judgmental.

If the problem is particularly sensitive or difficult, consider the powerful technique of asking the person who is causing the problem for assistance in solving it. A good approach is to start the conversation with:

> "Could I get your help with something? I have a problem I don't think I can solve on my own, and I am hoping you can help me out."

This approach puts the other person in a receptive state of mind. For example, when a manager's behavior is creating a problem for an employee, the employee faces a delicate situation. The employee can address the issue by starting the conversation as above, and then following up with a neutral description of the problem:

> "I like getting my work done efficiently, and last-minute requests for changes really decrease my productivity. Can you help me develop a system that would allow me to make the changes you need as far in advance as possible?"

With some managers even this approach might hit a brick wall, but it is often surprisingly successful, and it is certainly better than a pleading or accusatory approach.

BUILD A PARTNERSHIP TEAM

When building a team to address a long-term problem or an ongoing series of problems, you should consider the character and problem-solving skills of potential team members. Seek to recruit teammates who are:

- **Optimistic and solution-oriented.** These are fundamentally the best teammates for solving any kind of problem. Whatever they may or may not have to contribute in terms of knowledge or experience, you can count on them to stay positive and help keep the process moving forward. One of the great benefits of TEAMWORK is the ability of team members to help each other stay in a Strong RESPONSE state; to remain determined, confident, and productive.

- **Supportive *and* challenging.** Teams always benefit from a good mix of positive encouragement and critical questioning. A teammate who constructively challenges assumptions and proposals by asking insightful, relevant questions has great value. Someone who can spot a crucial flaw in a proposed solution can often prevent serious trouble.

- **Complementary personality types.** Be sure to include a wide variety of problem-solving personality types. A team composed entirely of Thinkers may generate a lot of good ideas that never get translated into action, while a Doer team might plow ahead with an inferior solution. Having both on your team will ensure that the problem gets solved, and that it gets solved right. Social types keep the team working together smoothly and happily, while Individuals are great for tackling tasks delegated by the group. Linear people keep everyone organized and on track, while Intuitive people can spot hidden opportunities and create outside-the-box solutions.

Try to exclude from your team those individuals who are:

- **Tar Pits.** These are the complainers and pessimists who respond to any problem by reciting their own tales of woe, and who react to any suggested solutions with doubt, ridicule, or apathy. Their pessimism will devour the team's productive energy.

- **Antisocials.** These people are habitually rude to others, or are overly sensitive to criticism. Few things bring a team down faster than the pettiness of a member who frequently insults, or is too easily offended by, other team members.
- **Potted Plants.** These individuals participate in the team's business only by showing up. Their passive presence lowers the team's average level of enthusiasm, participation, and commitment.
- **Yes Men.** These people are more concerned with pleasing or flattering others than with seeking an effective solution. They can lead the team astray by enthusiastically supporting a truly terrible idea, especially if the bad idea is proposed by a person in a position of authority.

Once you know who you want on your team, request their participation in a sincere and friendly manner. Act the way you want your team members to act: optimistic, energetic, and solution-oriented. People are more eager to help someone who is positive and upbeat. The more enthusiasm you exhibit, the more willing others will be to join you.

Consider offering tangible rewards to encourage participation in your team. Providing refreshments is an inexpensive way to create a positive atmosphere and make team members feel that you appreciate their efforts. If you are in a position to provide special privileges, gifts, comp time, or a financial incentive, determine what would give team members a sense of being appropriately recognized and rewarded.

Describe the commitment you are seeking: when the team will start work, how much effort will be required, and how long the project should take. For example:

- If you are rounding up a group of friends to help you move, you might say, "Could you help me move into my new apartment next Saturday? It's great, a bigger place for about the same rent. I'll have everything packed, so it's just a matter of lifting and carrying. We're starting at ten a.m., and if everyone shows up we should be done by four. I'll have plenty of drinks and snacks on hand."
- If you are creating a process-improvement group at work, you might say: "We're forming a team to find ways of reducing turnaround time, and I'd really like your help. We have to cut at least a day out of the production schedule to stay competitive, and I'm sure we can do it if we get good ideas from people in each department. I've scheduled meetings on each of the next four Mondays, at ten o'clock. The final recommendations are due at the end of the fourth week."

Get Commitment. It's fine to spark interest in your project, and beneficial to create enthusiasm for it, but as any salesperson knows, you have to "close the deal." This is also true when building a team. You might know someone well enough that if he says, "That sounds good," you can be sure that he'll show up, but as often as possible seek a clear-cut acknowledgment like, "I'll be there," or, "You can count me in."

Lead Your Team

Communicate effectively. Teams always work more efficiently under a deadline, so let everyone know what the completion date is, even if it is just a target. If the deadline later needs to be moved, explain the reasons for the change.

When the team is discussing a problem, look for opportunities to agree rather than disagree. Develop the habit of saying, "Yes, and..." instead of, "No, but..." If someone says something, and you agree with half of it and disagree with half of it, focus on the part you agree with. Take the part you agree with, restate it, and build on it in the direction you want to go. When you do so, give credit to others even when you are substantially adding to their ideas by making a comment like, "I'd like to follow up on Bob's suggestion..." "Sue's comment gave me an idea..." or, "I like where Joe is heading..."

Also develop the habit of giving praise frequently and honestly. Often a simple, "Good idea" or, "Nicely done," will make team members feel their efforts have been worthwhile.

In lengthy problem-solving situations, provide regular progress updates. It might be a simple, "We're half done," "Only a couple of hours left," or, "All we need is a little more information." In other cases, use memos, posted progress reports, summaries, or minutes to keep the team updated on its progress toward the goal.

Do your share. Be sure to do your share of the team's work. A frequent source of tension in families and organizations is the perception that some team members are not pulling their weight, that they are benefiting from the efforts of the group but are not contributing enough in return. If you create a team and then expect your teammates to do most of the work, you will find it difficult to recruit members for future problem-solving.

Wrap it up. Bring the work of your team to a positive and decisive end. Be wary of the temptation to squeeze extra work out of your team by enlarging the stated task or taking on another problem altogether. When the problem has been solved, it's time to thank your teammates, praise their efforts, and explain the results. Then dissolve the team. If you later receive any praise or recognition in your role as the leader of the team, give credit to your team members and pass the praise along to them.

YOUR LIFE TEAM

Your life is significantly influenced by the people with whom you spend the most time. Over time, you will tend to think, feel, and act more like they do. In particular, your ability to solve problems can be greatly enhanced by their support or diminished by their negativity.

A key step in taking control of your life is consciously choosing who you want as members of your *life team*. This means purposefully building a circle of people who will provide you with encouragement, assistance, and sound advice in your problem-solving efforts. It is team-building as a deliberate, lifelong strategy.

You can begin building your life team by evaluating your current relationships – family, friends, acquaintances, and coworkers – in terms of how much they contribute to or detract from your fulfillment. Consider everyone you know, even those with whom you do not have strong relationships, as potential members of your team.

For each person, ask yourself:

- Is this person a positive or negative influence in my life?
- Does being with this person bring out the best in me, or does it draw me into bad habits and unproductive thinking?
- Does this person support and encourage me in my pursuit of fulfillment, or does this person ridicule and discourage me?
- Is this person a solution-finder or an obstacle-maker?
- Does this person serve as a role model of the life I am seeking to achieve, or as an example of what I am determined to avoid?

The answers to these questions will help you decide which relationships you should seek to strengthen and which you should bring to an end.

Consider dropping from your life team people who are:

- **Pessimistic,** who criticize your efforts to solve problems and argue that your solutions will be unsuccessful
- **Flattering,** who make you feel good superficially but add nothing to your progress toward fulfillment
- **Problem-oriented,** who focus on trouble and difficulty, and who draw you into contests to see who has the worst problems
- **Corrosive,** who bring out your worst by dragging you down to their level, and with whom you behave and think in ways you would rather avoid
- **Inert,** who are going nowhere and will be a drag on your progress as long as you remain tied to them
- **Undermining,** who continually sabotage your problem-solving efforts
- **Hypersensitive,** who are so easily offended that they cannot engage in mutually constructive criticism
- **Inconsiderate,** who erode your spirit with rude, belittling, or insulting behavior

Any friends or relatives who exhibit these negative behaviors and are unwilling to change have chosen an approach to life that you should not feel compelled to share. You can make a good-faith effort to help them improve their attitudes, but you may have to accept that some of them will remain trapped in their problem-suffering identities. Do not allow their pessimistic messages and bad examples to infect your heart and mind. It won't do either of you any good if you to stay stuck alongside them. Use RELEASE to effectively bring these relationships to a conclusion. There is at least some chance that the example you set by pursuing fulfillment will later inspire them to adopt a more positive approach to life as well.

Keep or add life team members who are:

- **Optimistic,** who are positive, encouraging, and forward-looking
- **Challenging,** who know how to give constructive criticism, ask insightful questions, and raise valid concerns
- **Solution-oriented,** with whom you enjoy discussing and creating great solution ideas
- **Complementary,** who fill in the gaps in your solution-finding toolbox because they are good at the kinds of problem-solving that are a struggle for you, or who truly enjoy the tasks that you find unpleasant
- **Inspiring,** who bring out the best in you, or who embody your fundamental beliefs
- **Interesting,** who have valuable knowledge or experience and like to share it with others
- **Supportive,** who encourage and energize your problem-solving efforts
- **Interested,** who are curious about everything, with whom you can productively discuss any kind of problem or topic
- **Fun,** who make you laugh and make problem-solving seem like play

Discovering and sharing solutions with teammates like these is natural and effortless. It is easy to enter the flow state in their company. Deliberately find and cultivate such individuals at work and in your personal life.

You really can choose with whom to live your life: your friends, your partner or spouse, the company for which you work, and the relatives and coworkers with whom you form the strongest relationships. Turn your life team into an asset, rather than a hindrance. This is a key strategy for *leading your life* rather than *allowing life to happen to you*.

Conclusion

You can magnify the impact of your problem-solving resources and increase the likelihood of your success by joining and forming teams. Problems that would be impossible for any person to tackle alone can be readily solved through team effort.

Belonging to teams provides you with opportunities to share your knowledge and skills with others and to benefit from their expertise in return. Great problem-solvers are eager to help others and are open to receiving help in turn. Make regular use of phrases like "I'd be happy to help" and "I could use a hand with this." Solving problems with others hones your skills, broadens your knowledge, and strengthens your identity as a problem-solver.

Teamwork: Summary

- **Life is a team effort.** We are most successful when acting cooperatively, due to the problem-solving efficiency of shared effort and shared rewards. You are a member of many groups that can act as teams.

Delegation Teamwork

- **Benefits of delegation.** Delegation allows you to reallocate your resources to solving the problems that matter the most, spend more time doing the things you enjoy, finish necessary work, and concentrate your efforts on the things you do best.

- **Overcoming reluctance to delegate.** Delegate any problem that does not advance you toward fulfillment. If you are focused on making your vision a reality, you will delegate easily and frequently.
- **Downward delegation.** Delegate downward when you have the authority to do so. Be politely assertive and explain the task clearly. You retain responsibility for ensuring the problem gets solved.
- **Sideways delegation.** This involves convincing a peer to take over one of your problem-solving tasks. Make use of the many positive motives that others have for helping you.
- **Paid delegation.** Consider the value of your time when deciding whether to solve a problem yourself or hire it done. If you are firm in your desire to achieve your compelling goals, you will re-prioritize your spending.

Partnership Teamwork

- **Benefits of partnership.** Partnership helps you solve problems that would be impossible to tackle on your own, achieve shared goals, turn tedious chores into games, and make new friends.
- **Everyday partnership.** Request help from those who can provide immediate assistance, share the problem, and use constructive confrontation to address someone else's behavior.
- **Build a partnership team.** Look for solution-finding teammates and avoid obstacle-creating teammates. Request help sincerely and directly. Get commitment.
- **Lead your team.** Set deadlines and do your share of the work. Look for things to agree on, give praise, and share progress reports. Wrap it up when the problem is solved.

Your Life Team

- **Choose your team members.** Make conscious decisions about who will share your life. Distance yourself from those who negatively influence you and create obstacles. Seek out those who are positive influences and help you find solutions.

THE EIGHTH TOOL

CREATIVITY

INVENT YOUR OWN
BRILLIANT SOLUTIONS

CREATIVITY is an extraordinarily powerful solution-finding tool. As we mentioned in DISCOVERY, you don't need to come up with a creative solution for every problem you encounter. But sometimes nothing else will do. For example, when:

- You are facing a truly new and unique problem for which there is no existing solution.
- The solution that worked well in the past is now ineffective because circumstances or technology have changed.
- Yesterday's solution still works, but it is now possible to create a new solution that is even better.
- You have found an "okay" or partial solution and you want to find ways to improve it.
- You are just plain bored with doing things the same old way and want to try something fresh and exciting.

Prepare to be Creative

Here are five habits of thought and behavior that will make it easier for you to achieve consistent success as a creative problem-solver. The more you incorporate these habits into your life, the more success you will achieve when using the specific CREATIVITY techniques that are presented later in the chapter.

Be Ready for Setbacks

Being creative means doing something new; it means experimenting with new ideas, new methods, or new technology. Most new things simply do not work perfectly right away. In fact, sometimes they don't work at all! Unfortunately, many people feel an exaggerated sense of fear at the prospect of experiencing the setbacks that are an inevitable part of the process of innovation. As a consequence, they avoid trying new things in order to avoid the risk of feeling frustrated, disappointed, or embarrassed. But if you wish to be a great problem-solver, you must embrace setbacks as a "cost of doing business" in the CREATIVITY process.

Masters of problem-solving are not deterred by the possibility that their creative efforts may be unsuccessful. If you try a hundred solutions and they all fail, but then the hundred-and-first solution works, guess what: you just created a great new solution! So don't allow yourself to be paralyzed by the fear of failure. Move forward, taking comfort in the knowledge that repeated failure is the mother of eventual success. Give yourself an unlimited number of chances to find a solution that works.

Creating a new and better solution requires taking risks. At a minimum, you are likely to risk some of your time, money, and effort. **But the risk that stops most people from being creative is the risk of ridicule.** Anyone who tries something truly innovative is likely to be mocked, criticized, or laughed at by small-minded people during the process, even though the innovation may turn out to be tremendously successful in the end. So be it! Allow others to jeer at your willingness to be adventurous and bold while they live cautious and timid lives themselves. Just smile and say to yourself, "Oh well, that's how some people are." Many great new solutions seemed impractical or even ludicrous at first. If it had seemed logical, safe, and reasonable everyone would have been using it already. Breakthrough solutions come from overturning assumptions and defying current wisdom.

To help you persevere in the face of setbacks or ridicule:

- Use INSIGHT to put yourself in surroundings that accommodate and reward your creativity, so you do not end up as a creative peg in a conformist hole.
- Use RESPONSE to consistently generate Strong emotions like enthusiasm, confidence, and optimism.
- Use TEAMWORK to build a life team that supports you, rather than undermines you, in your efforts to create new and better solutions.

AVOID ANTI-CREATIVITY

As we discussed in CLARITY and FOCUS, the words you use to describe problems can have a big impact on your solution-finding success. Phrases like "It's impossible," and "It can't be done" may sometimes be true (although not nearly as often as most people assume) but their habitual use can erode your ability to think creatively. Consider the message that statements like these send to your subconscious. How likely is it that your subconscious will help you find a solution when you've just told it that there is no point in trying? If you do this often enough, you may establish a self-identity as someone who finds it impossible to even *try* to solve challenging problems.

SOLUTION POWER

Bear in mind that yesterday's impossibilities are today's realities. There are examples throughout the history of invention:
- Talk to someone on the other side of the world? "Absurd!"
- Fill an office building with cool air on a hot summer day? "It can't be done!"
- Squirt cheese out of a can? "Impossible!"

Phrases like, "You can't do it that way," or, "We've always done it this way" also have an inhibiting effect. Often we allow our thinking to be constrained by assumptions and traditions, by the unwritten rules of a relationship or an organization. Examine all assumed rules about what you can and cannot do in any problem-solving situation. Rules should only exist to help solve or prevent problems, so when they end up getting in the way of a solution consider breaking them, changing them, ignoring them, or eliminating them. Don't let yesterday's solutions become today's barriers.

LEADERSHIP AND THE IMPOSSIBLE

One of the roles of a leader is to make the impossible possible, and then make the possible inevitable. I have seen many situations in which everyone in an organization except the leader *knew* that something was impossible, but the leader insisted on moving forward anyway and they got it done. In fact, it is surprising how often accomplishing the "impossible" turned out to be not only possible, but actually pretty easy. Looking back on it, the only really hard part was for the leader to convince everyone else that they should at least give it a try. In any organization with great leadership, accomplishing the impossible happens all the time, and becomes taken for granted as business as usual.

Even if you are not in a position of formal leadership, you can still act like a leader. If nothing else, you can *lead your own life*. So go ahead and achieve the impossible. It may seem a bit odd at first, but after you've done it a few times you'll get used to it and it will come to seem quite normal, even routine.

-Reagan

Here's a sneaky, and very common, anti-creativity phrase: "I have no idea." It is easy to fall into the habit of saying it rather casually, but consider what a disempowering message you are sending to your subconscious. Just say it out loud a few times: "I have no idea. I have no idea. I have no idea. I have no idea..." Does that sound like something you would say in a Strong problem-solving state? Is it possible that if you say it often enough, even if you say it light-heartedly, your subconscious might conclude that you are someone who truly has *no ideas*? Some people seem to go out of their way to create the impression that they are utterly devoid of thoughts or information. How many times have you heard someone say, "I have absolutely no idea" or, "I don't have a clue" in a way that proclaims, "I don't know, you should not have expected me to know, I don't want to know, and I'll never know."

In reality, you *always* have at least *some* idea how to solve any problem. Try using phrases that are more accurate, positive, and useful. When asked for a solution to any problem you can always:

- **Suggest a way to find a solution.** "I don't know, but you could find out by..." or, "I don't know, but I can tell you who probably *does* know..."
- **Eliminate wrong answers.** "Well, I can tell you a few things that probably *won't* work..." Identifying ineffective solutions helps to prevent wasting time and effort, and narrows the search for the best answer.
- **Guess.** "I'm not certain, but you could try..." Guessing is a quick way to tap into your subconscious and often produces surprisingly accurate and valuable ideas.

At the very least, just say, "I don't know." This conveys a relatively accurate message without being unnecessarily negative. There are plenty of things we don't know, but not that many about which we have "absolutely no idea."

Fill Your Mind

Stock your brain with all kinds of knowledge and experiences. You never know when a particular fact could come in handy, when a story from history could provide good guidance, or when an idea from another field could suggest a solution by analogy.

You may spend a significant amount of time commuting or traveling. Are you making the best use of that time? You could use your travel time to listen to news or informational radio programs. Audio recordings of books, including shortened executive summaries of many books, are also available. If you are using mass transit, you could read, watch videos, or go online.

Engage in random acts of life. Go to a live concert featuring a kind of music you don't generally listen to. Read a book that has gotten good reviews on a subject you know nothing about. Get a visitor's guide for your area and go to the local attractions you have never visited. Think of some people you would like to know better and invite them to lunch.

Talk *with* people. Make a habit of asking questions about what the other person knows, rather than just talking about what you already know. Even if you don't feel naturally interested in a person, process, idea, or topic, if you just scratch the surface you might discover some intriguing new information or insight.

Stay Connected

Remind your subconscious of the solutions you are seeking to create by regularly focusing on your compelling goals and connecting with your vision of fulfillment. Many people find that it works well to set aside time for a weekly "reconnecting" session and for shorter daily sessions. You can structure these sessions in the form of goal-setting, planning, contemplation, meditation, prayer or whatever technique works best for you. The simple act of routinely telling your subconscious what goals you are committed to achieving automatically increases the flow of great solution-creating ideas.

STAY RESTED

Consistently getting enough rest will make you a better solution-finder. Having adequate, regular sleep promotes emotional stability, intellectual clarity, and physical vigor. Although you may have experienced flashes of problem-solving inspiration while exhausted, it would not be wise to make that your primary problem-solving strategy. It is both unreliable and unpleasant. Many studies have shown the negative impact that sleep deprivation has on logic, memory, creativity, and judgment. Being sharp and clear-headed is the better approach to problem-solving.

Adopt a personal rule to never make an important decision when you are tired. This includes deciding to give up, feel hopeless, or draw a negative conclusion. Don't decide what something means, who you are, or whether a problem can or cannot be solved when you are fatigued. You can probably think of times when you were facing a problem and felt worn out and filled with despair, but after a good night's sleep the situation appeared more hopeful. Whenever you feel tired and find yourself thinking dark thoughts, just say, "I'm not even going to think about this now. I will consider this problem again tomorrow. If things still look this bleak in the morning, I will have plenty of time to feel badly about it then." The nice thing is, it will always look at least a little better, and sometimes a whole lot better, in the light of a new day. In fact, you will often look back on the night before and wonder what the heck you were feeling so down about. Plus, later in this chapter you will get tips on how you can use your subconscious to solve problems while you sleep!

CREATIVITY TECHNIQUES

Experiment with these great creativity-boosting techniques, even if you don't consider yourself a naturally creative problem-solver. You will almost certainly find some that will give you excellent results.

GO TO YOUR CREATIVITY PLACE

This is a simple technique. First, figure out where you usually are and what you are usually doing when you get your best creative ideas. Then, whenever you want to think creatively, go there or do that.

Where are you when you experience a natural flow of creative thinking? It could be someplace like:

- A coffee shop
- Your bed
- A park, sitting under your favorite tree
- Your office, before others have arrived or after they have gone

What are you doing when you get your best ideas? Maybe it is while you are:

- Taking a shower
- Driving in the car
- Going for a walk
- Talking with a friend

Don't worry about whether your answers to these questions seem silly. For example, some people come up with great solutions while applying polish to their fingernails or toenails. That's fine! The rule is simple: if it works, use it. And the more often you use it – the more often you generate creative ideas in a particular place

CREATIVITY

or during a particular activity – the more you reinforce its "magic," and the better it will work in triggering your creative powers.

Your personality type influences the kinds of locations and activities that you will find helpful:

- If you are an Individual problem-solver, you probably find that solitude is best. Do some gardening or take a walk around the neighborhood. Do whatever gives you time by yourself to concentrate on figuring out a solution or to clear your mind so your subconscious can bring the solution to you.
- If you are Social, your creativity is stimulated by interacting with others, so get on the phone with a friend or discuss the problem with a coworker. Sometimes just being among other people helps. Try taking your notebook and have lunch at a busy restaurant, or go to the mall and think about the problem while mingling with the crowd.
- If you are a Thinker, you probably work best in places that are quiet and low on distraction. Visit the library, take a warm bath, or go for a walk in a park. Or block out distractions with some Mozart or Bach, and let your thoughts be guided by the beautiful structure of the music.
- If you are a Doer, you thrive on action and movement. Turn up some energizing music, do a vigorous workout, or get to work implementing the first part of the solution while you continue to figure out the rest of it.
- If you are Linear, you probably think best in familiar surroundings, following an established routine. Try to maintain some space of your own at home and at work that you can keep neat and well-organized. Also have a supply of graph paper on hand, as it is great for creating a sense of order out of any set of facts, ideas, or figures.

- If you are Intuitive, you might benefit from a change in location or routine. Try some random acts of life like those mentioned in the "Fill Your Mind" section of this chapter.

> **SERENITY IN MOTION**
>
> I find consistent success coming up with creative solutions while running. Once I'm into the run I let my body and breathing go on autopilot. The rhythm of the running and the oxygenation that comes from deep, regular breathing really boosts my mental activity and lifts my spirits. This puts me in an ideal solution-finding state in which my thinking is both calm and energetic. I can explore the inner world of ideas, trying possibilities on for size and pondering alternative courses of action. Also, since I tend to be an Individual problem-solver, the absence of interruptions, conversations, and media distractions works to my advantage.
>
> *-Kevin*

A suggestion: wherever you are, whatever you are doing, be prepared to record your great creative ideas as soon as they occur. Keep a notebook, recorder, or PDA in your car, by your bed, and in your purse or briefcase. Make a note right away, before the moment of inspiration fades. "I'll remember it in the morning" and, "I'll write it down when I get home" have spelled the end of many strokes of genius. Use napkins, matchbooks, and even the palm of your hand as temporary keepers of your inspiration. Call your own answering machine and leave yourself a message.

USE SILENCE AND SOUND

The increasingly common practice of having a television or radio on all the time – at home, in the car, at work, in restaurants, at the airport – leaves little quiet space in life for creative reflection. Many people have become so accustomed to the constant distraction of news and music that they hardly know what it feels like to simply be alone with their own thoughts. Unfortunately, living with constant media noise drowns out a powerful creative ally: your subconscious mind. Try setting aside some regular quiet time in your daily routine. This will help alleviate the frantic "if only I had a moment to think" sensation that many people now feel. The absence of external noise allows you to hear the voice of your own thoughts, letting you think more clearly and plan more effectively.

You will be a better solution-finder if you can establish a comfortable relationship with silence, and therefore with the creative power of your own thoughts. Many great innovations have arisen from idle thoughts, unsettling realizations, peaceful contemplation, uninterrupted concentration, and even outright boredom. Make some space for them in your life.

When silence is not possible or desirable, be sure that what you listen to works to your advantage. You may find that blocking out unwanted sounds with white noise, for example by turning on a fan, will make it easier for you to focus your thoughts. You can also experiment with recorded nature sounds or background music. This can help you to relax while also subtly stimulating your creative thought processes. Of course, if you are at your creative best in a Strong & Active state, then pump up your creativity with music that makes you want to jump up, dance, and sing along. Periodically buy some new music to keep things fresh and help spark innovative new ideas.

HAVE FUN

People often assume that solving a tough problem has to feel like hard work, that they have to "get serious" and "buckle down." Unfortunately, adopting that kind of sober mindset shuts off creative thinking. Problem-solving doesn't have to be a grim and somber undertaking even when the problem itself is quite dire. Rather than match your mood to the nature of the problem, choose the RESPONSE state that will help you create the best possible solution.

SOLUTION POWER

One great way to stimulate creative thinking is by turning the problem-solving process into a form of play. Play is one of the primary techniques that children use for learning how to solve problems and succeed in the world. It is by playing that children discover how to overcome obstacles, plan ahead, handle setbacks, and work cooperatively.

When you play, you free your conscious and subconscious minds from the preconceptions and constraints of adult life, releasing your full creative potential. So instead of asking, "How will I achieve this goal?" ask, "How will I have the most fun while achieving this goal?" Instead of asking, "How will I overcome this obstacle?" try, "How will I make overcoming this obstacle seem like a game?" Some people have this idea built right into their vocabularies: "Let me play around with it for a while and I'll get back to you."

Another great way to make solution-finding more fun is to approach a problem with a sense of curiosity. We've talked before about the unique power of curiosity in the problem-solving process. Momentarily let go of your assumptions about the problem and start asking simple, fundamental questions with a childlike sense of wonder and exploration: "Where did this thing come from? Why is it the way it is? What makes it go? What is it made of? What would I find if I took it apart?"

You can also make problem-solving fun by turning your thinking upside-down. What's the *worst* solution you can think of? The silliest? The most expensive? The most inefficient? The most complex? What if you had to convince someone that it would be better if the problem *didn't* get solved? What could you do to make sure that you *never* reached your goal? Playing with the idea of doing the opposite of what you think you should do, or of doing it in some completely foolish way, will often reveal a deep insight or unique perspective that leads to a truly revolutionary solution.

CREATIVITY

Consider that humor often arises from putting two seemingly inconsistent ideas together in a fresh and surprising way. Doesn't that also sound like a definition of creativity? That is why using humor helps put you in a great state of mind for creative problem-solving. Fun and laughter can make problems seem less intimidating, allowing you to tackle them with enthusiasm instead of trepidation. Your brain becomes quicker, more nimble, and more open to innovative ideas when you are relaxed and enjoying yourself.

Never dismiss any creative idea as absurd or silly out of hand. When someone comes up with a really "crazy" or "dumb" idea, immediately grab onto it, explain why it is actually brilliant, and explore all of its possibilities. Often it will actually be a good solution, or at least part of a good solution, or it will stimulate a lot of openness, laughter, and out of the box thinking that rapidly leads to a solution.

FUN AT WORK

I like using mottoes as a leadership technique. Inventing and repeating simple sayings is an effective way to create a lasting awareness of key strategies and concepts in the workplace.

One of my favorite sayings is, "We believe in having fun *while* we work, we just don't believe in having fun *instead* of working." I teach employees this phrase beginning with the day they interview to join the company, so they know my philosophy from the very start. Inviting people to enjoy their jobs – to support each other, laugh together, and look for the humor and fun in the challenges they face – helps them work more creatively and productively. And since I have to work in the same building, I would much rather spend my days in an upbeat environment with people who enjoy each other's company.

The motto also reminds them not to cross the line into wasting time with socializing or horseplay. After all, in the long run we will all be the happiest if we do great work and build a prosperous company with secure jobs and advancement opportunities.

-Reagan

Think Big

Ask yourself some "What ifs" on a grand scale. What if:

- You would get a million dollars for solving the problem?
- You could ask anyone you wanted to help you, and they had to oblige?
- You had unlimited money to spend on a solution?
- You had all the time you wanted?
- You could build a laboratory, workshop, or factory and fill it with all of the tools and equipment you wanted?
- You would become world-famous if you solved the problem?

As vividly and thoroughly as possible, visualize how you would solve the problem under these circumstances. Then figure out how you can transfer those methods or ideas into your real-world circumstances.

For example, suppose you are trying to solve the problem of being overweight. You could imagine that you have just been cast in your first acting role as the star of a major movie, and in one scene all you will be wearing is a bathing suit. Filming starts in six months. Since this is your first role, you're not a rich movie star yet, so you can't hire a trainer or join a fancy health club. What would you do to get yourself in shape for that scene? Visualize the kind of enthusiasm, dedication, and commitment you would invest in a carefully selected program of diet and exercise. Make it as real for yourself as possible. Imagine how great it would feel when you achieved fabulous results in just six months. Then go ahead and do in real life what you imagined yourself doing to get ready for that movie. After all, isn't feeling great and being healthy in your own real life just as important, or actually much more important, than looking good in some movie?

CREATIVITY

In a similar vein, instead of wondering, "What would be a good solution to this problem?" try something like "What incredible solution would absolutely and completely solve this problem forever and ever?" or, "What solution would crush this lousy problem like smashing a peanut with a sledgehammer?" What an empowering mindset! Instead of making do with a solution that is just barely enough to take care of the problem, come up with one that will whack it clear out of the ballpark!

THE *SMASHING THROUGH* MINDSET

When Reagan and I were young our father enjoyed teaching us parlor tricks. One day he announced that he could break a walnut with his bare hand, and challenged us to figure out how to do it before he showed us. Reagan and I took turns squeezing, twisting, and prying at walnuts as hard as we could, to no avail. Then Dad put a walnut on the kitchen table and with one quick slapping motion crushed it flat with the palm of his hand!

We thought this was a swell trick, but when we tried it ourselves, we still couldn't do it. When we slapped the walnut it felt like a rock, and we bruised our palms without producing a single crack in the shell. Then Dad explained that the real trick was to ignore the walnut and focus on slapping the surface of the table beneath it. What a difference! We weren't hitting any harder, but suddenly we could crush the walnuts almost effortlessly.

This technique can be an empowering approach to problem-solving. Instead of aiming your solution-finding efforts *at* an obstacle, aim *through* it. Instead of chipping away at the problem, smash it to bits!

-Kevin

THINK SMALL

In times of plenty you can afford to use expensive or resource-intensive solutions. You can take your time researching and planning, creating optimal processes, and gathering all necessary resources. Inevitably, though, you will find yourself in situations where time and money are in short supply and you are forced to innovate. What is interesting is that the cheaper and faster solution you then develop often turns out to be a much *better* solution. In retrospect, you can see that the time-consuming and expensive approach was actually sloppy. Being forced to find a more efficient way often produces a cleaner and more effective outcome. So even when you are not under financial or time pressure you can use the *think small* mindset to generate superior solutions.

So, what do you have on hand? What do you have available to you right now that you could use to solve your problem at little or no additional cost? Not just how much time and money, but what skills, equipment, supplies, teammates, and information? What if you had to prepare a meal for a dinner party using only what is in your kitchen right now? Would you despair, or could you put on your chef's thinking cap and astound yourself and everyone else with a great meal?

If you are a do-it-yourselfer, you have probably spent time rummaging through the odds and ends in your garage or workshop, mentally seeing if something you happen to have on hand could be used for an entirely different purpose. How many times have you used leftover lumber, jars of old hardware, and the tools you have accumulated from past projects to make a quick fix or even to create something entirely new?

A prime example of this make-do attitude, of creativity under extraordinary restrictions, is the story of Apollo 13. A series of malfunctions severely damaged the ship during its flight to the Moon, putting the crew in great danger. The astronauts and ground crew had to create complex technological solutions using only the parts that happened to be on board the cramped space capsule, under intense time pressure and with the lives of the crew at stake.

Challenge yourself: even if you have plenty of time to solve a problem, why use a time-consuming solution? What if you had to have the problem solved in a month, or next week, or tomorrow, or in ten minutes? What if you had to solve it with half the money you actually have available, or with no money at all? What if you could only use what you could find in your car, office, or purse? It can truly be said that necessity is the mother of invention, because it is such a great stimulant for creative problem-solving.

THINK BY ANALOGY

Start with what you know best: your interests, skills, and areas of expertise. Maybe you're good at cooking, dancing, fixing car engines, playing video games, or writing reports. How is the problem you are facing now similar to the ones you encounter in those pursuits? What methods, tricks, rules, and shortcuts do you use in your areas of expertise that you could apply in some way to this problem situation?

For example, suppose you are good at proofreading or editing. Think of the meticulous mindset you use when you do that work, and the techniques you use to ensure that you catch all the errors and improve the writing. Can you use that same meticulous approach to analyze every aspect of your current problem? Sit down and rewrite the problem in the form of an essay, being sure to capture every important detail. This will clarify your understanding and get you started on finding an effective solution.

Here are some more examples of thinking by analogy:

- If you are a sports fan, consider how your problem is similar to a problem that might arise during a game. How would your favorite player or coach respond?
- If you are a history buff, draw a parallel between your problem and one or more historical events. How would Churchill, Edison, Ghandi, or Alexander tackle the matter?

- If you are a cook, think of creating a solution like developing a new recipe. What ingredients will you need for your solution, and in what proportion and sequence?

The demands of modern life have led to increasing specialization, which has led in turn to decreasing awareness of potential solutions from other fields. Today more than ever, it really pays to have an open and curious mind, to search out and absorb the lessons of history and of all categories of knowledge. An entrepreneur who understands military strategy, psychology, and carpentry, for example, has many valuable solution-creating skills that he can apply to business problems. Football players have experimented with yoga, ballet, and the martial arts in their quest for balance, flexibility, and conditioning. So broaden your horizons, cultivate diverse interests, and fertilize your thinking with facts and techniques from as many fields as possible.

You can develop analogies by considering your problem in light of the following factors:

- **Category.** What is the general category of your problem? Let's say it is people management, which is basically getting others to do what you want. What else involves getting others to do what you want? How about parenting, athletic coaching, animal training, military leadership, and advertising? If you know how to raise a child, train a dog, or coach a little league baseball team, you already know many of the basic principles of business management.

- **Tools.** What tools do you enjoy using? Which ones do you use most often, and which ones work best for you? How about a pocket knife, dictionary, screwdriver, scissors, map, spatula, telephone, shovel, camera, vacuum cleaner, hammer, or copier? Reflect on what it is about your favorite tools that makes them so effective. Then consider how you could incorporate those qualities into a solution. If you could create a tool to solve your problem, what would it look like and how would it function?

- **Emotions.** How does this problem make you feel? Irritated? Fearful? Disappointed? Let's say it was "irritated." What else makes you feel that way? Bugs flying around your head? What would you do about that? You might shoo them away, swat them, or spray them. You might cover yourself with repellant to make yourself unattractive to them, or wear a hat with netting to keep them away. You might set out traps, spray the whole yard, or encourage birds or bats to devour them. Is there anything about these solutions that triggers an idea for solving your current problem?

> THINKING BY ANALOGY
>
> One of my most satisfying creations was *Rampant Rockets*, the comic strip featured in my online magazine. At the beginning of one drawing session, I found myself in a situation familiar to any artist: sitting at the table, staring at a blank piece of paper, and wondering what I was going to put there. As I was staring at the paper, pen in hand, searching and wondering, I thought, "There's tension here, as though something is waiting to happen. This feels like the moment before a lightning strike, when a difference in electrical charge is building between the ground and the clouds." In that moment, the paper became a grassy field, and I was up in the clouds looking down. I knew something needed to happen, that there was an idea in my brain that the field of paper was demanding. So I just let it happen – CRACK! – a key phrase leapt out, and that was the spark that ignited the rest of the strip.
>
> -Kevin

MAKE IT A STORY

If you were telling the story of a particular problem to a young child, how would you explain what caused it and what kind of solution you were looking for? Telling the story in simple terms can clarify your understanding. Storytelling can also help you to identify the source of the problem – the beginning of the story – and to put all the events of the situation in sequence. Then, of course, you get to add your own "happy ending" of how the problem will get solved.

Similarly, have you ever noticed that it can be easier to think of solutions for other people's problems than for your own? So, imagine that someone else has your problem and has come to you for advice. Pretending that you are advising someone else who has an identical problem allows you to depersonalize the issues and look at them more objectively, with less emotional interference. Give that imaginary person your best advice on how to proceed, and then follow it yourself.

Employ Your Subconscious

Your subconscious processes all of the sensory information you receive before passing some of it along to your conscious mind. In the process of filtering, sorting, matching, and discarding information, it frequently encounters interesting relationships: subtle changes, peculiar similarities, striking novelties, and recurring sequences. If these relationships are interesting enough, your subconscious tells you about them through the voice of intuition.

People often ignore intuitive messages. This is because their conscious minds cannot see the logic in them, or because the intuitive voice is too soft to be heard above the din of everyday life, or because they are too busy with other things and do not pay attention. You can benefit greatly by learning to listen for and carefully consider these internal messages. Be on the alert for solution ideas that come to you out of the blue. They often appear when you are engaged in some routine physical activity and your mind is idly pursuing its own paths, as when you are doing the dishes, taking a shower, driving, or jogging. You are also likely to receive these messages when your busy conscious mind is de-activated, as when you are meditating, falling asleep, or just waking up.

You don't have to wait and hope for these intuitive messages from your subconscious. You can learn to tap into your intuition any time you need assistance. To do so, you need to get your busy, noisy conscious mind out of the way and become receptive to the simpler, quieter messages from your subconscious mind. If you have been pounding away at a problem and feel like you're not making good progress, just stop *trying* to find a solution for a while. Let go of the problem on a conscious level and give your subconscious an opportunity to pass along some intuitive advice.

You can let go in many ways and to varying degrees. It can be as simple as just getting up from your work and taking a short break. Consciously decide to stop thinking about the problem for a few minutes. Take a deep breath, get a drink, or step outdoors. Any change in location or position can be helpful: stand up, stretch, lie down, sit cross-legged, or do a few calisthenics. Get your breath flowing and your blood moving. Try the "Breathing by Numbers" exercise in Appendix A.

Activities that require you to focus your conscious mind on a simple, diverting, physical task are a good way to clear the channels so your subconscious can send useful messages to you. At home you can shoot baskets in the driveway or throw darts in the basement. Teach yourself to juggle, or to do tricks with a yo-yo. It doesn't have to be anything fancy. Shooting rubber bands into the trash can for a few minutes works great!

Take a longer problem-solving break with a physical activity like running, biking, or aerobics; or with a household task like washing the dishes, doing the laundry, or gardening. Anything that focuses your attention away from the problem can be effective. One good way to take a break is to just get up and take a walk whenever you feel stuck. You don't have to put on any special shoes or clothing, or go anywhere in particular, just head out the door and walk around the block once or twice. Activities like these function as shortcuts to a meditative state, but you don't have to think of it that way; just let it work. Simply do the activity without any effort to focus or direct your thoughts, and let your mind drift. Your subconscious will give you the ideas you need.

If circumstances allow it, and you feel the need for a longer break from the problem-solving process, put your efforts on the shelf for a while. Take a mental vacation from the problem for a few days, weeks, or months. When you come back to it, you may find that your subconscious has been working on it the whole time, and has some fresh insights and ideas waiting for you.

One thing *not* to do is turn on the television. Many people automatically reach for the remote control whenever they want to take a break, but watching television puts you in a "receive only" mental state that shuts off your subconscious mind along with your conscious mind. It drowns out intuitive messages and prevents your subconscious from processing information and ideas in search of a solution. And once the TV is on, that ten-minute break often turns into several hours of aimless channel surfing.

You can also use your subconscious to solve problems while you sleep. As you prepare for bed, let go of the problem that you have been focusing on, and allow yourself to relax. It helps to say something like, "I ask my subconscious mind for a solution to this problem." Some people find that solution ideas most often come to them as they are drifting off to sleep, some receive their ideas in the form of dreams, and others find ideas waiting for them upon awakening. Sometimes the subconscious delivers a clear, complete solution. Other times it provides only an intuitive hint in the form of a feeling or a hunch. Be alert for these messages, record them immediately before they fade, and carefully consider their meaning.

BRAINSTORM

Brainstorming means generating a large number of potential solution ideas and recording them as fast as they occur, without any attempt to evaluate or analyze them. This can be done on the spur of the moment or as part of a formal problem-solving process, and it can be done alone or in a group.

Brainstorming on your own is a great way to loosen your mind and generate creative ideas. First, get CLARITY on your problem and write it down. Then get yourself into whatever Strong RESPONSE state is most likely to trigger a free flow of ideas and start recording whatever comes to mind. You can use pen and paper, a voice recorder, a keyboard, or whatever else works best for you.

The important point – and this is true for all types of brainstorming – is to suspend all censorship and all criticism. If a thought arises, no matter how ridiculous, impractical, or trivial it might seem, record it without comment. Any conscious judgment of the value of an idea immediately inhibits the free flow of additional ideas. Your subconscious idea-generating engine does not respond well to being judged!

Write down what you *wish* you could do, even if you know you can't. Put down what *should* work, even if it hasn't in the past. If an idea makes you laugh, put it in. Make a note of silly, expensive, poetic, outrageous, dangerous, boring, impossible, and borrowed solutions. Even record an idea that is just a different wording of a previous idea. Everything and anything goes! Keep it up until you feel bone-dry, take a break, and then generate more ideas.

The point of brainstorming is to give yourself a wealth of ideas with which to work. Temporarily turning off the critical filters of your conscious mind allows for an outpouring of creative ideas. After the ideas have been generated, it is time to re-engage your analytical thinking. You can group the ideas, rewrite them, perform cost/benefit analyses, compare them to see which seem most promising, and experiment with them. The more ideas you can generate through the creative process of brainstorming, the more raw materials you will have from which to choose, and with which to build great solutions.

Use randomness. One fun way to stimulate brainstorming is by using randomness. First, find a way to generate a random concept or word. For example, you could open a book, magazine, dictionary, or thesaurus and, without looking, place your finger on a page. Make note of the word, phrase, or image under your finger. Tell yourself that whatever you found, no matter how strange, holds the secret to solving your problem. Then create a solution out of the "clue" that the word or image has given you.

For example, suppose your problem is being late for work, and you point to the phrase "rubber bands" in a magazine. How in the world could rubber bands be the key to a solution? Well, start by brainstorming about all the qualities and uses of rubber bands. They are cheap, flexible, and disposable. They come in many colors, sizes, and thicknesses. They are useful for keeping things together and for holding something in position. They are fun to play with, to stretch and shoot, and to use as rings or bracelets.

Now figure out how these qualities of rubber bands could be applied to solving your problem.

- They're flexible: Is it possible that rigidly adhering to every step of your morning routine makes you late on days when something unexpected happens, and that you could get to work on time by skipping a step as needed?
- They're disposable: Could you buy quick-fix breakfasts in disposable containers, cutting down on preparation and cleanup time?

- They keep things together: Would it help to have one place where you put all of your daily necessities each evening – your wallet or purse, keys, planner, briefcase, or backpack – so you never have to hunt for them in the morning?
- They're fun to play with: What could you do to make getting up and getting ready more fun? How about waking up to some great music instead of an alarm or the news, or trying a new kind of coffee or tea? Maybe you could create a game in which you reward yourself with some special treat after work on Friday if you are on time every morning that week.

Don't just generate one or two ideas and stop. Keep playing with the random idea and generate as many solutions as possible.

Team brainstorming. Including others in your brainstorming efforts can greatly improve your chances of finding a solution. With the right people, you not only get more ideas, you get ideas that no one would have thought of on his or her own.

Plenty has been written about how to organize and conduct group brainstorming sessions, particularly in business settings, so we won't go over that territory in detail. Here are the key methods for making any group brainstorming session most productive:

- Use the TEAMWORK tool to assemble a diverse and enthusiastic group of participants. Include children in family brainstorming and front line staff in business brainstorming. Exclude negative, judgmental, low-energy people even if they hold important positions.
- During the brainstorming session all participants must be on an equal footing, from file clerk all the way up to CEO. It can be difficult for an authority figure to step down into an equal partnership role, and for an entry-level staff person to step up into one. However, in order for participants

to cooperatively generate ideas, they must feel that they are (at least temporarily) operating at the same level. If there is a sense of hierarchy or authority during a session, then some lower-ranking people won't participate because they will feel intimidated and stifled. Higher-ranking participants may feel inhibited because of a sense that someone in their position should not risk "saying something foolish."

- Try using some of the other CREATIVITY techniques as idea catalysts during your group brainstorming sessions. Make it a game, have fun, or turn the problem into a story. Create analogies by completing the statement, "This problem is like _____."

As in individual brainstorming, do not allow any analysis or censorship during the actual brainstorming phase. The goal is to produce as many ideas as possible, so all suggestions must be welcomed and all participants must feel comfortable and inspired to pitch in. Even one critical comment can derail the process and interrupt the energy of the session.

Try including people who have no prior knowledge of the problem. Don't contaminate them with too much information. There can be an advantage in not having any preconceived ideas of what is possible and what is not possible. Just give them the basics, the minimum objective facts of the situation and the goal or goals. Be very careful not to shoot down their ideas with "yes, but." Make sure that you don't quickly turn their fresh eyes into tired eyes.

CREATE A BETTER SOLUTION

In DISCOVERY, we talked about using ready-made solutions rather than creating new ones, and about using workable solutions instead of searching for perfect ones. For everyday problem-solving, that is great advice.

Now, however, we're talking about solving tougher problems and about creating better solutions. So, even if you've discovered an adequate solution to your problem, how about challenging yourself to make it better? Take that pre-existing solution and find a creative way to improve it by at least ten percent, then look for opportunities to do even more. Treat the solution as a starting point and see if you can make it a hundred percent better, or use it as launching pad for an entirely new solution. In other words, don't view finding the solution as the end of DISCOVERY, but as the beginning of CREATIVITY.

Go for both and then for more. You will often be given the message that you must choose between two desirable outcomes. For example:

- You can be a tough parent *or* a loving one.
- The work can get done faster *or* more accurately.
- You can have low price *or* high quality.
- The workplace can be fun *or* efficient.
- You can have a good time *or* have moral standards.

Develop the habit of rejecting these kinds of tradeoffs. When you are faced with an either/or choice, your first answer should be "both." With CREATIVITY you can often build solutions that allow you to achieve both outcomes. Then the next step is to go beyond "both" and look for what would be *more* than both or *better* than both. For example, most people assume that cheaper must be slower or lower-quality, but in reality it is often possible to be better, faster, *and* cheaper. Many businesses based on the assumption that people will buy an inferior product at a lower price fail, while almost all businesses based on the assumption that people will buy a better product at a lower price succeed.

Conclusion

The word "creativity" is often associated only with artistic talents like acting, drawing, or music. However, creative problem-solving is a more universal skill. Everyone possesses important creative qualities. In fact, we humans are defined in large part by our ability to adapt, to find new and unexpected ways to get past obstacles and meet challenges. To be human is to be creative.

Therefore, everyone should be open to using the CREATIVITY tool. People who are inclined to be logical, practical, and orderly are often given the message that they are not creative. That is nonsense. If you are thinking, "I don't have a creative bone in my body" it is time to get that idea out of your head and out of your way. Remove that "non-creative" label from your self-identity, pick two or three techniques from this chapter, and start using them. The great solution you are seeking may be waiting for you right now.

If you consider yourself to be a naturally creative problem-solver, you can use the techniques in this chapter to build on that strength. Creativity is not just a gift, it is a skill that can be learned and improved. Consider people who are naturally good athletes: only a few make the commitment to raise their abilities to the highest level by strengthening their muscles through exercise and refining their technique through coaching and practice. Similarly, you can use the methods in this chapter to become a champion of creative problem-solving.

Creativity: Summary

Prepare to be Creative
- **Be ready for setbacks.** Accept the risk of frustration, disappointment, or ridicule as a natural part of innovation.

- **Avoid anti-creativity.** Be cautious of phrases like, "It's impossible," "You can't do it that way" or, "I have no idea." They send unproductive messages to your subconscious.
- **Fill your mind.** Stock your brain by using travel time productively, engaging in random acts of life, and talking *with* people instead of *to* them.
- **Stay connected.** Regularly refocus on your vision of fulfillment and your compelling goals.
- **Stay rested.** Get enough rest to be at your solution-finding best. Refrain from making important decisions when you are tired.

Creativity Techniques

- **Go to your CREATIVITY place.** Use the places and activities that support your creative thinking.
- **Use silence and sound.** Regular quiet time helps you listen to your intuitive, creative voice. Use sound – particularly music – to enhance your creative thinking.
- **Have fun.** Play, curiosity, and humor loosen the reins of your creativity and produce great solutions for even the toughest problems.
- **Think big.** Stimulate your thinking by imagining some grand "what ifs." Overpower the problem with a *smashing through* mindset.
- **Think small.** Look for solutions that require the fewest resources, particularly time and money. Create solutions using only what's on hand.
- **Think by analogy.** Start with the problem-solving that you do best, then apply those methods to the problem at hand.

- **Make it a story.** Turn your problem into a story in order to understand it better. Get perspective by imagining that you are advising someone else who has the problem.
- **Employ your subconscious.** Listen to your intuition – the voice of your subconscious – for problem-solving ideas. Take a break from the problem to give your subconscious time to work on it.
- **Brainstorm.** Temporarily turn off your critical thinking in order to generate a wealth of potential solutions.
- **Create a better solution.** Take a "found" solution and make it better. When faced with an either/or alternative, choose both.

THE NINTH TOOL

DETERMINATION

OVERCOME PROBLEMS
THROUGH COURAGE & PERSISTENCE

If you have used the first eight tools and still haven't found a satisfactory solution to a particular problem, then you're dealing with a tough one. Fortunately, as humans have demonstrated countless times and in astonishing ways, you have it within you to forge a path through what may feel like an impossible situation.

DETERMINATION is the tool to use when you must move forward in the face of fear, when you are setting out on a long hard road, when you must achieve success despite great adversity.

For example, you would use DETERMINATION if you were:

- An artist, inventor, or entrepreneur, trying to make your dream a reality
- A severely injured patient beginning the rehabilitation process

- An actor, apprehensive about going onstage for your first starring role
- A worker with three jobs, steeling yourself to make it through the next shift

In situations like these you must find the *courage* to move forward and the *persistence* to press on until you have achieved your goal.

COURAGE

COURAGE AND FEAR

Understanding fear. The most common obstacle people face when dealing with a really serious problem is the Weak emotion of fear. As we have said previously, fear is an unavoidable part of a fulfilling life. Consider that:

1. Fear arises whenever we perceive a risk of physical or emotional danger.
2. We instinctively know that the unknown may carry a risk of danger.
3. Living a fulfilling life includes trying new things, deliberately seeking out and facing the unknown.
4. Therefore, repeatedly encountering fear is a necessary aspect of leading a fulfilling life.

For some people, repeatedly risking danger is exciting. They seem born to be adventurers and risk-takers, and enjoy activities and situations that most others would find terrifying or overwhelming. But what if you are not one of these natural daredevils? In reality, everyone feels fear; it is just that different people fear different things. What may seem terrifying to you might seem like fun to someone else, but that person may be petrified by a situation that you would find quite enjoyable.

Consider the following situations:

- Giving an important speech in front of a large audience
- Telling another person that you have fallen deeply in love, and hoping that person feels the same way about you
- Climbing a sheer, rocky cliff hundreds of feet above the ground
- Attending a dinner party at which all the other guests are successful, sophisticated, and witty
- Spending a week at a remote cabin with no television or telephone
- Becoming the CEO of a large corporation that has been experiencing significant difficulties
- Having to care for a newborn infant by yourself for one full day

Any individual will view some of these situations as terrifying problems to be avoided and others as exciting opportunities to be sought out. No one is truly a coward. We each feel confident about different things, and we each must face the challenges of our individual fears.

Understanding courage. Courage is not the absence of fear, but the ability to act in the face of fear. You are courageous when you feel fear and proceed in spite of it. Courage is the quality that allows you to stand your ground despite the impulse to run and to move forward despite the instinct to hide. It allows you to embrace the experience of fear, so that rather than shrinking from it you can master it and build a fulfilling life.

Courage is not an unalterable trait; it is a habit of thought and behavior that can be consciously learned and improved. Countless individuals have achieved personal greatness by learning to master their most deeply-felt fears. For example, it is remarkable how many successful actors and singers have had to overcome terrible stage fright in order to build their careers as entertainers. You too can strengthen your courage, conquer your fears, and achieve your compelling goals. Your character is shaped by how you consistently act. By consciously choosing to face your deepest fears, rather than shrink from them, you can turn courage into your habitual, natural response to the sensation of fear.

Prepare yourself for courageous action. It is a good idea to prepare yourself properly before beginning any important endeavor. For example, if you are serious about your performance in a sport you select the right equipment, warm up your muscles, and make sure that you are emotionally motivated and mentally sharp. If you prepare in this way before running a race or playing a round of golf you get better results, have more fun, and suffer fewer injuries.

You can likewise get better results if you prepare yourself to be brave before tackling an intimidating problem. Let's look at some techniques you can use to get ready for courageous action.

Conquer Fear

In RESPONSE we discussed how Weak emotions like fear can be put to good use as messengers and as motivators. However, when you are facing an especially difficult problem you may experience an *excess* of fear, more fear than you can productively use for insight or motivation. This excess fear can interfere with your ability to solve the problem by triggering the instinct to fight, flee, or freeze. Here are some techniques for neutralizing excess fear:

Analyze the fear. Fear represents the dark side of human emotion. It is often an exaggerated, irrational reaction to a problem. You can overcome it by using the power of human reason.

Subject your fear to the careful scrutiny of logic and analysis by using the *intellectual and analytical* version of the Strong & Still RESPONSE. Cut fear down to a reasonable sense of prudent concern by reviewing the facts and weighing the true risks and opportunities. From this vantage point, the situation will seem interesting rather than threatening.

Any time you find yourself feeling afraid, check to see if you have been describing the problem with fear-generating, ineffective words like "disaster," "unbearable," or "hopeless." If so, you can redefine the problem using courage-generating words like "challenging," "serious," or "fascinating." Choose to define the problem in a way that is useful to you, rather than in a way that frightens you.

Let the fear pass by. Serenity, composure, and acceptance await you at all times and in all circumstances. Attain the *meditative and spiritual* form of the Strong & Still RESPONSE by using prayer, introspection, or relaxation. You do not need to allow fear to harm or entrap you; let it simply pass harmlessly past you. After all, it has no real substance; it is just a ghost that frightens the unwary with an illusion of ferocity. Observe it with curiosity and detachment.

All of the problem-solving strength that you need is within you right now, and all the problem-solving tools that you need are in this book. If you apply your inner strength and the *Solution Power* tools to any problem, you will find a solution.

Laugh the fear away. Fear doesn't stand a chance against the pure joy of the *exuberant and playful* version of the Strong & Active RESPONSE. So go ahead and sing, laugh, and dance! Fear thrives only in the shadows, so throw open the windows of your soul and let in the bright light of celebration and happiness. When times get really tough, you can choose to cry or you can choose to laugh. Laughing is better!

> **COURAGE AND COMEDY**
>
> The early responses to *Solution Power* showed us that not only did people want to read the book, they also wanted to hear us speak about the material. While we were both enthusiastic about doing the presentations, I realized that I had much less experience in front of a crowd than Reagan did. Although I had given a number of creative writing workshops, Reagan had many years of experience speaking regularly to audiences on business, legal, and leadership topics.
>
> I started looking for a way to quickly take my public speaking skills to a higher level, and I saw that a local comedy club was hosting "open mike" nights. Perfect! Standup comedy is the "toughest act in show business," the most challenging form of public speaking. I figured that if I could master standup comedy, any other kind of presentation would seem easy by comparison.
>
> I knew that this experience would require a *lot* of courage, that it would require me to push well beyond my comfort zone. I visited the club, met the manager, watched a show, and observed the crowd. This gave me a good feel for what it would take to successfully perform in that environment. I worked up a short routine and practiced it over and over in my living room. The more fun I had with the routine, the more clearly I could visualize myself generating an enthusiastic reaction from the audience, and the more confident I became.
>
> I did my first show, and it was a great success. Of course, some of the material I thought was terrifically funny didn't get quite the response I expected, but other lines had them roaring with laughter. Plus, I enjoyed the whole experience immensely. I also received the two ultimate signs of success: I got invited back and I got more stage time.
>
> *-Kevin*

Confront the fear. Fleeing or hiding from fear only increases its power over you. When you stand your ground and confront it, fear will turn tail and run, just like any other big-mouth bully. So generate the *relentless and unswerving* or *dynamic and forceful* versions of the Strong & Active RESPONSE, and tackle the fear head-on. Go ahead and get angry at the fear! Although anger is counterproductive in many problem-solving situations, it can be an effective weapon against excess fear. Turn loose a volley of virtuous fury, not against any individual or against your circumstances, but against the feeling of fear itself: "I have had it with you! You cannot harm me, and you will not stop me! You are not welcome here! Get out!"

Discover the limits of the fear. (Caution: If you have a history of anxiety or panic attacks, do not use this exercise.) Fear is most debilitating while it is escalating in intensity. It can seem like there is no upper limit on how intense the feeling will get. The perception that the fear could grow ever stronger is almost unbearable, and can feel overwhelming. In reality, emotions have a "maximum volume," a level of intensity at which they peak and then automatically begin to decline. This is true for all emotions, both positive and negative.

You can make any problem seem less threatening by proving to yourself that the fear it generates has a limited duration and a maximum level of intensity. Think about a serious problem you are currently facing, paying particular attention to everything about it that is frightening. Focus on the feeling of fear as it arises and grows. Make no attempt to shut it off or control it in any way; in fact nurture it, make it as strong and intense as possible. Allow yourself to become as terrified by this problem as you can possibly get.

As the fear grows, begin to observe it with a sense of curiosity. "I wonder how intense I can make the fear, and how long I can make it last?" You will be amazed at quickly the fear will hit its maximum level and then "get tired" and start to fade. No matter how hard you try, you will not be able to make the fear increase without limit, nor sustain it for long at its maximum level.

Now you know that you can handle the highest level of fear that this problem can generate. It wasn't much fun, but it also didn't cause any lasting harm. This exercise reveals that fear is not the all-powerful force it sometimes seems to be. It is only a transient sensation, a set of emotional and physical reactions that can fade as quickly as they arise. Once you have "de-fanged" fear in this way, it will lose much of its power over you. The next time fear starts to grow you can simply say: "Oh, you again. Well, you don't scare me anymore so you might as well just go away."

Turn to your team. Be open to support and encouragement. Tackling tough problems on your own is a good discipline, but you don't need to face overwhelming challenges alone. It is in times of crisis that your life team has its greatest value. Have the self-assurance to seek assistance when you are in greatest need of it.

Draw on your beliefs. Drawing strength from your fundamental beliefs will help you proceed in the face of a fearsome challenge. Many people find that their religious or spiritual faith is their strongest ally against fear. You can benefit from the certainty that you have a relationship with something bigger than yourself, and bigger than the source of any fear.

Consider the powerful role that your faith can play in inspiring you to take courageous action. Whether you believe in God, in your own inner light, or in a connection to the power of the Universe, you have help on your side that is vastly greater than any problem you may confront. If it fits into your belief system, remind yourself that the problem is part of a larger plan, that it has been given to you for a reason and that it would not have been given to you if you were incapable of facing it. It is meant to help you learn, to grow, or to achieve your destiny.

Look to your heroes. As was suggested in CREATIVITY, identify role models who inspire you. Learn as much as you can about them, beyond their popular image and well-known quotes. The more you know about them, the more often something they did or said will come to mind and provide you with comfort and confidence when you are struggling for a solution.

This doesn't mean you should try to *become* that person, but there is a special inspiration that can be drawn from the example of real people who faced real problems. In what ways did they display courage? How did they respond when confronting fear? What might they do if they were in your situation? Model your level of courage on theirs. We are fascinated with stories of triumph and heroism in large part because it gives us hope that we have similar potential within ourselves.

A MODEL OF COURAGE

At many times in our adult lives we have taken strength from the example of one of our heroes, Winston Churchill. He is best-known as the Prime Minister of Britain during World War II, but his whole life is a story of steadfast courage in the face of adversity, of turning daunting defeats into astonishing victories. He saw action on many battlefields, escaped from a prisoner-of-war camp, was widely blamed for one of the worst debacles of the first World War, won and lost numerous political offices, prophetically warned the world about the rise of Hitler, and then led the brave struggle that saved our world from tyranny. In addition, he was a successful and prolific orator, reporter, artist, and writer.

Reflecting on his life often helps us forge ahead in times of trial. The massive challenges he faced put our troubles in perspective, the fact that he often triumphed against long odds gives us hope, and the way in which he always rebounded from defeat helps us persevere. Above all, his irrepressible zest for adventure is a shining example of how to live life to its fullest.

-Kevin & Reagan

GET MOTIVATED

Use *the fork in the road.* This exercise is based on comparing your Weakest and Strongest possible RESPONSES to a particular problem.

First, envision the worst that could happen if you hide from the problem or make only timid attempts to solve it. What are the possible consequences for you and for those you care about? Don't just *think* about it, really *experience* it by vividly imagining a future in which you did not summon the courage to get the problem solved. Have you let somebody down? Are you stuck in a bad situation? Have you missed out on a golden opportunity? Are you drifting farther away from your vision of fulfillment?

Notice what emotions you are feeling. Do you feel a sharp sense of regret, of being disappointed in yourself? Are you angry and frustrated at your failure to take effective action? Remember that negative emotions can provide a strong "push" of motivation. The more vividly you can imagine how unpleasant this future would be, the more you will be motivated to avoid it by tackling the problem vigorously.

Okay, shake it off! Get up, stretch, breathe deeply, and let all that negativity wash away. *Do not stop the exercise at this point.* Recall (from CLARITY) that what you focus on is what you are most likely to get. So it is important to replace that negative vision of fearful ineffectiveness with a positive vision of decisive action.

Now envision a future in which you have boldly done what was necessary to get the problem solved. Vividly imagine the rewards of your wonderful achievement. Are you in terrific physical condition? Are your loved ones proud of you and happy for you? Have you eliminated your debts, doubled your profits, or achieved great career success? Were you able to give help to someone important to you, or have a positive impact on your community?

Notice the emotions that you are experiencing. How does it feel to have moved forward courageously and solved the problem? Are you relieved at removing a major worry from your life? Do you feel a deep sense of pride at achieving your ambitious goal? Are you experiencing a warm feeling of satisfaction? Do you feel like laughing or dancing with joy?

While you are in this wonderful state, look over at the "you" in that other future, the version of you who was dominated by fear. See and feel, with complete clarity, the difference between timidity and bravery, between ineffectiveness and achievement. Use this difference as a powerful source of motivation, combining a strong desire to *avoid* the undesirable future with a strong desire to *attain* the fulfilling future.

Finally, return to your present reality. Fully accept that you are, at this very moment, standing at the fork in the road. Drawing on the powerful motivation you have generated, *utterly reject* the path of fear and *fully commit* to moving forward on the path of courage.

Turn commitment into action. You can transform this powerful sense of commitment into immediate action and sustained achievement by using these techniques:

- **Put it in writing.** Record your commitment to solve the problem in your journal, planner, or on a posted reminder.
- **Change behavior.** Ask yourself, "What am I willing to do to solve the problem?" and, "What am I willing to *stop doing* in order to solve the problem?" Be firm with yourself, and make whatever behavioral changes are necessary to achieve your important goal.
- **Accept uncertainty.** If you delay action until conditions are ideal – until the stars are in perfect alignment – you will almost certainly miss important opportunities for success. Get moving even if you don't have all the resources you wish you had, or even if you cannot see the path to a perfect outcome with complete clarity. Be willing to proceed imperfectly, to keep moving forward even when things aren't going exactly as planned.

- **Speak effectively.** Use decisive language. Instead of sighing, "I guess I'll have to do something about this," firmly say, "I *will* take action to solve the problem *now*."
- **Take action now.** Whatever fears may have previously stood in your way will seem inconsequential compared to your confidence, strength, motivation, and commitment. Now is the time to take your first step on the path toward success. So do it!

PERSISTENCE

If courage is action in the face of fear, then persistence is sustained action in the face of disappointment or adversity. Only by continuing to strive despite repeated setbacks can you achieve your loftiest goals.

Many important problems can be solved only through sheer dogged effort. For some problems there simply is no creative shortcut, no easy way to slip around the obstacle. In cases like these, "There's nothing to it but to do it." You simply have to keep plugging away and do the work required, stubbornly moving forward until the last obstacle has fallen. As with courage, persistence is a skill that can be acquired and improved.

WORK HARD

The ability to work hard is one of the most reliable and effective problem-solving skills you can develop. While it is natural to avoid unnecessary exertion and discomfort, those who habitually seek to avoid *any* hard work severely limit their ability to solve problems. You will tackle any problem with confidence if you know that you can work as hard as necessary and for as long as necessary to get the job done.

Determination

Hard work is also a great antidote to feelings of discouragement. It is much easier to feel optimistic when you are working on a solution than when you are brooding about a problem or distracting yourself from it. The feelings of satisfaction and pride that result from sustained effort are much more rewarding than the seductive but fleeting payoffs of idleness and self-indulgence.

Seize opportunities to develop your ability to work hard for prolonged periods of time. For example, at some point in your life you will probably have to take a lousy job, not because it is a good match for your interests and talents, but just because you need the money. As you find yourself facing another tough day at work, consciously decide to turn the problem into an opportunity. Instead of simply getting through the day, treat the job as an exercise program for strengthening your persistence muscles. Learning how to handle nasty customers, meet "impossible" deadlines, get by with broken equipment, and keep working when tired will give you problem-solving strengths that will serve you well for the rest of your life.

BOXERCISE

The most physically demanding job I ever had was unloading trucks and sorting parcels at a distribution center for a national delivery service. We had to work very quickly, lifting and moving high volumes of packages that were often heavy and bulky. Once the conveyer belts started rolling, we engaged in an unrelenting and sometimes desperate struggle to keep up with the flow.

In order to gear up for this sustained exertion, I began to stretch out and warm up before the start of each shift. I also made sure that I drank plenty of water, since it was very sweaty work. At some point, it occurred to me that I was getting an excellent workout. I started thinking of my job as the "Hades Health Club," and viewing my work as an unusually demanding program of aerobic weightlifting.

This perspective really did make it easier to go to work each day and make it through the shift. After all, I was getting in the best physical condition of my life, and I was getting paid to do it!

-Kevin

Think about the people you know who can really hustle. Whenever a problem arises you can count on them to pitch in and tackle it with vigor. They are mentally sharp and in constant motion; there is a spark in their eyes and a bounce in their step. You can be one of those problem-solving go-getters! When a problem pops up that needs to be solved in a hurry, or if you just want to clear a problem out of your way so you can get on to more important things, use the Strong & Active techniques in RESPONSE to shift into high gear.

Sometimes, shifting into high gear is the *only* way to overcome a barrier and reach your goal, like when an important customer sends in a rush order, your team's best player is out of the game with an injury, or your plumbing has sprung a leak and your basement is filling with water. In situations like these, play hard and play to win! Reject the idea that you need to conserve your energy. Instead, see yourself as a human dynamo: the harder you work, the more power you generate. This simple change in perspective will enable you to sustain high levels of exertion for longer than you may believe possible.

STAY MOTIVATED

Enjoy solving the problem. Many people mistakenly assume that solving tough problems has to *feel* tough, that it has to be an ordeal. They may even harbor the perverse notion that the worse they feel about doing the work, the more credit they deserve for it: "Sure, you got your problem solved, but you *enjoyed* doing it. I had an *awful* time solving *my* problem." This is a trap; it creates a subconscious link between suffering and a sense of self-worth. The more miserable they make themselves, the more they feel worthy of praise. In reality, their achievements would be just as admirable, perhaps even more admirable, if they had found a way enjoy the problem-solving process.

So don't ever assume that solving a challenging problem has to feel like a burden. You really do not need to put on a grim frown, keep your nose to the grindstone, and mentally flog yourself into sustained effort. As often as possible, take pleasure from the process of reaching your goal. If someone says to you, "Great job! That must have been really tough to do!" you can smile and reply, "Thanks! I'm really happy with how it turned out, and I had a great time doing it!"

If the work of solving a particular problem is boring and drawn-out, see if you can use it as a form of meditation. You will more easily sustain your effort if you approach a repetitive task with serenity and acceptance. Put the problem in perspective: there are people all around the world who would love to trade places with you, who would be happy to have your life and be worried only about solving your problem. Be grateful that you are who you are, right now, doing what you are doing.

Life should not feel like a sacrifice, even when you are working hard to help others solve their problems. If you find yourself regularly "playing the martyr," you need a better perspective. Think about a mother whose mantra is, "I am sacrificing my own happiness for the sake of my children." How does that make the children feel? They may become burdened with feelings of guilt, resentment, and dependence. In addition, the mother has now established a subconscious link between suffering and love: the more unhappy she makes herself the more she proves her love for her children.

What a destructive cycle this is! The mother and the children would be far happier if she could adopt a new mantra: "I enjoy helping my children build a happy life." If helping others solve their problems is part of your vision of fulfillment, then you should *feel* fulfilled when you do so.

Use a "DETERMINATION buddy." Approach a trusted friend and explain your commitment to solving the problem. Ask your friend to support you in times of doubt or weakness, and to join you in celebrating your achievements. For some kinds of problem-solving, like getting in shape or quitting smoking, find someone with the same goal who will tackle the problem along with you. There is great strength in shared resolve.

One day at a time. Make long-term problems more manageable by solving them a week, or day, or even an hour at a time. For example, people often delay beginning a healthier diet or starting regular exercise because they aren't sure that they can stick with the program for the long haul. When you are puffing your way through your first one-mile run, it is hard to feel confident that you will continue to run three mornings a week, every week, for the next umpteen years. It can be equally hard to contemplate sticking with a new, healthier diet for the rest of your (longer and more energetic) life.

It is actually easier to sustain long-term effort by concentrating on short, specific periods of time instead of using an all-or-nothing approach. It's likely that you *can* find the discipline to eat better and exercise more *this week*. That doesn't seem quite so difficult. As you make progress, say, "I made it this far, and I'm doing fine. Now I'll take the next step." Every task you complete will strengthen your resolve. Schedule a time at the end of the week to appreciate your success and commit yourself for another week or even longer.

Make it a point to celebrate each milestone you reach, even the small ones. Go ahead, give yourself an actual pat on the back! Congratulate yourself with a "Good job!" or "Way to go!" Reward yourself with a fun activity or a little treat each time you achieve an interim goal.

Never Surrender

You have within you an inexhaustible source of strength and resilience. If a voice ever whispers in your mind, "You can't go on any longer, you have taken as much as you can take, you are near the breaking point," immediately respond with: "To heck with that! Life hasn't laid a glove on me yet! I can take this and ten times more. Bring it on!" Say it and mean it, and it will instantly become true. If your courage or energy ever begin to fail, simply ask yourself: "Am I surrendering?" You can always find within yourself an inextinguishable spark that will answer, "Never!"

Everyone experiences setbacks in life. At some point you will probably have to admit that a project will not achieve the desired results, that an innovation will not function as intended, or that a contest has been lost to a business competitor, athletic opponent, or romantic rival. How can you handle such situations without feeling defeated, or feeling like a failure?

First, recognize that the only true defeat would be to surrender your fundamental beliefs. **So long as you are true to your fundamental beliefs, any disappointment you experience is only a setback.** Even the painful realization that you cannot attain one of your compelling goals only means that you must set a new compelling goal, that you must chart a new path to fulfillment.

Therefore, when you experience a setback see it as a signal that it is time to change your strategy. Too often, people continue to butt their heads against a wall because they believe that any retreat would be an admission of defeat. In reality, flexibility and adaptability are important problem-solving traits. A willingness to change strategies actually helps you to pursue fulfillment with steady persistence. So whenever you encounter disappointment, give yourself permission to change your course of action. Step back, gather your strength, evaluate your options, reconnect with your fundamental beliefs, and chart a new course to fulfillment.

As you do so, take care in choosing the words you use to describe the situation. It is rarely useful to use phrases like "heartbreaking defeat," "crushing disaster," or "utter failure." It is more productive, and more accurate, to choose words like "setback," "detour," or "disappointment."

Just as important, be careful how you describe *yourself*. You are not "bad," "stupid," or "pathetic" just because you have not achieved a desired goal. People who attach such labels to themselves often think they are "being realistic," but actually they are just burdening themselves with a bunch of useless emotional baggage. If you are dissatisfied with the results you are getting, simply try a new approach. If your actions do not produce the intended results, ask, "Why?" from a state of curiosity. Then modify your actions and try again. Do not turn dissatisfaction with your results into destructive self-criticism. Accept that you are an imperfect human being, but do not damage yourself with anger, cripple yourself with remorse, or paralyze yourself with doubt. Give yourself permission to be disappointed, resolve to do better, and then move on. Allow yourself an unlimited number of chances to succeed.

Conclusion

Acknowledge and appreciate the determination that has gotten you this far in life. Then resolve to exercise it, to make it even stronger. The more often you take courageous and persistent action, the more you will find that no obstacle can stand in your path.

Time and again, ordinary people have triumphed in the face of great adversity. The essence of the human spirit is defined in moments when we reach beyond what we have achieved before, when we discover inner strength previously unknown to us, when we attain impossible victory through sheer willpower.

Determination: Summary

Courage

- **Courage and fear.** Fear is the most common obstacle to solving serious problems. Everyone sees some things as frightening. Courage is the ability to act in the face of fear. You can prepare yourself to take courageous action.
- **Conquer fear.** Use one of the many techniques for handling excess fear. Analyze the fear, let it pass through you, laugh it away, confront it, or find the limits of the fear. Turn to your team, look to your heroes, and draw on your beliefs.
- **Get motivated.** Use the *fork in the road* exercise to generate powerful motivation, then make a commitment to take courageous action.

Persistence

- **Work hard.** Hard work is a great all-purpose problem-solving skill. Use Strong & Active techniques to shift into high gear.
- **Stay motivated.** Enjoy solving a difficult problem rather than suffering through it. Find a DETERMINATION buddy, and solve the problem one step a time.
- **Never surrender.** Be true to your fundamental beliefs, and view disappointments as setbacks. Be willing to adopt new strategies. Take care in how you describe the situation and label yourself. Give yourself unlimited chances to do better.

The Tenth Tool

Release

Separating & Letting Go

RELEASE can be the first tool you use, or the last. When used first it helps you avoid getting entangled in unnecessary problems, so you never have to worry about solving them. When used last it helps you resolve intractable problems that cannot be solved using the other *Solution Power* tools.

RELEASE helps you to solve a problem by *separating* from it and *letting go* of it. Separating from a problem means creating distance between yourself and the root cause of the problem, for example by quitting a lousy job, selling a malfunctioning car, or ending an unhealthy relationship.

Letting go of a problem means liberating yourself from the emotional attachments that have bound you to it. It means realizing that the obstacle you must overcome is *your wish that things could be different than they are*, and that your goal is to accept that what you originally desired cannot be attained.

Separating

Avoiding Unnecessary Problems

The best way to solve an unnecessary problem is to avoid getting mixed up with it in the first place. This can be done by using RELEASE as the first tool. Doing so helps you bypass low-priority problems that would waste your problem-solving resources.

You have probably known people who seem to be *trouble magnets*, who are always getting ensnared in foolish, messy, or unimportant problems. They continually get involved in relationships with the wrong people, saddle themselves with responsibility for other people's problems, and stick their noses into issues that are none of their business. Clearly, this is not a path to fulfillment. These individuals keep themselves so busy dealing with low-priority problems that they don't have any time left over to deal with the problems that could make a real difference in their lives.

As we saw in INSIGHT, other people make the opposite mistake. They act like *timid mice*, trying to avoid facing *any* problems, including the ones they need to solve in order to attain fulfillment. This is a self-defeating strategy, one that leads to a small and unrewarding existence. You can only live a fulfilling life by taking on challenging but important problems.

You may also know people who are neither trouble magnets nor timid mice. They seem to have a knack for striking just the right balance. They slide past unnecessary problems without a backward glance, yet they continually discover and dive into problems that are great opportunities in disguise. They radiate an "I steer clear of trouble" aura that acts like a force field discouraging others from even trying to draw them into foolish difficulties. At the same time, they are the ones others naturally go to for help when a problem of real importance needs to be tackled.

All of these people – the trouble magnets, the timid mice, and the opportunity-seekers – are being guided by their intuition. So why do some people receive intuitive messages that they should get mixed up in all kinds of trouble, or meekly hide from all problems, while others receive helpful intuitive messages that guide them to success and happiness? It is because intuition is based on self-identity. Trouble magnets have a problem-*suffering* self-identity. Their intuition tells them to seek out a constant supply of messy, unsolvable problems to reinforce their identity as victims. Timid people have a problem-*fearing* self-identity. Their intuition warns them that all problems are dangerous and that no risk is worth taking. Intuitive messages provide poor guidance when they are shaped by an unhealthy self-identity.

So the key is to build a problem-*solving* self-identity that will generate healthy, trustworthy intuitive messages. The good news is that if you have used PRIORITY to create your fulfillment action plan you are already ninety percent of the way there. All you need to do now is consistently pursue your plan. Doing so will naturally build your problem-solving self-identity. Your intuition will reliably steer you away from trouble and toward opportunity when it is guided by your fundamental beliefs, compelling goals, problem-solving projects, and vision of fulfillment.

The more you trust your inner voice, the more sensitive you will become to the early warning signs of trouble (and also to the first hints of hidden opportunities). Whether you are on a first date, test driving a car, or interviewing for a job, listen to your heart. Don't ignore gut feelings that something is not quite right, because those messages are trying to help you stay on course toward fulfillment.

If a situation does not feel right, give yourself permission to say, "no," "that's not for me," or, "goodbye." You can figure out exactly what was wrong later if you want to, but don't feel that you owe any explanation at the time. It is perfectly all right to simply say, politely and assertively, "We're just not a good match," "I just don't want the car," or, "This is just not the right job for me."

> **GUIDED BY INTUITION**
>
> One day, while I was in my early teens, I was walking along the street with a friend when we met another guy – a friend of my friend – coming the other way. The three of us talked for just a few minutes, but my intuition immediately told me that this guy was heading for trouble, and I did not want anything to do with it. I had no interest in getting to know him better.
>
> I met him again about ten years later, when we were both first-year students at the same law school. We immediately hit it off and became good friends. It took us a while to realize that we had met once before. He confirmed that my intuition had been correct: at that time he had been entering a troubled period in his life during which he engaged in risky and unhealthy behavior. He recalled sensing that I was not interested in the kinds of activities he was getting involved in, and therefore he had not been interested in getting to know me, either. At that point in our lives, my intuition was steering me away from trouble while his was steering him toward it.
>
> It was fascinating for both of us to reflect on how accurately we had been able to "read" each other in just a few minutes of casual conversation. It was also interesting that when we met again ten years later, our reactions were very different. We rapidly formed a bond of friendship that continues to this day, and he is one of the finest people it has been my privilege to know.
>
> -Reagan

WHEN TO SEPARATE FROM AN EXISTING PROBLEM

What if you are already stuck in a messy problem? You can either stay with it and keep trying solve it, or you can separate from it and leave it behind you. Use one or more of the following methods to decide which is the right thing to do.

Get CLARITY. Apply all the techniques of the CLARITY tool to the situation:
- Define the problem as "I want *goal* but *obstacle*."
- Be absolutely honest with yourself, stripping away all excuses and illusions.
- Take complete responsibility for making your own decision to either stay or depart.
- Let others own their own problems. Don't let your choice be influenced by an unhealthy urge to rescue someone.
- Monitor your thoughts and speech for ineffective words like "unbearable" and "terrifying." Replace them with accurate, effective words, like "difficult" and "challenging."
- Get perspective on the situation. Consider what advice you would give to someone else in this situation.
- Put the problem in writing. This will help you clarify your emotions, motivation, and expectations.
- Identify the real root of the problem; maybe you have just been dealing with the symptoms.
- Create a problem-solving project. Whether you are going to stay and solve the problem or leave the problem behind, a written plan will help you do so successfully.

Ask your teammates. When you have to decide whether to stay in a problem situation or to separate, it is very helpful to have a solid life team you can turn to for support and advice. If you have teammates whose judgment you trust, and they advise you to leave or to stay, give careful consideration to their opinions. Don't reflexively reject their point of view simply because it is not what you wanted to hear at the moment. This single step could, for example, prevent many unhappy marriages.

In the end, of course, you are responsible for making your own decisions. If your fulfillment plan compels you to act contrary to all advice, you must take that path. Often the greatest achievements are accomplished by those who stayed true to their own ambitions and convictions even when no one else supported the choices they made. Just be sure that you have a clear understanding of why you believe their advice to be mistaken. Accept the possibility that you may later hear, "I told you so."

Rise above win/lose thinking. Are you reluctant to leave, or unwilling to stay, only because you think it would look like someone else had "won" and you had "lost"? You may find yourself thinking something like, "If I leave they'll call me a quitter" or, "If I stay then she'll know she won." If so, re-examine your motivations. Do you really want your life to be governed by some kind of imaginary competition? Who exactly is keeping score, anyway? Allow yourself to pursue fulfillment, and let others deal with their own perceptions of winning and losing.

Answer separation questions. Answering the following *separation questions* will help you make the best decision. If you answer "yes" to one or more of these questions, you can feel confident that separation is the wise and appropriate thing to do:

- *"Is this a destructive problem?"* If continuing your efforts to solve the problem could damage you, separate from it as soon as you can. This is particularly true of poisonous or abusive relationships. If you fear for your safety, or for the safety of someone in your care, you don't need to do any more decision-making: move away from the abuser as quickly as possible. This is true whether the abuse is physical or emotional, and whether the abuser is your spouse, another relative, your boss, or anyone else with whom you have a relationship. Please seek help. Do not allow fear to become your prison. Remember that you can choose who will, and who will not, remain as members of your life team.

- *"Is this an unfulfilling problem?"* If solving this stubborn problem would not advance you toward fulfillment, separate from it.
- *"Have I tried my best?"* If you have tried the other nine problem-solving tools to no avail, then it is time to use RELEASE. One of the benefits of the *Solution Power* system is that it is comprehensive. If the first nine tools have not achieved a solution, then you can feel truly confident that you have tried everything and it is time to move on. This gives you peace of mind that there really is no option except to separate from the problem. You will be able to look back and say, "I did all that I could, to the best of my ability."

Act with strength. Your decision to stay or separate should be based on Strong emotions rather than Weak ones:
- Separations that are driven by Weak emotions like anxiety, despair, anger, jealousy, or guilt are often unhealthy attempts to "run away" from important problems. These separations seldom succeed because the Weak emotions are likely to continue until the problems generating them are confronted and resolved.
- Separations that are motivated by Strong emotions like decisiveness, optimism, love, self-respect, or inspiration are likely to be healthy decisions to move away from toxic or stagnant situations. These separations are more likely to succeed because Strong emotions naturally guide you toward fulfillment.

When choosing whether to separate from a problem, use the following exercises to make a decision that is based on strength. If you are facing a serious problem you may experience powerful emotions when you do these exercises, so set aside a time to do them in private.

SOLUTION POWER

1. First, imagine staying in the situation, continuing to deal with the problem and trying to find a solution to it. Envision this vividly. As you do so, become aware of how you feel. Are you feeling fearful, ashamed, pessimistic, ineffective, or bitter? Or are you feeling assertive, determined, enthusiastic, joyful, or proud?

2. Clear your mind. Now imagine moving away from the situation and leaving it behind you. Again, vividly envision what this would be like, fully projecting yourself into the scene. Become aware of your emotions. You may feel a surge of anxiety at first, because change is often a little unsettling. Let that initial impulse pass, and take note of whether Weak or Strong feelings emerge in the end.

3. Again, clear your mind. Now focus your attention on the following specific Strong emotions:

    - Confidence
    - Courage
    - Assertiveness
    - Optimism
    - Self-respect
    - Enthusiasm

    Fill your heart with each of these wonderful feelings, using the RESPONSE techniques for generating Strong emotional states. You will likely find yourself standing tall, breathing deeply, and feeling energized. What a glorious feeling! While you are in this powerful state, consider the problem. What is your first image? Do you see yourself tackling it with renewed vigor, or putting it behind you and striding into a better future? Don't analyze your reaction, just notice which choice feels right from a position of strength.

At the conclusion of these exercises, you should have a good sense of which choice is linked to Strong emotions:

- *Shun the path of Weak emotions.* Don't give in to them, either by running away from a problem you need to face or by staying stuck in an unhealthy trap. In particular, if you find that you are staying in, or fleeing from, a situation primarily because of fear, you may want to seek advice and assistance. Get the help you need to make a good decision from a position of strength.
- *Follow the path of Strong emotions.* It is your path to fulfillment. Resolve to do what the best and strongest version of you would do. Make the choice you would make when you are at your best.

How to Separate From an Existing Problem

Have a *go to*. Separations often fail when people know that they want to get away from their current situation, but they don't have a plan where they want to be instead. For example, someone may impulsively quit a bad job without having a new and better job lined up. So it is vital that you identify a *go to* in addition to your *leave from*. Choose a positive goal or destination and head toward it, rather than just heading away from your current situation. It would be a shame to finally separate from your current problem only to end up in another situation that is just as bad or even worse.

You don't need to wait until you come up with the *perfect* plan, or the *perfect* place to go; that can be paralyzing. Your *go to* does not have be the ultimate destination of your dreams. It only needs to be better than where you are now, a healthy step that takes you further down your path to fulfillment.

Separate on your own terms. Separate from the problem at your own time, in your own way, and for your own reasons. Some people delay separating from a problem because they are afraid of what others might think or feel if they do so. Remember that you are pursuing your own envisioned future, and that your decision to separate is based on your fundamental beliefs. The fear that others might judge you or feel hurt is not a sufficient reason to change your decision. Don't wait for others to give you their permission or approval, and don't allow others to burden you with guilt. If you have allowed someone else to take too much control over your choices in the past, take that power back into your own hands now.

Separate with honor. You can prepare the way for a separation by explaining your decision to those who might be affected by it, to the extent that you feel is necessary and appropriate. Behaving respectfully empowers and elevates you, even if you are dealing with rude or unreasonable people. Maintain a Strong RESPONSE state and don't let yourself get drawn into petty bickering or pointless arguments. If you have truly made the decision to separate, any further debate or dispute is simply pointless. It is your decision to make, and you have no obligation to persuade others to agree with it before you move away from the situation.

You might say something like, "My intent is not to upset or betray you. My intent is to make a decision for myself that will be best for everyone in the long run. I understand how you feel, but I also respect my own opinion and perspective, and I have made my choice."

Take action. Set a separation deadline. Ask yourself: "How long am I willing to put up with this problem if nothing changes? Am I willing to be in this same situation a year from now, a month from now, or even next week?" Give yourself a clear and specific answer; don't settle for, "I don't know." It is tempting to postpone difficult actions, to avoid moments of personal responsibility and accountability. It can feel much easier in the short run to let yourself drift along. However, you must accept your obligation to direct your own life. No one will set the deadline for you, so you must set it for yourself.

It may help to approach the separation deadline from both ends. For example, you might say, "Certainly I can hold out for another month, but definitely not for another year." Work inward and pick a final date. Then use that deadline as the starting point for a problem-solving project. Maintain self-discipline in meeting the project's interim deadlines and the final deadline.

Think how good it will feel to look back and thank yourself for having the courage to make this important change in your life. Don't keep yourself in limbo, fantasizing about escaping from the situation without taking decisive action. Stop second-guessing or procrastinating. When the time to separate has arrived, do so.

LETTING GO

The process of letting go helps you deal more effectively with separation. In CREATIVITY, we discussed the technique of temporarily letting go of a problem. This meant taking a mental break with the expectation that you would soon return to the problem and get it solved. However, when we talk about letting go in the context of RELEASE, we mean permanently freeing yourself from all emotional attachments to the problem. We mean letting go of your desire to overcome an obstacle that cannot be overcome, or to achieve a specific goal that is truly unobtainable.

This is true whether it is a separation that you *choose* or an *unwanted* separation such as a loss. Sometimes things are lost that cannot be regained: a possession, a job, a game, a relationship, or a business. This includes experiencing the death of a loved one, which is the most final and unyielding of all human problems. Your beloved cannot be brought back, nor ever truly replaced.

Letting go of such a loss does not mean that you must put all aspects of it out of your mind. For example, if an important relationship has come to an end, you should continue to cherish the warm memories of your time together. But you will have to accept the loss – you will have to let go of your deep desire to have that relationship back – in order to resume your path to fulfillment.

> ### SHE WALKED AWAY
> It was one of those special moments, a mental snapshot that is as clear in my memory as if it had happened yesterday. My older daughter, Sarah, had just recently learned how to walk, and she was mighty happy about it. She was standing in the middle of the hallway in our home. It was a warm, sunny day, so she was wearing only a diaper. I was sitting on the floor at the end of the hallway. I said, "Come to Daddy!" and she began waddling toward me, beaming. I had my hands outstretched to her, but at the last second she decided that she had somewhere else to go. She wheeled around, giggling, and I can still see her little diapered behind trotting away.
>
> It was the first time that she had purposely turned away from me, and I knew right then that she was already starting on her road to independence. I was filled with a bittersweet vision of the future, of the hundreds of little separations that are a necessary part of raising a child into a capable adult. Parenting is filled with moments like these, when tears are mingled with pride, when our wish that our children could remain forever young is balanced against our knowledge that they must always continue to grow. There is nothing we can do but savor the pride and accept the tears. We all must find our own ways of letting go.
>
> *-Kevin*

The burden of desire. We saw in INSIGHT that desire is usually a positive and motivating force. It is what keeps us moving and growing, it is what makes life interesting and rewarding, and it is what compels us to seek out and solve challenging problems. In the problem statement, "I want *goal*, but *obstacle*," the "want" is your desire.

As we discussed in the Introduction, a problem is solved when what you *have* matches what you *want*. Most of *Solution Power* has been about how to accomplish that by overcoming obstacles and achieving your goal. In other words, you solve most of your problems by changing what you *have* to match what you *want*.

Letting go takes the opposite approach. When it is simply not possible to change your circumstances to conform to your desire, you must relinquish the desire. You must find a way to change what you *want* to match what you *have*. This is the process of acceptance, of letting go of a desire that has become a burden.

Letting go is not an act of weakness, but of strength. It is rejecting the Weak emotions of despair or bitterness and finding the serenity to accept that which cannot be changed.

How to Let Go

Forgive. If you harbor any feelings of guilt, blame, bitterness, regret, or resentment, you must relinquish them. So long as you cling to these Weak emotions, you will be bound to the problem by an unhealthy attachment and you will remain wounded by the separation. Attempts to get even or hold a grudge usually harm everyone involved without accomplishing any useful purpose. At the time of any separation, seek to *forgive* and to *accept forgiveness*. Part ways with goodwill and good wishes.

Pray and meditate. Rely on your spiritual beliefs and religious practices to help you attain acceptance; seek relief through prayer, meditation, or worship. Use the *meditative and spiritual* exercises in Response to achieve a state of serenity and composure. Let go of the desire that is no longer needed and no longer productive. Place the problem in the hands of a higher power, and trust in that power to give you strength and peace of mind.

Mourn. It is natural and healthy to experience a period of mourning after a separation. You are probably familiar with mourning in the context of dealing with a death, but it is helpful and appropriate to mourn in any situation that feels like a loss. You might need to mourn the failure of a business, a loss in a competition, or the end of a relationship. Even a positive separation can be the occasion for a feeling of mourning, as when your child ventures into the world as a young adult or when a promotion takes you away from coworkers with whom you have enjoyed working.

Mourning is a healthy process for handling the grief that frequently accompanies separation. When facing grief:

1. **Acknowledge it.** Grief is a natural reaction to loss, and therefore a natural part of life. If you feel sadness after a separation, don't ignore it. Recognize and respect it.

2. **Experience it.** Allow yourself to *feel* the uncomfortable emotions that often accompany separations, instead of trying to smother or suppress them. This will help you to process them and let them go, and to learn that you are capable of handling the consequences of a loss. As a result, it will be easier for you to take promising risks in the future.

3. **Express it.** Act appropriately on your feelings of sadness: cry, express your sorrow, and give voice to your regret. The destructive ways of suppressing those feelings – such as drinking, withdrawal, and hostility – almost always lead to more problems. Look to your life team for support and comfort.

4. **Give yourself time.** Mourning is a cleansing and healing process, and should be given an appropriate amount of time. Neither rush it nor indulge in it. Cry until you are done, then begin moving forward with your life again.

> ### MOURNING WITH LAUGHTER
> We cried at Dad's funeral.
>
> He had traveled far and accomplished much in his life. He was the adopted son of illiterate immigrants, and led a spare existence as a child. After serving in the Army in Europe during World War II, he went to school on the GI Bill. Having been a stutterer in his childhood, he took an interest in speech therapy. He and Mom met in college out in California and married soon after. When he finished his Master's degree, they moved to Minot, North Dakota, where he helped build the State College's new Department of Speech Pathology and Audiology, which went on to gain wide recognition for its excellence. He also earned his doctoral degree from the Mayo Clinic. A PhD college professor – not bad for a farm kid from Michigan.
>
> Dad was a demanding teacher, but in a way that serious students respected. He helped countless children and adults overcome speech impediments, including those born with cleft palates and those who had lost their vocal cords. Dad became a widely-known and well-respected member of the community. He maintained high standards, helped a lot of people, and always tried to do what was right. He is the only person we've ever known who spoke with perfect grammar in everyday conversation. We always knew he loved us deeply.
>
> So, we cried at his funeral, and felt somber and disconcerted. His childhood best friend, Andy, had flown in from Michigan, and he came home with us afterwards. We sat in the living room and began to reminisce. We told Andy about the time we tried to get Dad to quit smoking by packing his cigarettes with gunpowder. He told us about the time that Dad, *our perfectly-behaved Dad*, had swiped some steaks out of the officers' mess tent so his GI buddies could have a feast. We all began to laugh as we shared stories, and it felt good and natural. We were dealing with what we had lost by remembering the man he had been.
>
> *-Kevin & Reagan*

Say goodbye. You can gain a sense of relief by letting go with finality, so bring closure to your process of RELEASE by saying a final farewell. When dealing with an unwanted loss, keep in mind that saying goodbye to a valued relationship or to a cherished goal does not mean forgetting or diminishing it. By saying goodbye, you are bidding farewell to a problem, not to the memory of the person or to the importance of the goal. You are acknowledging that something you desired is gone or is unobtainable.

If you are separating by choice from an unfulfilling or destructive problem, part ways with as much goodwill as you can muster. Even if you are just separating from a bad habit, a worn-out old car, or a town you never liked living in, you can let it go with positive finality by using this *universal parting*: "Our time together is done. I wish you well. Goodbye."

Conclusion

Most separations, wanted or unwanted, can be treated as opportunities if you simply make the decision to do so. People have found ways of turning even the most painful losses into chances for renewed growth and greater contribution. If nothing else, you will emerge from your time of trial with greater strength, confidence, and wisdom.

Once you have separated and let go, it is important to re-open yourself to the joys and pleasures of life. A good way to do this is to reconnect with your fundamental beliefs and your vision of fulfillment. You may have to find new paths to fulfillment, perhaps by setting new compelling goals. Focusing on the future will make it easier to truly put the problem behind you and move ahead.

Allow yourself to once again experience the richness and pleasure the world has to offer. Open the door and step outside the stuffy room that once defined your problem. How wonderful it feels to breathe fresh air, to have light shoulders and a smile on your face. On with life!

Release: Summary

- **First and last.** RELEASE can be used first to help you avoid getting entangled in unnecessary problems, and used last to help you resolve problems that cannot be solved using the other *Solution Power* tools.

Separating

- **Avoiding an unnecessary problem.** Don't be a trouble magnet or a timid mouse. Develop your healthy intuition so you can make good problem-solving choices.
- **When to separate from an existing problem.** Make the best decision about leaving or staying by using separation techniques like acting with strength and rising above win/lose thinking.
- **How to separate from an existing problem.** Have a *go to*, separate on your own terms, separate with honor, and take action.

Letting Go

- **Unwanted separation.** A death can create unwanted separation, as can the loss of a relationship, a job, a game, or a business. Free yourself of emotional attachments to an unsolvable problem; liberate yourself from the burden of desire.
- **How to let go.** Forgive and be forgiven, pray and meditate, mourn, and say goodbye.

AFTERWORD

It is our sincere hope that each person who reads *Solution Power* will go on to lead a life rich with problems. That phrase might have seemed odd if you had encountered it before reading this book. After all, what could be good about a life with a lot of problems in it? But now we have seen that choosing and solving the right problems is the key to building a successful and rewarding life.

In fact, it would be a terrible curse to say, "May you have a life with no problems." It is only by facing challenging problems that you discover and develop your full human potential for insight, achievement, and adventure. We hope that you will find many ways to use the *Solution Power* tools to build a life rich with the problems and solutions that lead to your individual fulfillment.

APPENDIX A

Breathing by Numbers

This technique has a number of benefits:

- It provides a rich flow of oxygen to your brain and muscles, helping you think clearly and act with energy.
- It opens and relaxes your abdomen and chest, dispelling tension.
- It is meditative, relaxing, and calming.
- It moves your thoughts away from dwelling on the problem and helps you shift them in a positive direction.

Here is the technique:

1. Purse your lips and gently blow all of the air out of your lungs.
2. Breathe in through your nose, counting silently: "One, two, three, four…" Fill your lungs from the bottom up, relaxing your abdomen and letting it swell effortlessly, then expanding your chest out and up. Draw the breath deep down inside you, but don't inhale forcibly. Instead, allow your lungs to expand as you gently draw in the air. Stop counting when your lungs are comfortably full.
3. Hold your breath for a multiple of that number. Most people will find that two, three, or four times as long is about right. For instance, if you counted to six as you breathed in, you would now hold your breath for a count of twelve,

eighteen, or twenty-four. Find the pace that works best for you. If you get all red in the face, eyes popping and cheeks swelling, you will only add to your stress! Don't strain. Instead of thinking that you are blocking the air from escaping, imagine that the air is comfortably residing in your relaxed, open lungs.

4. Breathe out slowly through gently pursed lips, again using a multiple of the "breathing in" number. Two or three times that number should be about right. Completely empty your lungs of air.

5. Repeat this process as many times as you desire. If you find yourself getting dizzy or lightheaded, simply shorten the duration of the "breath holding" and "breathing out" steps. When you find the numbers that work best for you, you will be able to continue this breathing pattern for as long as you like, until you are fully relaxed.

You can use this technique when you need a break, when you feel stuck, when you are preparing to take action, when you are feeling apprehensive, or when you want to stimulate your thinking to generate an idea.

Beyond using this technique, develop the general habit of relaxed breathing. Many people have fallen into the habit of taking shallow, constricted breaths. Check your breathing during the course of the day, even when you don't feel particularly stressed. Is it tight or relaxed? You don't have to breathe *deeply* all the time, but you should breathe *easily* as much as possible. Maintain a relaxed center.

Appendix B

Belief Adjectives

You can use this list of adjectives as an aid in discovering your fundamental beliefs. Go through the list and record the words that resonate, the words that say, "This is who I am, this is who I am meant to be." Then continue the process of identifying your fundamental beliefs in FOCUS.

adventurous	affectionate	altruistic
ambitious	assertive	attentive
audacious	austere	aware
beautiful	benevolent	bold
brave	careful	caring
cautious	certain	cheerful
clean	comfortable	committed
compassionate	concerned	confident
confrontational	conscientious	considerate
contrary	contemplative	cooperative
courageous	courteous	creative
critical	curious	decent
decisive	defiant	determined
devoted	different	dignified
direct	discerning	discreet
dutiful	earnest	efficient
deliberative	eager	empathetic
energetic	enthusiastic	extravagant
exuberant	fair	faithful
fastidious	flexible	forceful
forgiving	free	friendly

generous, genial, gentle
giving, good, graceful
gracious, grateful, heroic
honest, honorable, hopeful
hospitable, humble, impatient
impulsive, independent, indulgent
inquisitive, inspirational, inspired
interested, intimate, introspective
irreverent, joyful, kind
lenient, loving, loyal
magnanimous, mature, meditative
moderate, modest, moral
motivated, mystical, neighborly
neutral, normal, obedient
optimistic, passionate, patient
peaceful, persistent, playful
polite, popular, positive
powerful, pragmatic, prepared
proud, prudent, pure
rational, reckless, reflective
relaxed, reserved, resolute
respectful, responsible, restrained
reverent, righteous, romantic
secure, sentimental, serene
serious, shrewd, silly
skeptical, sociable, solemn
solitary, sophisticated, spontaneous
steady, strange, strict
strong, studious, sympathetic
tenacious, tender, thankful
thoughtful, tolerant, triumphant
trusting, trustworthy, understanding
uninhibited, vigilant, vigorous
virtuous, warm, wary
weird, whimsical, wise
worthy, zealous

ANECDOTES

THE VALUE OF PROBLEM-SOLVING DIVERSITY — 38
Confident leaders create successful problem-solving teams by hiring a variety of personality types.

ADOPTING NEW PROBLEM-SOLVING TOOLS — 39
An Individual personality type sees the advantages of a more Social approach to personal problem-solving.

SOMETIMES PROBLEMS STINK, AND THAT'S OKAY — 47
Turning a "big, stinking, dangerous problem" into a "big, stinking, dangerous opportunity to learn."

SEEING PROBLEMS AS OPPORTUNITIES — 48
Successfully moving from legal counsel to COO requires *pursuing* risks instead of *avoiding* them.

STRONG RESPONSE HABITS AND SELF-CONTROL — 68
A dormitory fire shows the value of developing effective problem-solving habits in advance of a crisis.

BE CAREFUL WITH BLAME: A TIP FOR MANAGERS — 109
Leaders get much better results by focusing on problem-solving rather than on fault-finding or scapegoating.

MINIMIZING PROBLEMS: A TIP FOR MANAGERS — 113
Anytime someone says, "Don't worry about it," it's time to start worrying.

DESCRIBING PROBLEMS EFFECTIVELY — 117
In order to create and maintain team motivation, it is vital for a leader to accurately describe coming challenges.

SOLUTION POWER

USING HUMOR TO GAIN PERSPECTIVE   120
A worker who laughs at problems while working to solve them helps himself and everyone around him.

THINKING IN WRITING   123
"You have not truly had an idea until you have put it in writing."

THE VALUE OF FACTS   124
Detailed research into a long-standing problem reveals that the financial impact is too small to worry about.

SOLVING PROBLEMS AT THE ROOT   127
A professional solution-finder solves the problems of his son's untied shoelaces and uncombed hair.

FOCUSING ON OVERCOMING OBSTACLES AT WORK   146
The problem has been defined, the complaints have been aired. Now it is time for the team to focus on solutions.

LOVE ON A BUDGET   151
A tight budget, plastic eggs, and the best Easter basket ever.

BORROW IT, IMPROVE IT, AND PASS IT ALONG   202
Asking successful organizations for their ideas, then improving them and offering them to others.

YOU GOTTA BE YOU!   204
"There is only one way to be a good lawyer, and that is your way."

A SPECTACULAR FIND ON THE INTERNET   206
Two fireworks aficionados find instructions for a "creamer bomb" online.

A TIP FOR MANAGERS: REWARD COMMUNICATION   215
Handling the complaints of an angry employee in a way that benefits everyone.

INSIST ON GREAT SOLUTIONS   221
Taking a contractor to task for a lack of innovation.

LEADERSHIP AND THE IMPOSSIBLE   238
The hardest part of accomplishing the "impossible" is to convincing everyone else to just give it a try.

ANECDOTES

SERENITY IN MOTION — **244**
An Individual problem-solver finds that running creates an ideal solution-finding state.

FUN AT WORK — **247**
"We believe in having fun *while* we work, we just don't believe in having fun *instead* of working."

THE SMASHING THROUGH MINDSET — **249**
Crushing walnuts with one hand as a metaphor for solving a problem completely.

THINKING BY ANALOGY — **253**
A cartoonist summons lightning to answer the challenge of a blank page.

COURAGE AND COMEDY — **270**
Standup comedy as the ultimate crash course in public speaking.

A MODEL OF COURAGE — **273**
Winston Churchill, an exemplar of courageous leadership and personal daring.

BOXERCISE — **277**
Welcome to the "Hades Health Club," where aerobic weightlifting classes are always in session.

GUIDED BY INTUITION — **288**
An adolescent hunch to steer clear of trouble proves accurate and helpful.

SHE WALKED AWAY — **296**
One sunny day, a daughter toddles away toward independence.

MOURNING WITH LAUGHTER — **299**
Dealing with the loss of a father by remembering the man he had been.

INDEX

A

achievement level. *See* Priority
Active reactions. *See* physical reactions
addiction, 71, 140, 173
Alexander the Great, 251
analogies, 200, 240, 251–53, 260
anger, 53, 54, 58, 60, 62, 69–72, 82, 103, 105, 113, 282, 291
   managing, 69, 72–75, 130, 143, 145, 215
   using productively, 270
anti-creativity, 237–39
anxiety, 50, 54, 60, 67, 78, 86, 106, 139, 271, 291, 292
   managing, 120, 130, 143, 187, 223
assertiveness, 53, 55, 84
   advantages over hostility, 69–72
   definition of, 70
assumptions, 38
   questioning, 123–24, 184, 225, 237, 238
avoidance. *See* problems, avoiding

B

barriers. *See* obstacles
behavior, 159
   and emotions, 61, 81–85
   changing, 98, 102, 223–24, 275
   habits of, 63, 68, 72, 80, 111, 129, 139, 145, 236, 267
   instinctive, 66
   manipulating, 69
   responsibility for, 92
   Strong. *See* Strong behavior
   Weak. *See* Weak behavior
beliefs, 155
   and language, 112
   fundamental. *See* fundamental beliefs
   spiritual, 297. *See also* faith
blame, 65, 105–10, 297. *See also* fault
brainstorming, 156, 222, 257–60
breathing
   and Creativity, 244, 255
   and Strong Responses, 81, 85–91, 292
   and Weak Responses, 81, 82
   technique, 86, 305–6
business. *See also* leadership
   failure, 96, 261, 281, 295, 298
   management. *See* management
   starting a new one, 42, 131, 169, 220
   success, 13, 43, 60, 83, 100, 261

C

career. *See also* job
   advancing, 42, 72–73, 103, 169, 171, 189–91, 204, 247, 268
   changing, 18, 45

313

choosing, 34–37
difficulties, 78
catastrophizing. *See* problems, catastrophizing
Churchill, Winston, 251, 273
communication, 55, 56, 67, 73, 84, 199–201, 215, 217, 219, 227
courage, 53, 268, 281, 295
  strengthening, 60, 268–76
criticism, 226, 230, 257
  constructive, 231
  destructive, 282
  handling, 84, 118, 212
cue, 78, 143, 148. *See also* warning
curiosity, 53, 63, 116, 127–30, 200–201, 246, 269, 271, 282

D

death, 45, 76, 157, 295, 298
defeat, 281–82
desire, 53, 79, 182, 221, 275, 285
  letting go of, 14, 295–300
desires, 40–43, 155, 180
diversion level. *See* Priority

E

Edison, Thomas, 251
emotional reactions, 51, 53–54, 213, 272
emotions
  and behavior, 61, 81–85
  and focus, 61, 142
  intensity of, 53, 79, 271–72
  Strong. *See* Strong emotions
  Weak. *See* Weak emotions

F

failure, 65, 78, 140, 189, 236, 274, 281–82, 298
faith, 53, 153, 156, 157, 171, 272, 297

fault, 59, 139. *See also* blame
fear, 41, 43, 52, 53, 54, 57, 58, 67, 74, 77, 81, 106, 173, 265, 290, 294
  and courage, 267–68
  managing, 118–20, 183, 236–37, 268–76, 291–93
  understanding, 266–67
fight. *See* instinct
flee. *See* instinct
flow, 188–89, 191, 231, 241, 242, 257
Focus
  fulfillment level, 155–62
  goal level, 149–55
  obstacle level, 143–48
  problem level, 136–43
Ford, Henry, 42
forgiveness, 53, 60, 223, 297
freeze. *See* instinct
fulfillment, 42, 43, 45, 92, 128, 142, 160–62, 165–66, 170–72, 173, 178–79, 188–91, 221, 229, 266, 275, 281, 286, 290, 293, 296
  and delegation, 212–13
  and fundamental beliefs, 155–60
  definition of, 155
  vision of, 187–88, 212, 240, 274, 279, 287, 300
fulfillment action plan, 162, 179–88, 220, 287, 289
fulfillment level. *See* Priority. *See* Focus
fundamental beliefs, 178, 187, 191, 231, 272, 281, 287, 300
  acting on, 155, 160–62, 170, 188, 189
  and setting goals, 180–85, 294
  identifying, 155–60, 180, 307
  surrendering, 281

G

Ghandi, Mohandas, 251
goal, 13
goal level. *See* Focus
goal question, 149, 150, 167, 168, 169, 170
goals, 70, 74, 146, 147–48, 172, 175–78, 185–86, 189, 210, 217, 279, 280, 285, 293, 295, 297, 299
  and career advancement, 189–91
  and fulfillment, 155, 187–88
  and responsibility, 105, 109, 142
  compelling, 58, 180–85, 187, 191, 211, 221, 240, 268, 274, 275, 276, 281, 287, 300
  creating, 152–53, 180–85
  high-priority, 43, 160, 175, 178
  identifying, 96–105
grief, 54, 298

H

habits, 38, 57, 95, 96, 99, 128, 138, 212
  developing, 15, 39, 47, 51, 58, 69, 72, 78, 100, 104, 115, 129, 136, 142–43, 145, 171, 196, 223, 227, 261
  Strong, 61, 63, 68, 152, 160, 199, 207, 236–41, 267, 306
  Weak, 61, 62, 67, 71, 85, 103, 105–8, 112–16, 138–42, 229, 237–39, 300
help
  asking for, 39, 76, 198–201, 203, 218, 223, 224, 227, 248, 289
  getting, 49, 102, 112, 197–98, 202, 203, 205, 209–32, 272, 290, 293
  giving, 41, 48, 63, 102, 110–12, 159, 170, 171, 188, 191, 201,

202, 210, 218, 222, 225, 230, 232, 274, 279, 286
hostility, 54, 57, 62, 69–72, 80, 81, 107, 298
humor, 47, 120, 247

I

instinct to fight, flee, or freeze, 57–58, 66–72, 81, 266, 267, 268
intuition, 84, 123, 215, 254–55, 287–88

J

job, 44, 103, 128, 150, 213, 247, 276–77, 295. *See also* career
  choosing, 13, 34–37, 46, 100, 287
  difficult, 67, 266
  unpleasant, 96, 285, 293

L

language, 112–17, 142, 199–201, 276
leadership, 109, 171, 189–91, 227–28, 238, 247, 252. *See also* management
  and personality type, 36–39
  and responsibility, 214
  and risk, 48
life team, 219, 229–32, 237, 272, 289, 290, 298
loss, 73, 295–300

M

management, 70, 107, 113, 117, 214–16, 247, 252. *See also* leadership
marriage, 44, 60
  improving, 13, 97, 100–102

troubled, 59, 69, 76, 78, 96, 289
minimizing. *See* problems, minimizing
motivation, 14, 48, 53, 60, 64–66, 136, 179, 184, 187, 268, 273–76
  clarifying, 102, 289, 290
  from Weak emotions, 79–80, 274
  push and pull, 79
mourning, 298–99

N

necessity level. *See* Priority
Nietzsche, Friedrich, 47

O

obstacle level. *See* Focus
obstacle question, 145
obstacles
  bypassing, 149–52
  identifying, 98–105, 121, 132, 154, 285
  immovable, 295–97
  overcoming, 105, 108–10, 143–48, 203, 246, 276, 282, 295
  smashing, 249
opportunities, 37, 50, 51, 71, 111, 128, 177, 216, 220, 225, 232, 261, 267, 269, 274, 275, 277
  and intuition, 286–88
  goal-level, 152–53
  obstacle-level, 146–47
  turning problems into, 11, 39, 40, 44–48, 69, 92, 160, 176, 189, 190, 277, 286, 300
opportunity statement, 47
opportunity, definition of, 44

P

parenting, 42, 44, 59, 75, 97, 101–2, 110–12, 125, 137, 153, 171, 177, 188, 204, 206, 215, 216, 252, 259, 261, 279, 296, 298
personality type, 17–18, 40, 51, 83, 243
  and leadership, 36–39
  and life choices, 35–37
  appreciating other types, 37–38, 225
  descriptions, 24–31
  Doer, 21, 28–31, 32–33, 34, 36, 37, 38, 39, 40, 55, 56, 57, 83, 162, 225, 243
  getting the most from, 34–39
  Individual, 19, 24, 26, 28, 30, 32–33, 34, 36, 39, 83, 210, 223, 225, 243, 244
  Intuitive, 20, 24, 25, 28, 29, 32–33, 34, 35, 36, 37, 154, 225, 244
  Linear, 20, 26, 27, 30, 31, 32–33, 34, 36, 37, 225, 243
  problem-solving examples, 32–33
  questionnaire, 18–22
  Social, 19, 25, 27, 29, 31, 32–33, 36, 39, 83, 223, 225, 243
  Thinker, 21, 27, 32–33, 34, 36, 37, 38, 39, 40, 55, 56, 58, 83, 154, 162, 225, 243
physical fitness, 13, 59, 60, 97, 100, 144, 274, 277
physical reactions, 51–53, 54, 272
Priority
  achievement level, 169, 175–78
  diversion level, 167, 172–73
  fulfillment level, 170, 178–91
  necessity level, 168, 173–75
problem level. *See* Focus
problem statement, 99–100, 121, 132, 144, 149, 296
problem, definition of, 13
problem-fearing identity, 287
problems. *See also* setbacks
  achievement-level, 169, 175–78, 183, 190

INDEX

admitting you have, 75–79, 103–4
analyzing, 52, 120, 121–32, 142, 251
ancient vs. modern, 67–69
as part of life, 41, 43–44, 303
attitude toward, 18, 46, 50, 96
avoiding, 41–44, 57, 63, 64, 76, 77, 80, 103–4, 110, 113, 119, 173, 267
catastrophizing, 112–13, 114–17, 140
challenging, 41–44, 74, 92, 117, 131, 147, 178, 183, 206, 237, 279, 296, 303
choosing, 165–66, 303
complaining about, 44, 106, 107, 140, 141, 146, 225
complex, 56, 67, 122, 131, 197
creating, 42
dangerous, 42, 57, 66, 68, 126, 181, 183, 250, 266, 287
defining, 96–105, 146, 269, 289
describing, 112–13, 114–17, 224, 237
destructive, 290, 300
difficult, 48, 55, 56, 61, 63, 72, 84, 99, 104, 116, 141, 183, 190, 196, 222, 224, 245, 265, 268, 272, 278, 285, 288
diversion-level, 167, 172–73, 187, 189
focusing on having, 59–62, 136–43
frightening, 85, 183, 267, 268
fulfillment-level, 170, 178–79, 178–91, 211–13, 221
gathering information about, 123–24
important, 39, 43, 66, 79, 165, 220, 276, 286, 291
kinds of, 11, 84, 167
long-term, 154, 169, 175, 177, 185, 190, 224, 228, 280

low-priority, 43, 211–13, 221, 286, 291
minimizing, 113
necessity-level, 168, 173–75, 190
of others, 110–12, 254, 286, 289
putting in perspective, 46, 62, 102, 118–20, 203, 215, 246, 273, 277, 245–47, 289
putting in writing, 121–23, 289
recurring, 65, 80, 141, 175
root, 125–30, 289
secondary, 125–30
serious, 44–45, 52, 68, 76, 79, 102, 103, 112–17, 169, 172, 225, 266, 271, 291
stinky, 46–47
turning into opportunities, 11, 39, 40, 44–48, 69, 92, 160, 176, 189, 190, 277, 286, 300
unnecessary, 43, 285, 286–88
unsolvable, 287
visualizing, 119–20
problem-solving, 15, 49, 209
  enjoyable, 55, 84, 231, 245–47, 279
  natural strengths, 17–18, 22, 34–38
problem-solving identity, 137–38, 145, 152, 155, 232, 287
problem-solving personality type. *See* personality type
problem-solving project, 122, 131–32, 145, 176, 179, 185–86, 287, 289, 295
problem-solving resources, 43, 166, 171, 173, 174, 176, 186, 211, 232
problem-suffering identity, 139–43, 230, 287
procrastination, 108, 110

317

R

reactions. *See* emotional reactions.
See physical reactions
relationships, 65, 170, 177, 199, 238
   and the subconscious, 254
   building, 84, 124, 187, 203, 223, 232
   ending, 127, 230, 285, 290
   evaluating, 229–32
   losing, 295, 298, 299
   unhealthy, 45, 130, 285, 286, 290
resources. *See* problem-solving resources
Responses
   choosing, 72–75
   Strong. *See* Strong Responses
   Weak. *See* Weak Responses
responsibility, 104
   and delegation, 214
   assigning, 132
   avoiding, 92, 141, 294
   for solving your own problems, 105–10, 142, 144, 289
   transferring, 219
risks
   avoiding, 48, 73, 109, 183, 236, 287
   considering, 269
   taking, 48, 76, 156, 213, 236, 266, 298

S

self-control, 52, 57, 66–72, 74–75, 81
setbacks, 39, 145, 236–37, 246, 276, 281–82. *See also* problems
solution debt, 198, 218
solution resources, 202–6
solution, definition of, 14
solutions
   analyzing, 257
   focusing on, 59–62, 69, 70, 77, 146
   habitual, 68, 99
   having fun with, 246, 257
   improving, 196, 201, 235, 260–61
   ineffective, 65, 67, 80, 102, 221, 225, 235, 239
   inexpensive, 250
   paying for, 219–21, 249
   pre-existing, 261
   putting into action, 60
   rejecting, 141, 226, 230
   sharing, 36, 195, 197–202, 231, 232
   win/lose, 49, 106, 107, 290
   win/win, 49
Still reacations. *See* physical reactions
Strong behavior, 85–91, 267
Strong emotions, 53–54, 92, 156, 197, 237
   and assertiveness, 69–72
   and decision-making, 291–93
   and focus, 59–62
   and motivation, 79
   and personal growth, 62–63
   and responsibility, 108
   and self-control, 66–69
   and Strong behavior, 85
   triggering, 85
Strong Responses, 109, 136, 156, 237, 245, 257, 292, 294, 297
   advantages of, 59–72
   choosing, 83–84
   generating, 85–91, 114, 225, 305–6
   Strong & Active, 55, 73, 84, 278
   Strong & Still, 56, 73, 84
subconscious
   alignment with conscious, 160
   and self-identity, 137–43, 145, 152, 160
   choices, 74, 93

definitions, 96
links, 61, 78, 142, 278, 279
power of, 56, 144
receiving messages from, 183, 239, 243, 254–56
sending messages to, 112, 137–43, 145, 160, 181, 237, 239, 240, 254–56, 257
surrender, 43, 89, 92, 161, 281–82
symptoms, 125–30, 148, 289

T

thanks, 151, 158, 197, 214, 218, 228, 279, 295
tool, definition of, 14
tools, 12–13, 78, 248, 250, 252
and personality type, 17, 34
habits of using, 14–15
learning new, 18, 36, 38–39
list of, 9
trouble, 39, 43, 63, 76, 102, 103, 107, 139, 158, 230, 273
avoiding, 225, 285, 286–88

V

vision of fulfillment. *See* fulfillment, vision of

W

wants. *See* desires
warning, 76, 81, 287. *See also* cue
Weak behavior, 71, 81–83, 103, 107, 139–43, 215, 216, 223, 230, 288
Weak emotions, 53–54, 57, 58, 72, 92, 96, 266, 268, 297
analyzing, 130
and behavior, 81
and blame, 105, 108
and decision-making, 291–93
and focus, 59–62
and forgiveness, 297
and hostility, 69–72
and language, 112
and motivation, 79–80, 274
and mourning, 298
and personal growth, 62–63
and self-control, 66–69
and suffering from problems, 136–43
managing, 74–75
using as cues, 77–79
Weak Responses, 115, 212, 268
avoiding, 81–83, 180
disadvantages of, 59–72
Weak & Active, 57, 73, 81, 107
Weak & Still, 58, 73, 82, 108

We'd like to hear from you!

Contact us at **www.pufall.com** to
- ♦ Share a great problem-solving story or tip
- ♦ Purchase additional copies of *Solution Power*
- ♦ Get information about our *Solution Power* presentations

www.ingramcontent.com/pod-product-compliance
Lightning Source LLC
Chambersburg PA
CBHW070554100426
42744CB00006B/271